DISCIPLE'S GUIDE
TO
RITUAL MAGICK

ABOUT THE AUTHOR

FRATER BARRABBAS TIRESIUS is a practicing ritual magician who has studied magic and the occult for over forty years. He believes that ritual magic is a discipline whose mystery is unlocked by continual practice and by occult experiences and revelations. Frater Barrabbas believes that traditional approaches should be balanced with creativity and experimentation and that no occult or magical tradition is exempt from changes and revisions.

Frater Barrabbas also founded a magical order called the Order of the Gnostic Star and is an elder and lineage holder in the Alexandrian tradition of Witchcraft.

DISCIPLE'S GUIDE
TO
RITUAL MAGICK

A BEGINNER'S INTRODUCTION
TO THE HIGH ART

FRATER BARRABBAS

Chicago, Illinois

Paperback ISBN: 978-1-959883-35-7
Library of Congress Control Number on file.

Published by:
Crossed Crow Books, LLC
6934 N Glenwood Ave, Suite C
Chicago, IL 60626
www.crossedcrowbooks.com

Printed in the United States of America.
IBI

OTHER BOOKS BY FRATER BARRABBAS

Mastering the Art of Witchcraft (Crossed Crow Books, 2024)
Sacramental Theurgy for Witches ((Crossed Crow Books, 2024)
Transformative Initiation for Witches (Crossed Crow Books, 2024)
Talismanic Magic for Witches (Llewellyn, 2023)
Elemental Powers for Witches (Llewellyn, 2021)
Spirit Conjuring for Witches (Llewellyn, 2017)
Magical Qabalah for Beginners (Llewellyn, 2013)

FORTHCOMING TITLES

Liber Nephilim (Crossed Crow Books)
Mastering the Art of Ritual Magick (Crossed Crow Books)
Abramelin Lunar Ordeal (Crossed Crow Books)
The Magical Norary Art (Crossed Crow Books)
Liber Artis Archaeomancy (Crossed Crow Books)

DEDICATION

This work is dedicated with love and admiration to the Goddess Tyannia, my beatified muse!

ACKNOWLEDGEMENTS

I give special thanks to Soror Rekhetra for the title pages and Parts I and II page illustrations, and to Keith Ward for his images and diagrams of the Magickal Devices.

CONTENTS

PART I
THE PHILOSOPHY AND
KNOWLEDGE OF MAGICK

PART II

The Grimoire

AUTHOR'S NOTES TO THE REVISED EDITION

It has been almost twenty years since I first wrote this book. It was also the first book that I had ever published. I remember getting copies of it after it had been published and I was thrilled to have my writings in print. I had a lot of ideas about ritual magic back then, and I had performed some incredible magical workings for the last two decades that were not written in this book. My objective in writing this book was to present my ideas to beginning students so that I might later be able to share my more advanced lore with them.

Yet, in the span of years since the time this book was published, I have changed and grown considerably. Back then, I was a middle-aged man seeking to make my mark on the world of magic and occultism. I had little previous exposure to that world, since I also had very little Internet presence with which others could engage. I guess you could say that there was a kind of naivety about me and that I had no idea what the rest of the occult world was avidly discussing. Perhaps the most important person in my literary life at that time was Taylor Elwood, who was running a branch of Immanion Books and who gave me my first chance to not only publish my work, but to also get to know my community. It was exciting and a shock, to say the least. I was not prepared for this exposure, and while some welcomed me to their Internet cloud community, others saw my work as derivative and not particularly interesting. Also, my opinions about the state of the magical and Pagan community were decidedly wrong (and even a bit pessimistic).

One thing that I should make clear is that I had completed two decades of powerful magical workings, so I had some pretty intense lore that I am only now, twenty years later, revealing to my reading public. My first book, *Disciples' Guide to Ritual Magick,* was written to introduce my potential audience to the basic technology of the kind of magic that I performed. It was based on an earlier work that I never published, titled *Pyramid of Powers,* and a fair amount of that text was cannibalized to write this book. It allowed me to assemble a manuscript in 2006 that I was to submit early the next year for editing, and after a period of time, publication. I wanted to write a new book that had the same objective as my old unpublished work: to introduce people to my methods of writing and performing rituals. I wanted to give my readers a working system of magic based on the fundamental structures that I had been using since the late 1970s.

At the same time as I was completing this work, my life began to drastically change. Whether I knew it or not, I was about to experience the end of my first long-term relationship (if you consider twenty-four months long-term, but it was for me), an economic crisis, and the transitioning into a new corporation for my day job. There was a lot going on, and I also had the management of a coven that had just expelled its High Priestess. There was so much drama and turmoil in my life at that time that I am astonished that I managed to get through it all and also publish my first book. Everything was made more difficult because of the stress and the problems that I was encountering, yet I persevered. That is the background that I was experiencing when I wrote this book.

Because I had taken much of the text for *Disciples' Guide* from the *Pyramid of Power* and reformed, revised, and even rewrote some of it, it seemed that there was not much left to write on this topic of producing a beginner's system of magic. I used the Grail mythos to decorate and empower the rituals in the book, since it represented the first level of degree material for the Order that I had helped to found. Our emblem was the Grail, and each level of degree material redefined it in a different occult context. The first level material was based on the Arthurian legends, and it had a kind of Pagan and Christian spiritual context. I thought that taking this kind of approach would be attractive to a wider audience, even though it represented a technology and a creed that I didn't actually follow. My personal magic was much more advanced and spiritually witchy, but what I wrote in my book was simpler and had a more modest objective. Even though I had taken materials out of the *Pyramid of Power,* there was still quite a lot of material that hadn't been used. And while the rituals were set up with a specific spiritual perspective, the rituals in the *Pyramid of Powers* were generic and could be completely modified.

After consulting with my friend and publisher, Taylor, I decided to resurrect the remaining lore in the book *Pyramid of Powers* and use it to write a new book titled *Mastering the Art of Ritual Magick* that presented to the reader a completely generic system of magic, covering the same basic foundation as *Disciples' Guide,* but with a body of text that would show how a generic set of rituals could be customized using a key made up of a series of tables of correspondences. What *MARM* did was show how to take a set of rituals and make them into a personal magical system. This was the objective for the original manuscript, *Pyramid of Powers,* and once I completed writing and publishing the three-volume work of *MARM* I felt that my objective had been met. The ritual lore for both books was basic and neither represented the kind of magic that I was working on at the time. However, because both *Disciples' Guide* and *MARM* shared the text of a previously unpublished manuscript, they were linked together, and I made comments in *MARM* that referred to pages and chapters in the *Disciples' Guide,* and vice versa. If you purchased *MARM,* then for a full explanation of my ideas, you also had to purchase *Disciples' Guide.* They were a pair of books somewhat dependent on each other for lore, and they needed to be used together to fully realize my magical perspective. I didn't plan on linking these two tomes to somehow sell more books, it just happened because they had a single source.

Now, years later, I was given an opportunity to either remove these books from the publishing world, or to revise them and republish them. Since both of these books represented lore and methodologies that I no longer either used or even promoted, I had the opinion that I should let them quietly disappear from the market. However, over the course of a few years, I discovered during interviews and podcasts that both books had a following, especially *MARM.* My new publisher was keen to revise and republish *MARM* and so I extracted the text from a galley-ready PDF and started to edit it. What I found is that there were so many references to *Disciple's Guide* that I knew I also had to revise and republish it as well, since I realized once again how linked these two books were. So, here we are in the present times, with *MARM* and *Disciples' Guide* fully revised and edited.

When I wrote this book, I had just completed reading several books by Ken Wilber. I was most definitely under his spell, and I used his work to try and give more credence to my own perspectives on ritual magic. There are a lot of quotations and distillations from his work in this book, and I feel that it represented a time when I was branching out to gaining knowledge from other sources. However, in the last twenty years, I have found that Wilber's books and ideas haven't aged very well, especially within the practices of magic. His exclusive use of Freudian psychology and his narrow and unyielding viewpoints about topics where he was not an expert have tarnished his otherwise obvious brilliance. While I still use some of his ideas in my magical metaphysical beliefs and perspectives, I have gotten over with my intellectual fascination with him.

Overall, I decided to leave the lore and my ideas from that time long ago in both *MARM* and this book. They represent a time capsule of where I was, both intellectually and from a practical magical standpoint. Many of the ideas I had from that time I no longer follow, and much has changed in the world since then; all of it transformed me. I am an accomplished occult author with over twelve books written, something that I would have found hard to believe back in the early 2000s. While I may have evolved since that time, I still believe that the material in this book serves an important purpose. It is a beginner's book, which is unlike most of the books that I have written. This book also gives the reader a complete system of magic that they can use. It also serves as a suitable introduction to the book *MARM*, which will show how to build a basic system of magic from scratch. I am happy to revise these two works and present them for future readers to explore and experiment with the art of ritual magic, using rituals that will allow them to bend the laws of probability and achieve constructive changes in their material world.

—Frater Barrabbas, May 2024

PREFACE

This book was written for the beginning magician: an individual who at least knows something of this topic but isn't as experienced as a practitioner of the high art of ritual magick. We all have to begin somewhere, and this book assumes that the reader or ardent student is contemplating their entrance into the practice of magick. It's my desire to make the student and reader of this book into an accomplished ritual magician and an initiate rather than just another jaded dilettante. My desire is quite ambitious and perhaps even foolish, but I believe that this book, if read and practiced diligently, will do just that!

My ideal student will have read other books about magick. This will enable them to compare and contrast what I have written with other books on this subject. There are a lot of books written about magick, and some of them are good and some are deplorable.[1] Someone could easily ask the question, "why should there be yet another book that would teach the beginning seeker how to work magick?" Surely, the subject matter must be covered ad nauseam by now! I admit, without even a hint of embarrassment, that there are a lot of books on this subject, but I believe that this book truly delivers the methods and practices of ritual magick into the hands of the seeker unlike any other book in or out of print. The proof of this statement is found in the second part of this two-part book, which contains a grimoire of eight complete rituals that can be used to assemble a magickal discipline.

I define ritual magick as the Western occult methodology of gaining access to the domain or world of Spirit and its higher states

---

1   A list of some of the best of these kinds of books is found in the bibliography section of this book under the heading "Magick."

of consciousness via specific practices, techniques, and rituals. The practices involve learning to control and shape the mind. The techniques are used to engage Deity as an extension of oneself, and the rituals consist of a body of lore that generates personal power and meaning within a sacred space. We will cover each of these topics in greater detail in this book.

Two terms that I have used above—*grimoire* and *magickal discipline*—are the key to the uniqueness of this work. Most authors of magickal books seem to be happy to give the seeker a few simple rites to whet their eager desire for practical work. Yet, none seem to consider that the magician works magick using a discipline. A magickal discipline is defined as a regimen of occult practices and methodologies that assist the magician in developing the ability to perceive and act within the domain of Spirit. A magickal discipline requires a body of rituals or practices of some sort and the directions to perform them, called a *grimoire*. A magickal discipline also requires a schedule for working these various rituals, specifying their order and periodicity; it is the combination of practices and timing that makes it an active discipline. Offering a few simple rites to the student without the context of a practical discipline indicates that a discipline is not needed. It's like saying that a person can be a competent athlete without a regimen of practice and physical exercise. An untrained and unpracticed athlete is one who either quickly gets hurt or performs poorly at their sport. This is, of course, a ridiculous train of thought when considering athletics, and, less obviously, when considering ritual magick. Magickal discipline is very important to the mastery of the practice of ritual magick, and without it, magick has no context in which to operate, and will probably fail to produce the results that the erstwhile magician desires. This book seeks to fix that omission and that is, by itself, its greatest claim to uniqueness.

My second reason for writing this book is to include important parts of a larger work that I wrote but never published. The reader will find a few references to a three-volume book entitled *The Pyramid of Powers*. This three-volume work was written by me over a decade ago for the intermediate practitioner of ritual magick. I assumed that there were enough books for the beginner, and that a new book dedicated to the more advanced magician was an important addition. After completing all the writing, editing, and preparing it for publication, I sent out samples and cover letters to the various publishers. I later realized by the stack of rejections I received that the publishing world did not agree with my assessment. Since that time, I have come to understand that their point of view was the correct one. I must admit that not publishing it was something of a disappointment to me, but it was also a learning experience since that large work allowed me to write extensively on the topic of ritual magick and clarify my thoughts.

I decided some time afterwards to write a more scaled-down work for the beginner, using some of the same text and approach that made *The Pyramid of Powers* a truly monumental work. That book also had a grimoire of rituals, but allowed for their customization so they would be able to fit into the magickal system developed by the intermediate student. Some of the sections of that work were written so well that I didn't feel it was either constructive or prudent to rewrite them, so I decided to borrow some of the text from those books to expedite the writing of the current work.

My other reason for writing this book is to promote a magickal organization that I and several other individuals started back in 1988. This organization was called the Order of the Gnostic Star, or, more esoterically, the E.S.S.G. (*Egregore Sancta Stella Gnostica*). I have put the first two years of the magickal curriculum of that organization on a website available to anyone who has Internet access. The URL for that web site is www.gnosticstar.org, and that should assist the curious in their quest. I can safely say that the first two years of lore for the E.S.S.G. represents the most simplistic rituals of that organization, concerned with Elemental and Talismanic magick. The next year in the curriculum concerns itself with theurgy, invocation, and the practice of magickal evocation. There is at least a total of seven years of this curriculum currently written. It is my hope to eventually make all that lore available to the public through a combination of publishing and putting material out on the Internet; but for now, the current work and the Order's website will have to suffice.

The structure of this book was created in a very deliberate and methodical manner. The first section of this book concerns itself with the definitions, mechanisms, devices, techniques, and symbology of the ritual magician, laying the groundwork for the second section.

The second section contains the actual practical work of the ritual magician, including the techniques of mental discipline as well as the basic seven rituals that are used to formulate a magickal discipline.

In reading this work, one may notice a certain degree of repetition, and I would like to address that issue. Because this book contains sections from the *Pyramid of Powers* series and has text that I have written exclusively for this book, there might be some redundancy found in the various sections of this work. I hope that the reader will excuse me if a certain point is repeated two or three times in the course of the work, particularly since it won't be repeated in the same manner.

I begin this book with both a keen inspiration and deep dedication for the work and the study of the practicing ritual magician. May you, the reader, and I, the magician, combine our knowledge and experience in this work, making clear and useable what is often obscured by secrecy and superstition, and marred by arrogance and hubris.

—Frater Barrabbas Tiresius
A Disciple of Ritual Magick, Autumn 2006

Part I

THE PHILOSOPHY AND KNOWLEDGE OF MAGICK

CHAPTER ONE

MAGICIANS AND MAGICK IN THE POSTMODERN EPOCH

When I was teenager and attempting to learn the art of ritual magick from the ground up, I believed that there was an existing social organization of magickal practitioners and deep occultists who would one day invite me to be a participating member of their august body. Certainly, when I visited my favorite occult bookstore in Milwaukee, I met many whose knowledge of the occult towered over mine. They might've been members of that secret organization. I imagined that these superior students of the occult were keeping an eye on me and would, in time, recognize my efforts and aid my spiritual and magickal process with the legacy of their greater wisdom.

Except for the four years that I was a member of a particularly high-magick Alexandrian Witch coven, I have found that most occult organizations seem to concentrate on nothing more than a basic level of magickal practice. The small but popular movement that once existed in the 60s and 70s, where people were learning to truly master the art of ritual and ceremonial magick, seems to have evaporated over time. The early seventies were a time when many individuals, including some very brilliant minds, explored the occult sciences with renewed vigor and creative insight, but those times have been superseded by a period of cynicism and mediocrity. Only a handful of the members of organizations such as the A.A., the O.T.O., the new Golden Dawn orders, the O.T.A., various independent practitioners, and a few that are involved in high magick versions of Witchcraft and Neo-Paganism have been faithful to the discipline and practice of ritual magick in the Western Mystery tradition. The majority of Western occultists and followers of the New Age have judged ritual magick to be too arcane, too arduous, or even irrelevant to the practice of an esoteric spirituality. Some, such as New Age Theosophists, have even declared the practice of magick evil and profane.[2] Many adherents of Wicca and Neo-Paganism have dropped any pretense to the serious mastery of ritual magick altogether and either practice a greatly watered-down and ineffectual variety of spell craft, or don't practice magick at all, which is rather odd, considering the supposed pronouncements of the Goddess of Witchcraft to her followers in the Charge of the Goddess. So, the practice of ritual magick in the present time is seriously lacking, if not extinct.[3]

How did this decline occur, why did it occur, and what can be done to reverse it? Perhaps another question should be voiced: "Is ritual magick even relevant to the new millennium?" If ritual magick is in decline, then solid practitioners of magick are also scarce, leaving only the dilettante and the poorly trained as the majority of magicians today. If one were to examine the most recent books on the subject, magick has become either the domain of the pretentious elitist who is more prone to talking and writing about the topic than practicing it, or the rank beginner, since little is shown of actual magickal inquiry and there's nothing that's either new or cutting edge. There are exceptions, of course, but they are few and mostly obscure. The subject matter of books seems to indicate that students are only interested in what has already been documented, rehashing the writings of Aleister Crowley, Israel Regardie, Walter E. Butler, Dion Fortune, Franz Bardon, William Gray, Gareth Knight, Kenneth Grant, Manly P. Hall, and others from those great past generations of path finders and creative occultists. The writers of today can't hold a candle to these luminaries of the twentieth century, and with the exceptions of Nigel Jackson, Peter Carroll, Phil Hine, L. Denning and O. Phillips, "Poke" Runyon, Lon Milo Duquette, Frater U.D., and a

---

2   One need only compare the writings of Elizabeth Clare Prophet with that of Blavatsky or even Alice A. Bailey, where Prophet censures the practice of magick while both Blavatsky and Bailey conditionally accept it. Yet all of these authors make a distinction between white and black magick and appear uneasy about making it an important part of one's spiritual practice.

3   That was my opinion at the time, and it turned out to be quite untrue. I will leave these statements as an artifact of what I thought back then.

number of lesser-known authors, little truly new material has surfaced. Many writers have focused on preserving the traditions of the Golden Dawn and its successors or attempted to rewrite occult history to satisfy their secret agendas. The practice of new and challenging rites has, for the most part, ceased to exist. We are left with the writings of the great luminaries, a few books by some very sharp contemporary writers, and a lot of dreary disciples who have done nothing but restate and repeat what has already been thoroughly examined in past writings.

The question of whether magick is relevant to the new millennium should be tackled, but it wouldn't be justified if one were to examine how magick is practiced by most adherents today. If we define magick as a method of determining one's own process of psychic transformation and spiritual evolution, then it would indeed be relevant in today's world. Such a process of individual spiritual transformation would appear to others that a person had been initiated not by an officiating body or order, but by their own work and accumulated experience. Over time, they would independently evolve wholly and completely from novice to initiate. Ritual magick is the annexation of religious symbols, theologies, and religious rituals and ceremonies for the singular use of the individual, so they can become spiritually self-determined and self-directed. The old orthodox creeds and religious organizations, as well as the old secret orders and their progeny, are no longer adequate organizations to deal with the world as it now exists. What is needed isn't only a new kind of organization (an organization that is not an organization per-se), but also a new definition and practice of ritual magick: one that would affect not only its associated spiritual and magickal philosophies, but also its various rites and ceremonies.

The decline of the practice of ritual magick is the result of mediocrity and a lack of creativity. I might add that few present-day authors seem to be really practicing the art of ritual magick themselves. If they were assiduously practicing their art, they would have found new areas of creative insight and new practical methods for applying their theoretical knowledge instead of rehashing old material. The rituals that are presented in many, but not all, of the latest books on the subject demonstrate a very low level of actual practical knowledge. There is a dearth of complex systems or new types of ritual structures and methodologies. It seems pretty disingenuous if an author presents a completely new way of defining magick and then fails to produce actual ritual methods that are nothing more than a rehashing of rudimentary practices. What we have are some authors who have creatively derived new perspectives on the subject of magick but nothing new in the area of ritual practice and performance, and this would certainly label them as a type of armchair magician who has nothing to add to what is already an aging body of practical lore. This is one of the reasons for the decline of the practice of ritual magick. We are surrounded by mediocrity and the hosts of the preservers of magickal traditions now long out of date.[4]

People's attitudes and habits have also contributed to the decline of magickal lore in our present age. We need only to acknowledge the general decline of literacy (both reading and writing), the never-ending quest for the quickest route to immediate gratification, unwillingness to pursue personal self-discipline, and a complete lack of appreciation for the subtle and the nuanced to be made aware of what's lacking in people to properly practice ritual magick. It shouldn't be too surprising that people are unable to acquire the ability to work magick. All we need to do is to look at the world around us, what with all the incessant activity and distractions. People are trying to live in the ever-growing urban and suburban sprawl with its transportation nightmares, media saturation, and the intrusiveness of hyper-connectivity. Many are also trying to cope with the ultra-stresses of the postmodern world reeling in its political and spiritual bankruptcy. We appear too insensitive and are made seemingly deaf and blind by crass commercialism. The malaise of materialism and its associated cynicism, and the incessant over-trivialization of our values and cultural heritages, has sucked the marrow out of our existence. How can such a seemingly overly sophisticated, desensitized, cynical, and close-minded group of people ever be able to enter the ultra-subtle realms of magick and mysticism? The only answer to this question is that a person must experience a very painful and profound transformation—a powerful shock or jolt—to force them to break from their personal and self-absorbed preoccupations and biased perceptions even for a short time. Such a person would have to really want to experience that kind of drastic change for it to be a possibility. To become a practicing ritual

---

4   Since the time that this was written by me, I have found that the practice of magic in the West has been completely revitalized along a number of different fronts. My opinions were based on what I had seen in the early 1990s without a more intimate engagement with the magical community.

magician requires many years of work, many painful transformations, constant effort, and even some personal sacrifice.

In the United States, there are many who profess to believe in a Deity, and still more believe in a source of evil (Satan), but few have gone beyond the limited sectarian definitions of spirituality to really experience this subtle world with their eyes and minds wide open. To be able to experience magickal and mystical states of consciousness, one must have an open mind and inquiring soul, and not be biased by one's religious prejudices. Ideally, what's required to enter the world of magick is an inner domain or place of peace where a person can get away from the outer world and its distractions. A place within allows a seeker to divest themselves of all the perturbations of our postmodern world so they can sense the deeper nature of consciousness that is illuminated by Spirit. Once this is accomplished, they would then develop a methodology that could manipulate that perception of Spirit to allow the perception of magickal phenomena. A person needs to become disconnected for a brief period from the media frenzy of the world. Within that quiescence, they must reflect on their inner self and on the nature of one's spiritual being. Meditation is the tool to affect this change, but it's only the first stage to this pathway. Much must be done to aid the seeker in learning how to see and experience reality in a completely different way.

When following the regimen for a magickal discipline, there's no quick path to immediate gratification, no silver bullet that answers all questions or a universal panacea that quenches all thirst for knowledge. The valid seeker learns to be patient and practice these various meditation-based exercises for many months—even years—before they will experience the truly profound phenomena of magickal manifestation. This is because, contrary to popular opinion, all spiritual phenomena are very subtle, obscure, symbolic, and indicative of a deep structure embedded in the higher states of consciousness. Such a regimen of practice and the subtlety of the phenomena that underlies it would frustrate most seekers who have neither the time, sensitivity, nor the discipline to make the effort successful. Nonetheless, a seeker who sees the importance and relevancy of such a regimen and makes the time to practice it consistently will ultimately penetrate the mystery of transcendental magickal states of consciousness. A magickal and spiritual discipline is something that takes several years to master. The benefits are slow in coming, but quite profound when they arrive.

The modern magician is a person who not only realizes the importance of the knowledge and practice of ritual magick but also is willing to take the time to actually practice this discipline in a methodical and persistent fashion. They are individuals who obviously have very different priorities than the average person and are willing to undergo the necessary partitioning of their life to make the practice of ritual magick a fundamental focus of their existence. They are willing to forgo some of their social life and material ambitions to have time to study and practice their spiritual vocation. I am not advocating a complete break with the mundane world, but only a partitioning of that world to allow for a space where one's sensitive and subtle inner perceptions are allowed to manifest. The partitioning of one's life into areas for practical occultism and other areas that allow one to exist in this world (job, family, social life) is neither impossible nor harmful. In fact, it allows one to be more focused on the vicissitudes of life and find a better means to cope with change than any other method. One always has a place of peace and strength to retreat to emotionally heal, scrutinize, self-examine, and resolve life's challenges. However, it takes time to develop this internal partitioning. One isn't always poised or capable of dealing with stress in a state of disconnectedness in the beginning of the study of magick. Life can (and does) interfere with the student's progress, and the student must always make a huge effort not to allow crisis or calamity to deflect the daily, weekly, monthly, and yearly efforts for spiritual transformation. The spiritual and magickal discipline becomes the ultimate refuge from the madness and meaninglessness of our world, but it takes time to build this refuge and equip it with all that we need to continue to grow and evolve as spiritual and magical people living in a world ruled by science and secularism.

The practice of magick is a process that fuels itself and assists the magician to grow and discover new magickal and mystical lore about themselves and the world that they live in. A magickal practice is not static; it's highly dynamic. The magician works rituals that give them certain information and insights, allowing for creative speculation and the ultimate production of new rituals which, when performed, produce new insights and additional information. The quest for knowledge is the primary quest for the ritual magician, aside from the usual rites for health, wealth, and good fortune. The magician learns that their world is not made any easier using magick. In fact, it becomes a decidedly more complex and nuanced world, and the magician must learn to balance the reality of magick with the needs and responsibilities of their mundane life. A life made by magick is one that is more difficult to live, since the magician must maintain that place of perfect peace where the magick is produced while living a normal mundane existence with all of its stresses and inherent difficulties. Also, there's no great reward for the practicing magician, since neither riches nor fame are theirs for the taking; rather, they must find a greater inner satisfaction with their lot, having perceived the vistas of the great chasms and heights of the spiritual dimension, and articulated its reality to others. The magician is the high-tech Shaman of the twenty-first century, and in the not-so-distant future, the populations at large will become aware of their wisdom and deep insights, as well as their ingenuity in determining new spiritual perspectives that are helpful and necessary to the postmodern world. Such a person, if inspired to produce video images and music of their experiences, would be considered a media magician, since they would have forged their visions so that all would be able to view them.[5] The magician's ultra-creativity would make them able to fashion an endless variety of visions and insights, since that is exactly what ritual magick produces over time.

What is this *practice of ritual magick,* and how does that practice work? I have stated that someone who is practicing ritual magick would not only master their art and craft, but would also use a great deal of creativity to fashion new rites and occult lore. The magician works magick on a periodic cycle and performs magickal workings using the diurnal cycles of day and night, the cycles of the Moon and Sun. Through trance and empowered altered states of consciousness, they will immerse themselves into the magickal and mythical domain of Spirit. The periodic and consistent contact with that other world will profoundly alter and change their entire mode of being. They will have dreams, visions, and insights; converse with angels, daemons, gods and goddesses, and other spirits; and directly experience various domains within that World of Spirit. All these experiences will add to their knowledge and lore. They will not only learn about the world they live in, their path and destiny, and the destiny of the world during their time, but will also learn how to build better rituals and add new rites

---

5   While I saw this as a prophetic insight, it has yet to materialize twenty years later. I think it is more hypothetical than prophetic.

and ceremonies to their growing repertoire. Over time, they will fashion their own grimoire or workbook of rituals and workings and will possess a journal filled with the accounts of their amazing inner journey. They will have to make sense of it all, and so will also try to explain and understand the deeper nature of their magickal experiences. This will reveal even more of their greater world and their place within it. The path of magick is a glorious and fantastic one.

You might ask the question, "how does the author know these things about the practice and discipline of ritual magick?" Or perhaps even think, "who is this person to make these kinds of judgments?" I would reply that I am an experienced practitioner of this art, and I have faithfully and consistently practiced it for over thirty-five years. I have not plumbed its greatest depths and there is much more for me to experience and learn, even though I have practiced it for so many years. One could say that I am a product of my time, for I grew up in the 60s and 70s and adopted many of the trends and fads. But since that time, I have built up my knowledge and experience, taking this study and discipline far beyond the trendy fad that it appeared to be back then and seeing it mature into a deep and profound spiritual practice, one that has a timeless relevance and infinite scope.

Back in the early seventies, there were many—including myself—who sought out the path of magick, the Qabalah, astrology, Tarot, and various other obscure occult practices. Many books were written and published at that time to fulfill the exploding need for information. Some of these books were good, but most were just the same kind of superficial beginner's books that you still see on the bookshelves today. The classic books on magick were also being reprinted, and my comrades and I bought them all, read and studied them, and tried to make the practices work. Not all endeavors were rewarded with success, of course, and we had to continue our search and deepen our studies to develop the wisdom to distinguish the truth from fantasy or outright falsehood. Those of us who persevered discovered that it required a really serious commitment that went far beyond the hyped values and superficial motives of that time.

Those who continued found the great truths and profound visions that we believed were there, hidden by the trendy hype, slogans, and overly commercialized sound bites produced by the colorful self-appointed gurus of the time. That hype was like a smoke screen or a veil of disinformation that had to be pierced for one to realize the true value of a spiritual and magickal path. So many succumbed to the fantasy of the path of magick, not realizing how serious it actually was, but a few recognized the truths and realities behind and beyond that insipid dream and managed to produce their own spiritual and magickal disciplines. These new spiritual and magickal disciplines weren't entirely unique, since they were based on what was known and done in the recent past, but they were also fully vetted and useable, based on real experiences and practical knowledge.

Now, over fifty years later in the twenty-first century, those of us who maintained our path have discovered the enormous importance and value of the spiritual and magickal disciplines that we forged decades ago. We seem to have something important to share with others in this turbulent and directionless era. Perhaps simply by enduring the vicissitudes of those times, we've become the very masters and spiritual teachers that we've been seeking all these years. The irony of this fact does not escape me. I've written this book and a great deal of other documentation so others may discover—or even rediscover—what never faded nor failed for me and a few others. Ritual magick is a real and living tradition in this darkening postmodern age, and it supplies the seekers with the answers to combat the spiritual wasteland of this time. Ritual magick is the answer for all the unanswered questions facing the Western-based spiritual systems. We are in a crisis moment regarding faith and spiritual convictions. Yet ritual magic can be applied to any metaphysical system in the West, as long as it's based on esoteric principles and steeped in occultism. Other religious methodologies (most notably any form of orthodoxy) are completely incompatible with the tenets and practices of ritual magick.

The study and practice of ritual magick constantly produces new lore and techniques from the old lore. Magick is, by its nature, a heterodoxy, for it appropriates all the magickal and religious lore from the previous ages and synthesizes them into a new form and methodology, expressly tailored to the individual practitioner. It's a spiritual discipline that is the very essence of creativity, for it follows no creed nor obeys any dogma and allows the seeker to fully determine the nature of their inner self and the domain of the World of Spirit.

Ritual magick will never be a trendy alternative for the bored dilettante, just as the other serious paths are not for the superficial seeker. Yet it is my hope that people will get tired of the hype, sound bites, and media pandering of packaged spirituality, and begin to really start asking questions about fate, destiny, death, and the meaning of life, perhaps becoming interested in knowing the real answers to these questions. Orthodox religions can't answer these questions for the individual, even if they pretend otherwise. It's up to the esoteric paths to provide for this need, made so acute by the overall transformation of human consciousness that is now taking place in the world. The discipline of ritual magick is the best approach for the "psycho-spiritual voyager" of the new age of spirituality. The techniques are always changing, evolving, and growing, and represent the expanding awareness of the operator themselves. Acquiring ritual magick as the driver of one's spirituality represents the decline of organized religion and the death of orthodoxy.

The world is becoming ever-smaller and less homogenous. High technology and the omnipresent media are drivers of this cultural syncretism. As a result, we live in a world that is ever more pluralistic and heterogenous, where various cultural traditions (old and new) are available for consumption. This will cause the breakdown of the boundaries of all traditions, cultures, and even identities, allowing for the mixture of old and new ideas that will produce powerful media driven trends. We will become citizens of the world, and national identities will become unimportant. Global economies, audiences, consumer practices, and interests will become so varied and individuated that it will be impossible to have a specific definable source. Certainly, historical traditions in various cultures will always be observed and preserved, but they will be the quaint and rich artistic expressions of a mature world culture, and they will not have the power to divide people and cause the calamities of hate, murder, and war. This is our destiny in the not-so-distant future, and it represents the changes that have been unleashed by a number of factors, which I mentioned above.[6]

In the meantime, the world is consumed by its obsession with the preservation of traditional values, and the fear and paranoia associated with rapid and uncontrollable change. We will either implode into sectarian, cultural, and racial anarchy, or we will progress painfully and fitfully—but unavoidably—into a better world. The choice will be determined at an individual level, but ultimately realized at the global

---

6   We can see this happening today, nearly twenty years later. However, there is also a prevalence of misinformation and partitioning that is polarizing our society today.

level. The individual has more power to change the world than they might realize, since if enough people believe that they have that power and use it, the world changes. The syncretism and the spiritual heterodoxy of ritual magick represent the wave of the future. As a method of integral spirituality, it represents one of a host of holistic approaches to living and functioning in the new age century. But this can only occur if the people of this planet have a chance to make this determination, and do not succumb to fear, anarchy, isolation, and total destruction.

The world as it exists today is nothing less than an object lesson about what must be changed in all of humanity if we are to embrace our future and fully develop our potential as a species and a global culture. All our world's seemingly irresolvable problems become resolvable if—and only if—we approach the world and its issues with an open mind, unlimited optimism, patience, and a desire for justice and equality. Certainly selfishness, divisiveness, and self-absorption have caused most of the ills plaguing the world today. Adopting positive alternatives to these negative pursuits will allow the world to grow so that attitudes like selflessness, inclusiveness, and global awareness reach beyond the petty self and its persistent needs. The realization that everything we do today as individuals influences global culture as a whole will heal our species in a wondrous and almost miraculous manner. Such a realization of how we must change as individuals was unthinkable even fifty years ago but is now mandatory—such is the changed world we live in today.

If a person sought to enter the world of the practicing magician, how would they proceed? Where are the sources of information and methodologies from which to obtain the beginning knowledge necessary for these first steps? How do we judge what is true regarding this arcane subject when we do not even know much about the subject in the first place? Who can be our guide, teacher, and confidant, if the time for gurus and teachers is seemingly past? Who can we trust in this time of suspicion and darkness? Ultimately, we can only trust ourselves and our own intuition, and we must believe in ourselves enough to at least make some kind of beginning step. However, I believe that we can review what is generally known about magick from various literary sources and I can share in the knowledge gleaned from the many years of personal practice that I have gathered together.

I share this knowledge not to determine the only way to approach this discipline, but to illustrate one of several ways to acquire it. I don't make any claims other than that I'm a practitioner of ritual magick, and that all my claims should be examined in the light of objectivity and truth. To prove or disprove my points, one must be willing to test the instrumental injunctions that are given, perform the rituals in the manner directed, and determine their value for oneself. This is all that I ask of students: try the rituals and methodologies and see for yourself if they work as advertised. Experimentation is the only method that a true magician may use to determine validity in the world of spiritual experiences. Nothing can be taken for granted unless it can be experienced in some fashion. The test is always in the fashion of, "can it work for me? How can I incorporate it into my practices? And how I can share that information with other people?" Some ideals can't be tested, so their merit is either determined as being of a possible future value or discarded as irrelevant.

Determined seekers using this methodology won't fail, since they will be building up their knowledge over time. Eventually, they will be able to approach and determine even the most fundamental questions about life, such as the meaning of life, individual destiny, and even the significance of death, the immortality of the spirit, illumination, enlightenment, and the possibility of union with the Deity. These questions will be determined by experience and personal knowledge, and the answers will be unassailable and of great value to the individual. Since human spirituality is common to all human beings, the answers will not be so subjective and individual to the point that they don't apply to humanity as a whole. There will be ample common ground for individual seekers to gather, perform, and practice their magick in ever larger groups and associations.

What will be of greatest value will be the methods and techniques that such creative endeavors will produce, as opposed to the visions and vistas that they'll grant their practitioners. An example is the book *Vision and the Voice* by Aleister Crowley. While the reader is amazed by the complexity of all the visions experienced and written down through the invocation of each of the thirty Enochian Aethyrs, after reading several of them, the book seems to be less relevant to the reader than to the author who wrote it. It's far better for an occultist or magician to write up how they did their magick and let their readers perform the rituals and see what results occur. When magicians work magick and gain the illuminating results as visions and insights, they end up developing their own theosophies and occult perspectives from them. These many occult perspectives tend to revolve around the magician's personalized versions of the common mythopoetic and metaphysical themes, analogous to those found in the world religions of the past and present. While the visions themselves won't be particularly important, such work performed by a large mass of individuals will herald a major shift in world consciousness, where as part of a group, the average individual will approach and begin to apprehend the subtle and causal levels of consciousness, perhaps for the first time in history.

CHAPTER TWO

THE OFFERINGS OF NEO-SORCERY: RITUAL MAGICK FOR THE NEW AGE

We seek to define the nature of magick so we can understand and harness it. This is accomplished by stating premises about magick and elaborating on them.

The first premise of magick is that things in and of themselves have no intrinsic meaning or value, and that human beings create all the meaning and value that exists in the world. Humanity collectively controls all information that is believed in and acted upon. I must also stress that the creation of meaning is a profoundly creative process that everyone participates in, whether they realize it or not. Most values and definitions of reality are determined by our culture and aren't usually redefined by the average individual, who often accepts them without question.

The second premise is that the phenomena of magick is caused by an intrusion of the higher states of consciousness associated with Spirit into our normal conscious mind. The resultant field of conscious noumena is controlled or manipulated with a combination of specialized mind-states, such as trance, and various artifacts or fetishes, such as magickal tools and devices (like talismans and amulets). The source of all magickal phenomena comes from the human dimension of Spirit, and it is experienced as the various associated higher states of consciousness that emanate from that domain (psychic, subtle, and causal).

The third premise is that magickal states of consciousness are triggered by symbols of psychic transformation, so individuals who learn to master the techniques of producing these phenomena must first learn to creatively use these symbols as mind altering tools. Whatever way magick is practiced, it involves being exposed to the higher conscious states of the magician's spirit. This exposure, over time, will cause permanent changes in the practitioner, regardless of whether it is unconsciously or deliberately pursued.

The fourth premise is that the ultimate goal of all magick is union with the Absolute Spirit, whether the practitioner realizes this truth or not. The magician who is only interested in manipulating reality with their magickal rites will unknowingly be incrementally transformed over time until they suddenly realize a profound change. A magician who actively seeks union with the Deity will realize it sooner, and this will add a profoundly spiritual dimension to their magick.

The fifth premise is that the practice of magick is an integral spiritual discipline, which means that the student takes a holistic approach to its study, leaving no stone unturned and crossing numerous disciplines of both the soft and hard sciences, as well as the occult sciences. Magick also assists the student in the quest for self-realization and self-determination.

The first premise is probably harder to understand than the other four, so I will attempt to substantiate it below with several examples and a deeper analysis. Once this premise is fully realized, then the others naturally follow, and we can then operationally define magick in a very narrow sense.

The social and institutional world that we live in has been adapted to be secular and purged of all religious sentiments, except those that are most general to all faiths, particularly those of the West. As a sign of this secularism, even mainstream church organizations—such as the Protestant Methodists, Presbyterians, Congregationalists, Lutherans, Anglicans, and American Catholics—have lost their spiritual intensity and become social institutions that shepherd their followers through the sterile wastelands of an uneventful, productive, indulgent, mediocre, and boringly happy life. Such a secular mindset recognizes and deals with only the outer vicissitudes of life, and only then as social and political issues. The greater questions of spiritual significance are patiently ignored and omitted, since they are considered the domains of the abnormal and maladjusted. From cradle to grave, the world has superficially become quietly deprived of all myth and mysticism, made seemingly safe and shallow by the tenets of secular scientism, while the gyrations and eruptions of pop culture, civil unrest, and the violence of nature are depicted as aberrations or meaningless tragedies that terribly end peaceful and productive lives. However, this secular explanation of everything as an impersonal factor of statistics is disheartening to anyone who is seeking meaning and direction in their life. Secularism seems to attempt to quietly strangle the passion and vibrancy out of life. On the other hand, religious fanatics believe that everything is the affair of God Almighty, and even natural disasters are some kinds of moral punishment or judgment. The real truth, of course, is a path charted between the secularists and the religious fanatics.

A rational perspective of both the outer world and the inner world would state that the vast material universe consists of inchoate matter that is soullessly participating in the manifestation of physical laws from a Microcosmic to a Macrocosmic level. As human creatures with the synergetic phenomena of mind and spirit, we must perceive the world as determined by teleology, meaningfulness, and personal destiny. To see the world as meaningless and determined wholly by chance is to see a world without hope, compassion, direction, or understanding. Such a world view would cause anyone to lose their reason, to succumb to depression and despair. However, to see a world where every single event is determined by God is to adopt a medieval mythic worldview, just as problematic as the one ruled by empirical science. Both perspectives are correct, and both are incorrect. The occultist, whose inclination is to examine the deeper nature of things, determines that the correct perspective is that we create meaning and significance out of fictional interpretations, fabricating our reality and giving it a plot, a moral lesson, and heroes and villains. This is our essential nature as human beings, who must perceive and embrace both a personal and intimate encounter with the physical world and the domain of Spirit. We perceive meaning and divine intervention where it is relevant to us, knowing that it is purely our subjective perception and understanding, and accepting that as a fundamental truth. The Deity is not dead to matter or human intellect, but the Deity doesn't determine everything that occurs in the world. We make this determination ourselves, and so we function as a gateway for spirit and matter to interact with each other. This is a rational and metaphysical perspective, and one that plots a middle course between the philosophical tenets of religion and the mathematical theories of science.

When a fundamentalist preacher rants from their pulpit that an earthquake, tsunami, hurricane or tornado, volcanic eruption, drought, flood, pestilence, or plague are the direct effect of an angry and vengeful God, punishing humanity (and the world) for its iniquities, we must reject such logic out of hand. Does it make sense to perceive the hand of the Absolute Spirit in what are, after all, the varied phenomena of nature? An earthquake occurs as the result of jolting tectonic plates releasing pent up pressure in a manifestation of geological force. Such phenomena are soulless physical occurrences that have no meaning other than what we apply to them. We create meaning, but that meaning can't be perceived as an absolute truth. It can only be perceived as a personal and relative truth, albeit one that can be shared with other people. Such manifestations of nature can't be judged as evil manifestations of a supernatural intelligence, so we must adopt a rational perspective when examining religious propaganda.

The centennial influenza epidemic is a disease that is a cross-species virus that happens once every hundred years or so, with devastating results. The last occurrence of this pandemic in 1919 was not judged by historians to be a scourge sent by God, but many who lived through it would make a connection between the end of a brutal world war pursued with soulless zeal by humanity gone mad and the manifestation of a natural pestilence, set to kill millions more as a kind of divine retribution.[7] No wonder the following decade saw the chaotic intermingling of conservative religious fervor, right-wing fascism, and liberal anarchy. The madness of that period was attributed to the terrible horror and loss of life in the great war of the previous decade, as if piety, racial purity, or excessive consumption would erase it from the consciousness of the world. As a note, we are soon to be revisited by this pandemic and the state of our morals or piety will not stop it from occurring. Rather, it will be our medical prowess that will save the day. It will be interesting to see what is made of such a scourge in the twenty-first century if we fail to contain and eliminate it with our science. We have already seen the religious pundits make an issue out of AIDS, attributing it to God's punishment of homosexuals.

---

7   Of course, I wrote this before the COVID-19 epidemic hit the world in 2020. It was a modern pandemic, but it had a similar effect as the 1919 version, with the same social issues and government failure to correctly identify and then to allow medical science to effectively resolve it.

The disease cited above is a natural phenomenon that is not controlled by a supernatural agency but represents the possible manifestation of a viral world that is only now becoming understood. Yet, religious pundits will say all sorts of things to passionately paint the world with an overly simple palette, one that has a very religious and personalized bias and is very attractive to many people. These religious pundits are, in a sense, lying to all of us and themselves, and committing an egregious hypocrisy. Their perceptions are valid and represent the truth as they see it, but their beliefs aren't to be confused with objective physical facts. So instead of feeling guilty and wondering if perhaps the preachers are correct and God is pissed off at humanity, we can realize that we create all meaning in the world. We individually and collectively create the answers to the questions about why and wherefore regarding our experiences of life.

However, even if a lot of people share the same belief (such as "the Earth is flat" or "the Sun revolves around the Earth"), it doesn't make it an objective fact. This is especially true if it's related to human sentiment and personal values (i.e., religious, political, and cultural values). To science, there's no good or evil; there are only objective facts without any personal values. That's the real world, and we mustn't confuse our powerful experiences in life with any kind of absolute value or objective truth. With that being said, we can cease trying to determine or somehow verify the absolute value or truth of our beliefs. We can, instead, focus on the beautiful, creative process of making and applying meaning and personal significance in our lives. As we perform this task, we should always know that the progressive things that we create about ourselves and the world that we live in will aid us in our quest for self-fulfillment, but they aren't the same as absolute truths. Let us beware of that folly!

In summary, we are the great creators of all meaningfulness in the world. This becomes obvious when one uses a rational and occult perspective, seeing and agreeing with the truth of objective reality as determined by science and also accepting the subjective truths that are found within the deeper mind and the greater spirit of each human being. To us, then, there is good and evil operating in the world, and we color this world with our values and beliefs. The clever occultist knows that it's a creative process and doesn't confuse sentiments and beliefs with cold, objective facts. The world becomes more realistic when one keeps this perspective in mind, but it also doesn't become empty of sentiment and subjective values, which are vitally important to human nature. The magician knows this fact and uses it to create a powerful magick in their world.

Even if the world around us is void of meaning and hazardous in its chaotic and probabilistic manifestations, we at least can feel secure in our beliefs and faith in ourselves, however at odds with the forces of the world this might seem. We can believe that we will adapt and ultimately thrive, despite the gloomy projections and statistics that appear to indicate otherwise. From a personal perspective, the Deities light torches to show us the way through the labyrinthine maze of the myriad vicissitudes of life. From the perspective of science, we foolishly and daringly pit ourselves against insurmountable forces that rend the world and victimize humanity. What drives this folly of daring and madness is the magick of our own personal myths and the perception of our lives' meaningfulness against all probability. The real truth is that we're all heroes and heroines of our own mythic comedy and tragedy. To discover this reality is to take the first step into the world of the magician.

If we create our own personal meaning and share this creation with others, then we have the power to determine the meaning and significance of whatever we experience. If others agree with our magickal visions, created myths, and derived beliefs, then we have begun to objectify them to some extent and will realize them as part of the manifestation of our full potential self. If we create delusions or believe in lies, then others will judge us as deluded or false. There is a balance between what we can experience and determine as meaningful and between what we experience and what we can share with others. Truth is experienced within a subjective field but is measured through peer review and how our spiritual perceptions translate into intelligible and rational dialogues.

For instance, we can have a magickal experience where an entity tells us that we are the Deity, and we may internally affirm this to be a great truth, but we'd be wise to translate it rationally into the greater truth that all human beings, and perhaps even all things, are God, and that our experience is not exclusive to ourselves but universal to all. A foolish interpretation of such an experience would be to take it all literally and selfishly, believing that the experience somehow conferred an exclusive godhood on oneself. Sharing such a revelation with other magick users would quickly show the error of this kind of thinking, or the madness of it if one persisted in believing it even after it was rejected by one's peers. Truth may be subjective and relative to the ritual magician, but it's not exclusively so; there are universal truths and mechanisms for determining objective truth. These mechanisms of determining objectivity are similar to those used by scientists and must be used extensively by the magician to avoid erroneous assumptions and foolish ego-based exaggerations. (We'll cover the nature of these mechanisms later in this book.) The folly of arrogant pride and self-delusion is not exclusive to the magician, but seems to be more obvious, ludicrous, and tragic to outsiders than the usual personal excesses and flaws one finds in the seeker.

The occultist and ritual magician is one who takes full responsibility for the creation of personal significance and meaningfulness and even delights in the artful creations, experimentations, and personal embellishments. The magician creates personal meaning in a culture that has none, but instead of living in a mythic world of delusions where subjective values are taken as objective facts, they live in a world where science and religion have beautifully and harmoniously defined their own interrelated spheres and the transcendent aspects of life reside peacefully with the mundane and the scientific. It is a place where subjectivity doesn't attempt to invade objectivity, and objectivity doesn't invalidate the subjective. It is a middle course between extremes and is more relevant today than at any other time in the history of humanity. Our social and religious institutions have violated this careful balance between subjectivity and objectivity, so they're no longer able to assist the individual in creating personal meaning and significance. The discipline of magick offers the ability to create personal meaning and significance, to determine one's destiny and understand one's past. This claim must be examined so we may realize how important magick is to us in this new millennium and begin to define the nature of ritual magick (how it works and how it is used). Magick gives its practitioners the ability to evolve and grow their conscious minds, grasp the world through the transcendent perspective of Spirit, and ultimately discover conscious union with the Deity, enlightenment, and complete self-mastery.

The practice of ritual magick, as it's defined in this book, represents the cutting edge of spiritual experimentation, since it delineates the frontier of spiritual research in the Western Mystery tradition and can be approached as an integral study that assists the student in the quest for self-realization and self-determination. Magick is accessible to those living in the Western world, particularly those who espouse an occult and esoteric perspective within their spiritual and religious traditions.

Magick is not merely a mechanism for applying one's will to achieve results in the world, for it also includes a spiritual perspective and religious practices and is deeply involved in the realization of spirit in the material world. Some individuals practice magick as a means to an end, seeking to make things happen in the world without apparent overt actions, but I believe that such a perspective does little credit to the integral approach to life that magick fosters in the practitioner. I believe that the practice of magick is a holistic exercise and, therefore, merely acquiring a good life and all that denotes (self-mastery) is neither the chief nor only objective of the practicing ritual magician. I will define these other objectives later in this book, but clearly the principal objective must be some kind of evolution of consciousness.

In Aleister Crowley's book *Magick in Theory and Practice*, he defines magick as "the science and art of causing change to occur in conformity with will."[8] While I accept this statement as truth in the widest definition, I feel that it's too general. It includes many things that are not properly defined as magick. Crowley appears to be interested in broadening his definition so that magick seems to be a part of nearly every human volition. This does little to assist the student in understanding the true nature of magick.

Magick usually operates within a context of sacred symbology or through the agency of specialized mind-states (trance) and can be aided through the use of various devices, such as specialized tools, fetishes, spirits, gods, psychic energies, and techniques of transformative psychology. Magick makes things happen in the physical world according to the will or desire (intent) of the practitioner, but it does not obey any kind of rigid cause and effect rules. In fact, magick appears to be beyond all forms of causality, displaying a paradoxical trans-temporal quality that is analogous to very high states of consciousness. Magick seems to operate as a kind of super-linguistic phenomenon, generating connections and intensifying meaning where no such connections or meaning are possible. Magick, when it's used to specifically satisfy a need, operates on what is possible in the targeted intention, although

---

8   Crowley, Aleister, *Magick in Theory and Practice* (Castle Books, 1991) p. xii.

that intention may not necessarily be probable without the extra focus and significance it receives through the magickal process.

The term *magick* isn't to be confused with states of mind that are pre-rational or pre-personal as it's used in modern psychology. That type of "magic" is seen as an early childhood developmental stage where there's a confusion of image and object, thought and the perception of reality; where the world seems to actively take part in the projection of the ego, and where the concept of *other* than self doesn't yet exist.[9] This is a mind-state associated with young children around two years old, and isn't to be confused with the trans-personal and trans-rational states associated with magick. This is the reason that we seek to differentiate the spelling of magick, referring to it as *transcendental magic* when using the normal spelling.

Magick is a process where the transformative powers of our higher consciousness are stimulated and awakened, so that they impact the focus of our mundane mind. This amplifying and energizing our desires and intentions are at the heart of the magickal operation, causing transcendental and trans-rational phenomena to occur in a manner that would be classified as paranormal or even supernatural. Magick is an oblique application of the abilities of the self as it exists purely within the domain of Spirit, whether any kind of entity or spirit is used in the operation. There are certain symbols, mind states, and mythic constructs that seem to stimulate our usually dormant higher conscious mind. These are the symbols of transformation that Carl Jung referred to (but didn't elaborate upon) in his theories of consciousness. These symbols seem archaic only because they represent timeless triggers that bring about an immersion of transcendental consciousness necessary to a successful magickal operation. These symbols were first established and used publicly, for the supposed benefit of all, by organized religion, but were known about and used as part of the secret teaching and lore of the earliest spiritual technicians, Shamans. Shamanism discovered these symbols of transformation for its own purposes, but organized religion harnessed them to manipulate the masses. However, these symbols have always been a part of the repertoire or methodology of gaining a personal vista of the domain of Spirit, even though they have been disguised and embedded in the

---

9   Wilber, Ken, *A Sociable God: Toward a New Understanding of Religion* (Shambhala Press, 2005) p. 70–71.

religious symbols used around the world; in our postmodern times, their usefulness has been rediscovered by various groups and individuals for mystical and magickal uses.

The method of stimulating higher consciousness through the use of symbolic triggers represents a kind of language that's only intelligible at the deep structure of our conscious being (Spirit). That language, its use, and the transcendental effects that it produces are what I define as *the operation of magick*. These symbolic triggers can be accidentally discovered or deliberately utilized by any individual experimenting with occult techniques and practices. They represent latent qualities that all human beings share equally. Those individuals who are sensitive and able to perceive subtle nuances in their conscious modes of being are more capable of deliberately manipulating and controlling these symbolic triggers, which seems to be the only requirement. Yet all these symbolic triggers represent various expressions of our timeless perception of Spirit. They resonate as a kind of mytho-poetry describing the paradoxical and inexplicable. The mere consideration of these paradoxical concepts or events brings about the feeling of awe and a sense of the paranormal other, and we either shudder and quickly think about something else, or we unwittingly invite those sensations and perceptions of that world and enter a psychic space that is the place of mysticism and transcendental magic. We're taught to not allow ourselves to contemplate such things and to retain our rational self-control at all costs, but in doing so, we keep away an important trans-rationality that could cause us to really change and spiritually grow.

To make complete sense of these statements, we must consider the nature of the human mind and how it works. Conscious awareness can be divided into three states that relate to the body, mind, and spirit, although this is a gross oversimplification. Each of these three states represents a hierarchy of conscious awareness, where the mind is a higher order state than the body and the spirit is a higher order state than the mind. Each of these states has its own method of perception, so one could say that there's an eye of flesh, an eye of mind, and an eye of spirit. The three eyes symbolize that these modes of perception are grounded in three different states of awareness. The eye of flesh represents the pure, unbiased, and unedited perception and experience of matter as processed through the body. The eye of mind represents all the activity associated with the mind, which includes processing the eye of flesh's sensory data, as well as the mind regarding itself, which would represent pure abstractions such as the generalizations of values, beliefs, opinions, rules, law, philosophy, and mathematics—all of the sciences, hard and soft. The mind is a higher order state than the body and matter, so it can make assumptions and theories about that domain which seem well-grounded in the rational exponent of our collective existence. However, in the matter concerning spirit, the mind has a harder time making any sense out of it. This is because the spirit is a higher order state than the mind and cannot be reduced to mental models or theories, nor perceived through one's ordinary sensory organs. There's a manner in which the spirit may be perceived, but it doesn't involve the rational mind. When the mind attempts to describe the domain of Spirit, it can only do so by negation (describing what it is not) or by paradoxical analogy, which is nearly useless. Only symbols embedded in the domain of Spirit seem to be able to act as signposts of the mind, indicating some level of meaning and inviting us to contemplate them, but attempts at placing values on them always comes up short.

The reason that the domain of Spirit can't be grasped by the mind or sensed by the body is because it represents a state that is trans-personal, trans-rational, trans-temporal, and seemingly beyond the normal considerations for space and time, causality, and even identity. The mechanisms that allow the individual to perceive the domain of Spirit are embedded in practices such as deep meditation, contemplation, and its associated techniques of focusing on an ideal or nothing, rituals and ceremonies that use religious or occult symbols, and deep trance states. Individuals can use the adoption of altered states of consciousness, but somehow these states by themselves don't automatically engage spiritual consciousness, which is why the symbolic triggers are used. The combination of symbols and altered states of consciousness, used together, produce an influx of higher states of consciousness into the plane of normal consciousness, causing it to be momentarily transformed and, at times, inducing a state of internalized ecstasy. We can determine if such a hyper-normal state of consciousness has been achieved by the effect that it produces: a normal event or occurrence suddenly becomes transported and profoundly impacts the mind. Such occurrences are perceived as paranormal or as deeply moving, meaningful occurrences, representative of a major life event. All people have these experiences at certain points in their lives, even if they aren't deliberately sought, and they may be accompanied by insights and life-altering realizations. Organized religion has learned to use these kinds of events as a means to produce controlled manifestations of Spirit within a social venue, so that their adherents can base the validity of their faith on an experience. However, individuals also have the means to produce these phenomena for themselves outside of religious organizations, and they can deliberately use them to produce personal meaning and significance. These practices and methodologies, when used by the individual, represent the backbone for the techniques and mechanisms of ritual and ceremonial magick.

We exist in a world that is bounded by normal consciousness, and we should understand that this is the beginning state required for spiritual studies. The normal adult who is not suffering from any pronounced regressive tendencies or pathological behavior is functioning at a level that psychologists refer to as *formal operational* or *Mental-Egoic*,[10] typified by self-reflexive thought, introspection, the ability to think about thought itself (metacognition), and the ability to change perspectives and see another person's point of view. It's also engaged in cooperative group ambitions, motivating people to seek self-regard within their social group, and generally behaving in a rational, conventional, and conscientious manner. All people share in this state of mental development once they arrive at adulthood, unless adversely affected by physical or mental disabilities. This is the foundation where all occult training and teaching begins. According to modern psychologists, this state of consciousness represents the highest level that may be attained.

Yet, contrary to modern psychology and its theories, many Shamanic practitioners, religious mystics, and occultists from all geographic locations and receding far into the Paleolithic past have shown that there are higher states of consciousness than what is normally experienced in the foundational level of Mental-Egoic. These higher states have been documented and elaborated upon for many centuries—most notably by Hindu and Buddhist philosophers and mystics—but all systems agree that these states can be divided into three basic levels: the psychic, subtle, and causal levels of consciousness. All these levels occupy the domain of consciousness referred to as Spirit. The psychic, subtle, and causal levels

---

10 The term "Mental-Egoic" represents what psychologists refer to as the mind directed by the ego or identity.

are the higher states of consciousness that we've referred to above. They cause all the paranormal phenomena associated with religious practices, individual meditative and magickal operations, and personal revelations. An examination of these states will undoubtedly reveal the different levels of phenomena that one encounters when Spirit intervenes into normal consciousness. Most individuals experience the lowest, which is the psychic level of consciousness, when encountering their spiritual self. This is particularly true for accidental or purely exoteric religious encounters. Still others can deliberately cause the higher levels of subtle and causal spiritual consciousness to enter into their normal conscious minds, altering their realizations, perceptions, and experiences of reality. Over time, these experiences can even permanently change the individual. Since these higher states are shown to be trans-personal, trans-rational, and trans-temporal, they can't be considered regressive but represent our legacy for further conscious development beyond normality.

We've referred above to symbols of transformation. These must be covered to further develop our theory of magick. There are six basic symbols of transformation, and all other symbols are derived from them. They represent the various aspects of the effects of Spirit upon normal consciousness. These six symbols are the *point, line, circle, triangle, cross*, and *star*.

The point represents an event, position, definition, and quality of self.

The line represents a relationship between self and other and is defined as the conduit that exists between heaven and earth, or the place of spirit and the place of matter. The line connects as well as divides two things, and it can have a pointer at either end—or even both—denoting direction as well.

The circle symbolizes a domain (a world), and a point within a circle symbolizes our place or location within that domain or world. There are two spaces delineated by the circle: the inner space (that which is within the circumference of the circle) and the outer space (that which is outside of the circumference of the circle).

The triangle is a symbol of the nature of spirit, which represents the fusion of self and other, creating a new being, which is their union. The triangle is also a gateway, since a pathway is defined as the reconciliation of opposites, creating a third and alternative way. It's also the definition of a plane (three points) and a symbol of the three dimensions for objects that exist in space.

The cross represents the intersection of two lines, and so divides space into four quadrants, symbolized by the qualities of the four Elements, the four directions, and the four seasons. The cross symbolizes the joining of heaven and earth, feminine and masculine, and light and darkness to produce the manifestation of earth and all that it contains. The cross, like the triangle, can assume many variations that augment and extend its basic meaning and effect. The cross and triangle are used extensively in religious iconography, both in the East and the West.

The star is a symbol of transformation itself, wherein the self is opened up like a flower to behold the full awareness of Spirit in Self. The star assumes many forms, and each one has its own symbolic qualities. Examples of the star are the pentagram, hexagram, septagram, octagram, enneagram, decagram, undecigram, and the duodecagram. There are numerous others, but once a star has more than ten points, it becomes less distinguishable and, therefore, less significant.

In addition to the above six symbols, there can also be colors that possess an intrinsic magical significance, although most colors have a powerful cultural significance, especially if they are perceived as brilliant hues or vibrating patterns of light that are unique and startling to the eye. There can also be sounds, but these would be unique, profound, beauteous, and ecstatic sounds, like the chorus of angels or the celestial music of the spheres. There would be scents, too. They would be like the most exotic, intoxicating, and wondrous perfumes that had ever been smelled; like the rarest balms, ethereal fragrances and purest scents that transport one with a single whiff. All these things, including variations of the six symbols, wouldn't be more than passingly remarkable by themselves, but in the context of an altered state of consciousness, they become the triggers of higher consciousness. These are the mechanisms that cause the normal conscious state to be profoundly affected and overwhelmed with the higher consciousness of Spirit. One who is trained in these techniques can reproduce them, although, like most transcendental phenomena, no single manifestation of spirit is quite like another, so they are created events that are unique and can't be repeated in the scientific sense.

There are also archetypal ritual patterns that the magician uses to craft rituals for specific uses. Although there are numerous patterns representing a large spectrum of complexity and utility, the two most basic are the ritual pattern for acquisition and the ritual pattern for the mysteries, most notably the Lunar, Solar, and Initiatory mysteries. The ritual pattern of acquisition is the most simplistic ritual pattern and is the first learned by the student. This pattern is used to target specific desires and intentions on the physical plane and make them accessible to the magician, whether it be for material needs (such as money, job, or career), one's love life, or other types of magick affecting the material plane, such as healing, preserving, and, if necessary, protecting and defending oneself against attack or even cursing. The ritual pattern of the mysteries represents the magician's entrance and immersion in the powers of the lunar cycle, which determine and reveal latent deep psychic themes and issues in the magician's unconscious. The magician's exterior spiritual revelations are determined by the solar cycle. The Lunar mysteries represent the detailed phases of the discipline of magick when the magician performs the various ritual workings of deep, soulful, and personally revealing magick that follows the Moon in its monthly cycle. The Solar mysteries are the magickal celebrations that represent the seasonal milestones of the magician's progress and allow them to connect with the spiritual dimension of the earth at specific traditional times. The mysteries of the Moon and the Sun represent the astronomical clock that assists the magician in accomplishing all the lesser and greater works associated with the magickal discipline and the manner in which the day, week, month, and season are given a special spiritual emphasis.

The Initiatory mysteries represent the growth and development of the magician and their work since the disciplined practice of magick causes the magician to evolve and incrementally transform until major permanent changes in their consciousness are revealed. A magician doesn't work magick without learning and growing wise over time, and that wisdom is based upon the constant and iterative exposure to spiritual gnosis, a topic that we'll deal with later in this book. As an adjunct to the Initiatory mysteries, the magician also performs various types of divination techniques, and there's a ritual pattern for the performance of deep and insightful divination where the magician must seek answers to crucial life questions. There's a pattern for divination proper, using divination tools such as the Tarot, I-Ching, Runes, and Geomancy, and there's a pattern for performing a vision quest, which is a ritual that seeks to reveal the greater mysteries of the self, such as determining new directions and significant life changes.

We must also examine what the practice of magick entails, and what it can do to the student who takes upon themselves the serious and disciplined study and practice of this occult vocation. As we've already pointed out above, the practice of ritual magick allows the magician to determine their own destiny, creatively derive the meaning of their life, explain the various occurrences of their past considering current spiritual revelations, and, most importantly, define who they are from a purely spiritual perspective. Armed with such self-definitions, the magician is then capable of accomplishing anything possible with greater ease and overriding wisdom. One can see how much less difficult and troublesome life is when one proceeds through it with a higher degree of inner knowledge and certainty than normal. In our current age of secular institutions and religious organizations that cater to the masses and unwittingly deny the individual their sense of personal worth, meaning, and destiny, it's refreshing to know that there's a spiritual practice and discipline that helps the individual define themselves and garner personal meaning while determining their own destiny above and beyond the distractions and chaos of our postmodern world.

Some of the most important features of a magickal practice and discipline using the techniques of modern magick (neo-sorcery) are self-empowerment, self-mastery, spiritual realization, developing a spiritual discipline through the study and practice of ritual magick, determining personal destiny, forming egalitarian groups or collectives (Star Groups), developing one's own magickal lore, and inheriting the ideals and legacy of the Western Mystery tradition in the twenty-first century. These are all important considerations and are examined in greater detail below.

Self-empowerment is an important feature of magick, especially considering the disempowering effect of our current world, where only the rich and politically connected have any real power and the rest go begging. Certainly, magick is not a substitute for wealth and temporal power, if such are desired by the individual, but it's essential for an individual to find personal meaning and significance in the world. Wealth and power tend to become obsessive pursuits that abrogate all other considerations in life, and even if the pursuit for wealth and power is successful, such a life is greatly diminished in quality.

Magickal power is defined as the intense feelings and perceptions that one undergoes when having experiences that are profoundly meaningful and significant. When a magician has many such experiences in a very short time, then they experience what is called *empowerment* and feels very optimistic and capable of dealing effectively with life's issues. In order for a person to be able to maximize their potential, they must believe that it's possible and within their grasp. People must know themselves well enough to determine what's possible at any given time, and to take advantage of any opportunity that arises. A series of successes in life breeds its own optimism and self-mastery. The practice of ritual magick affords the magician the perception of empowerment: they aren't insignificant and powerless, and they have the power and ability to determine their future as well as realize their ultimate destiny. How this is accomplished will be further elaborated below, since it is the hallmark of sorcery that the magician becomes a person of power. Self-empowerment isn't a delusional objective for the magician. It's the way of the modern magician to exploit rends in the social fabric and cracks in the institutional facade.

The magician defines self-mastery differently than the average person, who may assume that it means some kind of self-control or restraint. Magickal self-mastery is defined as the freedom to determine one's own destiny without undue interference from one's family, friends, peers, social position and class, career, and long-standing personal values and life expectations. To become a magician is to be profoundly transformed and permanently altered, to sense the world in a manner that few have the capacity to understand or realize. Thus, to become a magician is to question everything that one ever assumed about life and to reject everything that's not part of one's spiritual process and path. Magick has the habit of turning everything on its head. It shows the superfluous nature of our blind aspirations and how our social world, friends, family, and even the media have contaminated our true identity and filled our heads with thoughts and ideals that aren't our own. Self-mastery is a purgative process of removing all extraneous things from the self so that it becomes pure and unadulterated, tuned to the subtle spiritual processes that most people can't even sense, and directed by a spiritual process that seems to miraculously see the way through the labyrinthian passages of our overly complicated postmodern world to a simple and essential way of life.

Spiritual realization is a process where we come to know our spiritual self through personal and direct contact, a form of immersion where the super-conscious dimension of our self becomes briefly united with our mundane self. Every time a magician works magick, they invoke into their being aspects of their higher self, the spiritual dimension that is normally dormant and quiescent. After a period of time, the magician becomes slowly aware of the spiritual aspect of themselves, and eventually, this dim awareness becomes a powerful wakefulness, where their spirit becomes fully conscious and merged with the mundane self and its normal conscious mode. Spiritual realization begins with powerful psychic phenomena and strange occurrences, but these are just the outer effects of an inner awakening. In time, the subtle—and, later, the causal—levels of consciousness come to dwell in the mind of the magician, and gnosis begets enlightenment, which begets complete at-one-ness with Spirit. The God/dess within becomes manifest in such a manner that others can perceive it, and the magician completes the transformation from initiate to adept to avatar. This, of course, is the ideal, and is only rarely fully realized. For most seekers on the path of magick, obtainment of the psychic and lower subtle levels of consciousness would be a great accomplishment, and one could certainly master life quite astonishingly by only making the first step on the rung to conscious evolution, existing permanently and without instability in the psychic level of consciousness.

The spiritual and magickal discipline that a magician adopts represents two different but analogous areas that the aspiring magician must develop. The magickal discipline is the periodic and continual study and practice of ritual magick and its associated exercises (such as meditation, divinations, and self-analysis). The diurnal cycles of day and night, the monthly cycles of the Moon, and the seasonal cycles of the Sun represent the outer periodicity for the practice of ritual magick. There's also the quest for personal meaning and significance, material acquisition and achievement, and self-realization. These are the areas of a magickal discipline, and one can see that they involve the practices and effects of ritual magick over time.

A spiritual discipline is a very different matter, and some magicians don't even feel that it's important and discard it as superfluous, seeking to reap the rewards of practicing magick without any spiritual considerations. We've already made a judgment about this kind of narrow- and single-minded approach to magick. Certainly, even an avowed atheist who happened to practice magick would, over time, find their entire perspective towards spirituality permanently transformed. To practice magick is to engage our spirit in the domain of higher consciousness, whether we realize that fact or not. A spiritual discipline involves the Self and its relationship to Deity and includes spiritual exercises and magickal rites that define and amplify that relationship. A spiritual discipline will enhance a magician's ritual magick because it causes the elements of higher consciousness that are engaged in the magick to be more intense and evolved, pushing the realizations from the psychic level to the subtle and even the causal.

The magician should develop a personal religious cult of themselves as God, and perform within it as its priest, congregation, and corporeal representative.[11] As this relationship between Deity and magician is developed, the magician becomes more profoundly altered and begins to assume more conscious aspects of their own spirit. The rites of alignment are what the magician practices and develops to facilitate a closer and immanent relationship with the nature of their Godhead, or God/dess within. Invocation, communion, devotion, and assumption are the rituals of a spiritual discipline that are assiduously practiced by the magician. The magician also performs meditations and contemplations on the nature of that Deity, which change and evolve over time. The merging of a magickal and spiritual discipline represents an integral approach to the practice of ritual magick advocated in this book.

Over time, a magician is able to determine their own personal destiny. This is an evolving process, and one that isn't usually answered with any immediacy. In order to know their destiny, a magician is compelled to know and define themselves, not in any tangible way, but only in a spiritual manner, to enter into the domain of Spirit more easily. The magician must develop a spiritual identity before even beginning to realize what they must do for their life's vocation. Developing a spiritual identity is something that lies within both the magickal and spiritual discipline of the magician and occurs through the process of gaining a greater perspective on themselves by realizing their spiritual dimension. This can only occur through an iterative exposure to magickal phenomena and the immersion and transformation of the magician's conscious mind by the powers and

---

11 Of course, it is prudent to elect a Deity that can be closely identified with by the magician. This is not to say that the magician merely worships themselves as a God, but that they approach an external Deity and make it become powerfully aligned and connected to them over time.

insights revealed through their spirit. What's progressively revealed is the magician's higher self, or *Atman,* and it's through this aspect of themselves that they realize their true nature and identity.

To foster this process, the magician adopts a magickal persona and identity that will link them to their perspective of Deity, becoming an important part of their spiritual discipline and personal religious cult. As time progresses and the magician continues to assiduously practice ritual magick, that magickal persona or identity will go through many changes and alterations, eventually becoming the vehicle for their higher self to manifest and superimpose itself over their being. Once the magician knows themselves, they can understand all that they have undergone as a preparation for that moment of realization. Then, they are also able to perceive and realize their role and ultimate vocation in life.

As we can see, without a true knowledge of the spiritual self, there can be no realization of one's destiny. That's why the spiritual discipline, in tandem with the magickal discipline, is vitally important to the development of the magician's higher self. If the magician practices magick without a spiritual discipline, then they will be forever handicapped in the quest for discovering their true self and their destiny until such a time that they do indeed adopt one.

Magicians tend to be insular creatures who practice their art alone, shunning groups as being too distracting, particularly since most magickal groups tend to be run by charismatic autocrats or elite insiders who exploit newcomers and outsiders. It's better to deal with one's own daemons than have to withstand the pious mediocrity of institutional occultism, which is the unfortunate characteristic of many occult organizations that have great intentions for practicing magick but many excuses and exaggerations when it comes to actually behaving like real magicians.

It's important for the magickal practitioner to undergo periodic peer review, and this cannot be accomplished if they are practicing in complete isolation. It's also been proven to be a great disadvantage to be wholly self-absorbed in the study and practice of magick without some recourse to others who are also practicing. It's the province of others to judge our work and ensure that we don't go through our spiritual process half-baked or descend into delusion and madness. The practice and study of sane magick requires an objective judgment from learned and experienced peers, and this is the only means through which a magician may determine if their visions and lore have the merit of truth. Spiritual truth is inherently subjective, and to judge if a revelation is valid also determines its universal appeal and intelligibility. Does the magickal lore derived by the magician make sense to other magicians? This is an important consideration since it's all too easy for the magician to step into delusion and assume the erroneous insight or false prophecy as objective truth.

Since it's hazardous for the magician to work alone without any kind of interaction with peers, the magician should form a loose confederation with other magicians. It would be the ideal situation if they choose to practice magick together, performing group workings and developing group lore, because they would collectively gain as a group from the combination of every member's strengths. However, the only kind of group that a magician who is truly practicing magick would deem to join would be a group that had little or no hierarchy, used only the most basic rules, and would be governed strictly by consensus. Each member of the group would be a respected equal partner regardless of their background and experience, and each would bring into the group their special abilities and talents, as well as their own spiritual perspectives and personal magickal revelations. The equal combination of all these magicians and their personal magickal systems would produce a group whose combined magickal lore would be rich in expertise and wide in philosophical perspective. Such an organization has a name: a *Star Group*.

A Star Group is usually a small and intimate group of practitioners, ideally no greater than a dozen. A smaller group allows the individual members the maximum amount of growth in the shortest amount of time, since a greater amount of attention can be granted to each member. Large groups tend to easily lose their focus and succumb to mediocrity, whereas smaller groups have the ability to remain flexible and creative. Each member can demonstrate their knowledge, since the leadership is periodically rotated, and no one gets to dominate all the time. Thus, each individual has a greater degree of flexibility and time to perform their art within the group, and to be critically appraised of their ability to translate their visions into something others can find valuable. The creation and building of a Star Group is beyond the scope of this work, since we are concerned with the individual practitioner and their development, but this topic is covered extensively in my book *Mastering the Art of Ritual Magic* (*MARM*), and I would refer the reader to that work when they are ready.

All magickal students begin their studies by adopting the rituals and lore found in occult organizations and books or by experimentation. The magician experiments and attempts, through trial and error, to build up their ritual lore so they can ultimately practice theurgy with a degree of competence. If we use the Tree of Life as an initiatory guide, we can easily determine the first five stages that a magician should pass through in order to prepare themselves for adepthood, a level of initiation where they would be an accomplished magician and ritual expert. The stages are represented by the four Elements, which we will cover more extensively later in this book, but for now, we can explain how they represent the stages that a magickal practitioner will pass through as they grow and master their craft.

The first stage is attributed to the element Earth, and the topical area for study is forms of Earth magick that work with the four Elements, and their composite hybrids, the Elementals. An Elemental is a magickal entity consisting of two Elements, where the base Element is qualified by an Element, such as the Elemental Water of Fire, where Fire is the base and Water the qualifier. The magician spends time learning the basics, studying forms of meditation, yoga, breath control, trance, concentration, grounding, and centering. They will also study the entire spectrum of related occult material and become capable of understanding the Qabalah, astrology, Tarot, occult metaphysics, and the basic ritual pattern for material acquisition using various simple power structures, imprinting them, and projecting them to their target via an appropriate link. They will also invest themselves in a spiritual and personal religious system, defining their perspective of Deity, collecting the lore associated with that Godhead, and building rituals to facilitate a powerful spiritual alignment. The first level has a great deal of material already written and ready for use, and the student will find no lack of ideas or lore. However, from the very beginning, the magician must adapt or rewrite any of this material that they choose to use, whether found in books or derived from magickal experiments. They shouldn't take rites straight from other sources and use them without first thoroughly understanding them, then editing them so they fit into their system of magick. All materials and lore should be digested in this manner before being used, including the information and lore written in this book.

The second stage is attributed to the element Air, representing the skills associated with planetary magick and talismanic magick. The third stage is attributed to the element of Water and is associated with theurgy (evocation). The fourth stage is attributed to the element of Fire, and is associated with sacramental magick, ecstasy, rites of illumination and self-determination. The fifth stage is attributed to the element of Spirit, and is associated with the first stages of adepthood, working the magickal system known as Archeomancy (the magick of the source) and the Bornless One invocation. Written materials cover basic talismanic magick via the Golden Dawn, but any current and reliable forms of theurgy are not found in books, except those by the founder of the O.T.A. ("Poke" Runyon) and perhaps a few others. Written materials cover the elemental degrees from Earth to Air; beyond that, the magician is on their own. However, if the magician has acquired a good and solid system and methodology of magick that lets them master the first two levels of magick, then they can certainly develop the rest, perhaps with some hints and ideas from various sources. This is certainly what I did many years ago with far less material than is now available.

The Western Mystery tradition is the spiritual context within which the magician learns to master the art of magick. One might well ask, "what is the Western Mystery tradition, and how does it relate to the magickal seeker on the path to mastering their art?" Since we in North America and Europe are part of the Western matrix of cultures, we have a common spiritual heritage in the Judeo-Christian and Islamic creeds. Although the Western Mystery tradition stems from that heritage, it's since moved on to include more recent variations of that philosophy, such as Theosophy, Neo-Paganism, and Wicca. These more properly represent that tradition than any previous forms of orthodoxy. It's in Neo-Paganism and Theosophic interpretations of Christianity (Esoteric Christianity) that we find the representatives of the forefront of this newly revised tradition. The Grail and Sangreal legends and lore, the re-emergence of the feminine as Mary Magdalene or Goddess worship, and the reintegration of Celtic and romantic Paganism into otherwise sterile Protestant Christianity has breathed new life into the Western Mystery tradition. These new topics and areas of spiritual development have emerged from an occult renaissance that has spanned two centuries, beginning in the early years of the nineteenth century. Occultists have brought the study of magick from the Middle Ages into the nineteenth and twentieth centuries, revising its lore to fit with those times and be more accessible to students, and now they are poised to begin the greatest revision for the twenty-first century.

The Western Mystery tradition has seen the re-emergence of earth-based spirituality and deep ecology, and the changing of the concept of Deity from one that was omniscient and apart from nature to one that is immanent and central to nature, representing a cyclic return to an older way, but not a regression to the Pagan practices of the Greco-Roman period. Where it might appear that the old faiths of Judaism, Christianity, and Islam are being supplanted by these new faiths, the older religious creeds are finding a new manner of expression through the revitalization of the esoteric interpretation of these faiths. Christianity has such esoteric organizations as the Swedenborgian Church, Martinism, Builders of the Adytum, Society of the Inner Light, and the Servants of Light. Judaism has its Kabbalah, Canaanite Paganism, and Jewitchery. Islam has the various Sufi sects. All of these organizations believe that the truth is hidden, subtle, and wrapped in mystery and paradox; thus, they'd find it foolish to take anything literally, since everything is obscured by symbolism and allegory. It's in such a spiritual environment that the study of ritual magick becomes more important and perhaps essential, since it represents the medium by which students can directly test their theories and ideas against the reality of the domain of Spirit. Faith gives way to experience and knowledge, and passive and pious mysticism gives way to active ritual performance and visionary gnosis.

What's been written and taught in the past in regard to the Western Mystery tradition has become a legacy for all future works and accomplishments. The writings of such individuals as Eliphas Leví, Papus, Westcott, Mathers, Crowley, Regardie, Fortune, Hall, Butler, Gray, Knight, Grant, and a host of others represent the literary legacy for students of magick and Western occultism. Far from being an empty and fruitless examination of the past, these scholars and practicing occultists left a great deal of written material that's relevant and can be used to build the base for the occult scholar and practitioner of today. Our quest is to bring this study and practice into this century, where it will be needed far more urgently than ever before. The thing that the student must remember is that these individuals distilled the teachings of a past age (the late Middle Ages and the Renaissance), and one need not question the legitimacy of their sources but assume that what they determined was correct and useful, as far as it goes, unless and until the student has recourse to examine the original source material from an historical perspective, and then (hopefully) in the original languages. Otherwise, it's prudent to move on from these writings from the past and forge a new practice of magick based upon the needs and the environment of today.

CHAPTER THREE

THE SEARCH FOR SPIRIT: AN EXPLORATION OF THE HIGHER MIND

DEFINITION OF A SEEKER

In my many years as an occultist and ritual magician, I've met and talked with numerous people about religion and spirituality. I've discovered that there seems to be two kinds of people and minds when it comes to spiritual considerations. Either a person feels quite comfortable with their chosen church and religion and they don't need to seek any additional knowledge or practices (the majority), or they are seekers who have abandoned their original faith in order to seek out answers and fulfill needs that their previous faith failed to satisfy (a rare minority). There are probably some people who could fit into both categories, but that state is invariably fleeting, since once a person is touched by the passion for the personal spiritual quest, there's no other challenge or pursuit that satisfies the thirst for gnosis. Those who aren't touched by the desire to seek out the meaning of life can't understand the urges, intuitions, and insights that guide the occult initiate on their pathway to total self-realization. From the point of view of the initiate, the rest of humanity seems asleep. They aren't haunted by that rare sensation that humanity has a deeper self which sees the world with a heightened spiritual sensitivity. The prosaic world of religious morality and orthodoxy is the dream-like refuge of the masses; it's their protection from the risky places of soul-loss and delusion. Yet these same sleeping masses are those individuals who await their time of wakefulness in turn, and the joy and ecstasy that state entails. We seekers aren't bound by archaic covenants nor shackled by religious superstition, and this makes us dangerous and irresistible. Religious orthodoxy is no more than one of many illusory barriers and seductive veils that must be overcome in the pure pursuit of spiritual evolution.

Religious congregants see their religion as the ultimate goal, their holy grail, but spiritual seekers see all religions as the beginning phase of their life-long training and nothing more. Some people are content to find their place in the world, to feel themselves as part of a public and exoteric spiritual community where they don't have to work at being spiritual—it is done for them. When organized religion is taken too seriously and in too limited a context or a literal manner, then the negative qualities of dogma and religious superstition take root. This affectation casts a veil over people's sensibilities, causing them to become religiously sectarian, mentally rigid (monological), and quite capable of persecuting those who do not share their narrow religious viewpoints. However, a good liberal education and a mind that is steeped in literacy usually allows for a greater flexibility in regard to one's spiritual studies and beliefs. We should be respectful of everyone's faith and spiritual beliefs if tolerance and compassion are to be the enlightened axioms of social intercourse. It's also important to understand world religion from a pluralistic perspective. A generalized knowledge of world religion fosters a greater understanding of one's own practices and beliefs and causes one to acknowledge the many differences and commonalities between the faiths of the world. It also fosters religious tolerance; coincidently, this attribute is an essential quality of Paganism, despite how some might practice it. It's also an important part of Neo-Pagan theology that all Deities are valid, so none are rejected.

The new faiths of earth-based spirituality promote the spiritual act of seeking, for they see the passage of spiritual transformation as a journey (the continuously reoccurring diurnal cycle of the transformation of the hero or heroine). Since the new faiths accept gnosis as integral to their evolving creed, they're engaged in practices that generate ecstatic states of consciousness. Through exposure to the domain of Spirit, seekers are forever attempting to verify their personal spiritual experiences. To this end, seekers are people who need to know far more than what is written down about the nature of Spirit and feel compelled to continue searching for a special knowledge that will satisfy their yearning for spiritual fulfillment. Spiritual seekers never stay within the boundaries of a single creed or religious doctrine; instead, they find truths in many religious beliefs, philosophies, and practices. They gather all these facets of truth together to create their own heterodoxy—an amalgamation of various spiritual beliefs, verified by personal experience or gnosis. The spiritual practices of the new faiths could be defined as a form of religious syncretism.

It's my theory that people who are true spiritual seekers are actually sensing something about the world that many others don't: the domain of Spirit encroaching on our mundane world. How else can we explain why someone would reject their own creed and family faith for something wholly and completely alien to them? Why would someone need to seek something that is not defined nor part of a normal religious canon if they did not sense that there was something actually out there, waiting to be discovered? Seekers are more sensitive and intuitive, and they are not afraid of where their thoughts and feelings may take them. Seekers seem to be almost fearless in their pursuit of what must be for them, a thing both unknown and unknowable. For most people, their encounters with the spiritual domain are limited to when they are born and when they die, and perhaps an occasional encounter when they have a near death experience or someone dear to them dies. Most people seek to avoid contact with the unknown, the paranormal, and the supernatural, wishing to bury themselves in their humdrum daily affairs as a method of self-protection. But for those who are seekers, whose spiritual path includes a discipline of working magick and seeking gnosis, their encounters with the paranormal are more frequent, even deliberate, and become a part of their not-so-ordinary existence, and often these experiences can and do have a profound, *transformative*, and life-altering effect.

The path of the spiritual seeker is one that is difficult, dangerous, and often filled with disappointments. There are no guarantees that the seeker will find the fulfillment they desire, but it's guaranteed that one will experience rejection and ostracization from one's peers. To seek what is indefinable and mysterious is perceived by others as folly at best, and at worst, they are threatened by it. There is an old popular saying, originally penned by the eighteenth century English poet Thomas Gray: "No more; where ignorance is bliss, tis folly to be wise."[12] This saying has been eulogized by later poets, quoted by various pundits, and even

---

12 Gray, Thomas, "Ode on a Distant Prospect of Eton College," *Poems*. (J. Dodsley, 1747) pp. 17–25.

partially quoted by rock stars (such as *Ignorance is Bliss* by the Ramones), but it boils down to one main issue—that it's better to be ignorant of one's fate than partially aware or foolishly motivated. The search for spiritual knowledge is a very serious undertaking and must be carefully promoted, lest one engage in self-delusion and even madness. The seeker chooses to assault the underpinnings of their sense of what is real and objective in order to realize what transcends reality and objectivity: the domain of Spirit itself. So, we must be warned of the hazards on the path of the spiritual seeker and pursue our objectives in a guarded, disciplined, and careful manner, knowing that once we begin this path, we shall find it of infinite breadth and endless in scope. The following poem by Alexander Pope amply illustrates this point:

> *A little learning is a dangerous thing*
> *Drink deep or taste not the Pierian Spring*
> *These shallow draughts intoxicate the brain*
> *But drinking deeply sobers us again.*[13]

(One is reminded of the *drinking* associated with Omar Khayyam's poetry.) A religion that accepts and promotes spiritual seeking is also advocating that their adherents undergo spiritual evolution. The constant exposure to paranormal worlds and the domain of Spirit causes the seeker to undergo continual transformation in an earth-based religious tradition, and thereby realize the very highest states of consciousness—those of the subtle and causal levels of being. Such a faith would believe that the barriers between Deity and humanity are very porous and thin, since the congregant often assumes the qualities and characteristics of their personal Deity (the God/dess Within). It naturally follows that those individuals who engage in an earth-based spirituality will ultimately evolve into enlightened seekers, known as the magi of a new Aquarian age, and this event will come to pass by default as a consequence of the simple nature of consciousness.

---

13   Pope, Alexander, "An Essay on Criticism" (1711).

INITIATION AND TRANSFORMATION:
RITES OF PASSAGE
AND SPIRITUAL EVOLUTION

Our mundane life is filled with changes, and our challenge is to meet and integrate those changes into our daily lives. Our failure to adjust to results is a poor adaptation to life. Most changes are part of the flux and flow of life, seemingly granting individuals good fortune and luck, as well as trials, misfortune, and tragedies. However, some changes are strategic and more significant, meaning that they represent an opportunity for individuals to better themselves and grow and expand rapidly, making themselves more aware of the self, others, and the greater world around them. These changes are perilous and take us outside of ourselves, subjecting us to strange forces, mythic archetypes, and processes that seem to have little to do with our daily lives. These strategic changes are called *transformations,* and they are usually triggered by life events that are more powerful, meaningful, and significant than what is normally experienced. It's said that a wise man heeds the advice of their transformations, and a fool ignores them.

When we choose an earth-based religious tradition, like Wicca, Witchcraft, Neo-Paganism, or a Magickal Lodge, often there's an associated rite (initiation) that's performed after we've gained a foothold in that tradition. That rite represents a passage from one state to another, from a state of lacking knowledge about that tradition to a state where we become knowledgeable. Rites of passage like these exist at various strategic moments of our lives, and mark points where we become knowledgeable about a new aspect of life, such as seining rites (baptism) for the newly born, rites of puberty and becoming an adult (such as getting a driver's license, getting laid, and becoming eligible to vote), marriage, parenthood, retirement or rites of eldership, and rites associated with death (such as wakes or funerals) to mark our passing from this world into the next.

Initiation rites can be social rites of passage, but they can also include a certain amount of personal transformation. Yet, rites of passage (initiations) and personal transformations are actually two different things. They should always be used distinctly since they denote different things, even though we often use them interchangeably. It's possible and even likely to experience both an initiation and a transformation, but it's not the rule; they are two different events and two different experiences. One can receive initiations into various social organizations (such as the Masons, Odd Fellows, Eagles, Elks, Lions, Liar's Club, and Greek fraternities and sororities) and not be in any kind of spiritually transformed state. That is especially true for non-esoteric organizations and quasi-religious social cliques. One can also undergo a powerful spiritual transformation and not be a zealous member of any particular creed. However, for esoteric organizations and true spiritual paths, an initiation and a transformation should occur simultaneously. In fact, that is the expectation in earth-based spiritual traditions, whether it's stated as such in the lore or just implicit in its practices.

Magick is the method and the means through which an initiation and a transformation occur simultaneously. Those esoteric organizations that support the practice of some form of magick are the organizations that have developed the means of continual personal transformation, which is also the obvious path of personal enlightenment and self-illumination. Those esoteric organizations who eschew the practice of any form of magick are completely fraudulent in their core philosophy and should be avoided by one and all. Without magick, there can be no growth, no spiritual evolution, and no hope of self-realization. The definition of magick is included in the broadest of practices and beliefs, but the focus of magick is always on the transformation of the individual so they may directly and periodically experience the Deity in all its mystery and manifested glory. Magick is the mirror that reflects the Microcosm into the Macrocosm and back again, thus developing the greater depth of the individual soul. Magickal rituals are the sacred practices of individuals who seek to experience the world of Spirit, for magick is the use of sacred symbols and rites for private instead of public purposes, and the goal is always a form of gnosis, which is the knowledge that one is a true being of Spirit.

However, in order to talk more intelligently about magick, transformation, and initiation, we need to define our terms and their associated meanings. Perhaps the simplest way to define our terminology is to examine these words as they appear in the dictionary, and then expand on their definitions. In this manner, we will proceed from the known to reveal new insights about these terms, and perhaps even reveal something that is unknown.

When we examine the definition for initiation, we find the following entries:

"**Initiation:** *the rites, ceremonies, ordeals or instructions with which one is made a member of a sect or society or is invested with a particular function or status.*"[14]

This seems to fit what we have said in previous paragraphs.

"**Initiate:** *to induct, facilitate the beginning of—to induct into membership by, or as if by special rites. Synonym: to begin. The condition of being initiated into some experience or sphere of activity—knowledgeableness.*"[15]

Aha! The word "knowledgeableness" is used in the second definition above, a point that we stressed previously. The knowledge that is spoken of can be *exoteric*, as that found in a fraternal order, or it can be *esoteric*, as that found in a magickal order. Esoteric knowledge is synonymous with gnosis (intuitive spiritual wisdom), so initiatory knowledge within an occult organization represents intuitive knowledge of the Deity.

As we can see in the above lines from the Merriam-Webster dictionary, an initiation represents a rite of passage, a gateway or lintel-crossing from one station in life to the next. One who is initiated possesses a kind of special knowledge, granted as a privilege and responsibility by an organization or hierarchy. When this rite is performed in an esoteric organization, the conferees of initiation are part of a spiritual hierarchy. However, in most cases, initiation is used to bring a candidate for membership formally into that organization. The purpose of such an initiation, in an exoteric organization, is to grant membership and not to profoundly alter one's consciousness. Anthropologists have traced the antecedent to these social organizations in the tribal Moiety, representing the precursor to all later secret societies. The Moiety, which is a social phenomenon where a tribe is divided into two parts and each group

---

14   "Initiation." *Merriam-Webster.com.* Merriam-Webster Dictionary, 2024. Web.

15   "Initiate." *Merriam-Webster.com.* Merriam-Webster, 2024. Web.

practices their rites in secrecy from the other half of the tribe, represents a basic human organizational behavior, and might even be traced backed to some precursor hominid instinctive behavior. A social organization or lodge, which conducts secret rites, with signs, passwords, and grips, can be conducted in a fashion that is no more spiritual or magickal than any other semi-public activity. Thus, it is not unusual to find individuals who are high initiates in various social orders, but who have not experienced any kind of psychological transformation.

We must examine the nature and definition of transformation in order to realize the true source of spiritual evolution; for obviously it is not through initiation alone that we are changed.

> "**Transformation:** *act or process or instance of transforming or being transformed. To change in composition or structure, to change the outward form or appearance of—to change in character or condition. Convert, change, to make radically different.*"[16]

The part of the definition of transformation that seems to be most relevant is the expression "to make radically different" and also "to change in character or condition." Transformation is defined as "a radical or profound change," but such a change could be either progressive and evolving or regressive and debilitating. Within the context of the occult, we refer to transformation as the means to achieving positive spiritual change within oneself.

To round out the definition of transformation, we have to include two other terms: *transcendence* and *teleology*. We include them because progressive transformation seems to cause one to sense the deeper structures of reality and being and to perceive that there is a final end or purpose to life.

> "**Transcendence:** *exceeding usual limits, surpassing—extending or lying beyond the limits of ordinary experience—in Kantian philosophy: being beyond the limits of all possible experience and knowledge. Being beyond comprehension—Exceed. Transcend: to rise above or go beyond the limits of, to triumph over the negative or restrictive aspects of, overcome, to outstrip or outdo in some attribute, quality, or power.*"[17]

---

16 "Transformation." *Merriam-Webster.com*. Merriam-Webster, 2024. Web.
17 "Transcendence." *Merriam-Webster.com*. Merriam-Webster, 2024. Web.

Those who choose the purely scientific view of reality have sided with Immanuel Kant in accepting that the transcendental quality of consciousness is beyond all possible rational knowledge and beyond comprehension, and therefore must be irrelevant to the acquisition of real scientific knowledge. Of course, those who have been trained as occultists know this to be a fallacy, for we who are seekers often experience higher states of consciousness while immersed in the domain of Spirit. We are also able to explain and even teach the practice of obtaining these states of consciousness to others, thus making them quite objective. The transcendental realm of Spirit is inexplicable, so it is represented as a kind of meta-logic or metaphysics that defies quantitative or qualitative analysis. It is also a domain of human experience that is universal in its potential, experienced by all, but seldom realized, except by a small minority of people. The word *transcendence* is used together with *transformation* to denote the kind of personal change that triumphs over all adversity and suppression, releasing the self to the greater and higher states of being.

*"**Teleology:** "Telos" (end) + "logia" (purpose). The study of evidence of design in nature, a doctrine that states that ends are imminent in nature, a doctrine explaining phenomena by final causes. The fact or character attributed to nature or natural processes of being directed toward an end or shaped by a purpose. The use of design or purpose as an explanation of natural phenomena."[18]*

Teleology could mean that, through a spiritual perspective, everything in the world has a purpose, a vocation, and a destiny. However, teleology has also digressed into such formulations as *intelligent design,* which is a stealthy re-packaging of creationism. I think that, by purpose or ultimate design, we must conclude that a subjective human process of creating meaning is taking place, and that it is not to be confused with objective physical reality. The meaning of life is not something that makes much sense when examined with the ruthless empirical eye of science.

The terms *transcendence* and *teleology* seem to refer directly to that domain of human activity called the Sacred. It seems obvious that to experience transcendence is to experience the world of Spirit, for it is

---

18 "Teleology." *Merriam-Webster.com.* Merriam-Webster, 2024. Web.

Spirit that transcends all that we might mentally conceive, and it is also the beginning and the end of all manifestation—the true source and destiny of all spiritual seekers. Thus, we also choose to examine the word *sacred,* since it seemed to be at the core of the terms that we have examined so far.

> **"Sacred:** *the power, being, or realm understood by religious persons to be at the core of existence and to have a transformative effect on their lives and destinies. Other terms, such as holy, divine, transcendent, ultimate being (or reality), mystery, and perfection (or purity) have been used for this domain. "Sacred" is also an important technical term in the scholarly study and interpretation of religions."*[19]

The word *sacred* represents the ground or basis for the domain of transcendental transformation. As such, it requires that all actions within that space be godlike and archetypal. All the above words—*initiation, transformation, transcendence, teleology,* and *sacred*—symbolize the process and the path of individual ascension, but throughout them runs the theme of the experience of Spirit. The world that is without time and space—that is trans-logical, trans-personal, non-dual, and myriad-dimensional—is the true multiverse of the Unity of All Being. It is this place of Spirit from which all manifestation came forth, imprinted with the synergistic potential to become conscious; it's that which all conscious individuals seek. They seek their ultimate union with the being-ness of Spirit, who is called a *God,* for lack of a better name. Thus, through the magickal artifice of emanation, involution, evolution, and union, the material universe, filled with dead inchoate matter, becomes imbued with life, consciousness, and, ultimately, Spirit. There are two cycles identified in this pattern, and they are the cycles of Transformation and Emanation: the intersecting paths of Light and Darkness, the realms of the Macrocosm and the Microcosm intertwined. The primary mystery that a magician faces is the mystery of their own being and its revelation as the *god/ess-as-self* within the World of Spirit. A wise magician must work magick that promotes and transforms themselves so that the realization of the

---

19 "Sacred." *Merriam-Webster.com.* Merriam-Webster, 2024. Web.

divinity within themselves becomes an objective reality. The name for this kind of magick is the *Great Work,* the magnum opus of magicians and alchemists, the obtainment of perfect spiritual illumination.

The process of spiritual growth is principally aided by a synthesis of transformation, transcendence, and teleology to cause strategic changes at important moments of our lives, so the progression of spiritual awakening and growth is personally significant and meaningful. Transformative initiations are a means whereby certain levels of trans-formation are objectified, but they can also facilitate the transformation process itself.

A DISCUSSION OF THE PARADIGM OF THE THREE EYES

From the preceding sections, we have identified three different domains of experience that contain the conscious being of humanity. These three domains appear to represent the material, mental, and spiritual worlds, representing the total field of the universe of human experience. From these three different domains of experience have been derived all the areas of knowledge, both exoteric as well as esoteric. The domains of matter and mind have had a necessary (evolutionary) and exclusive monopoly upon humankind, but the domain of Spirit has also had a profound impact on humanity as witness to the human propensity for spiritual knowledge and religious practices. However, a person will experience the pure non-dual dimension of being when the mind and body no longer dominate the individual, but are, instead, released within the transcendental domain of Spirit.

An analysis of the three categories of gaining knowledge, as presented by Ken Wilber, should allow a means of defining the domain of Spirit, first by contrasting it with mind and matter, and then by defining it through an appreciation of the transcendental conscious state of non-duality.[20] But first we have to define the spectrum of how we gain knowledge about the world, starting at the place where we interact directly with matter.

---

20 Adapted from Wilber, Ken, *Eye to Eye: The Quest for the New Paradigm* (Shambhala Press, 2011) pp. 2–35.

Three Categories of Knowledge

Below are the three categories of knowledge which conform to the three domains of matter, mind, and spirit. In selecting this simple technique to explain how humans perceive and organize their experiential world, Wilber allows us to define the domain of Spirit more tightly and qualitatively.

- **Eye of Flesh:** called sensibilia—physical reality of space, time, and objects—object empirical.
- **Eye of Reason:** called intelligibilia—mental plane and constructs—subjective phenomenal.
- **Eye of Contemplation (Spirit):** called transcendelia—transcendent reality—transcendental apperception.[21]

> *"[Mental constructs] are trans empirical and a priori…Logic is trans empirical…necessary and a priori for the manifestation of the natural/ sensory realm…the gross arises from the subtle which arises from the causal."*[22]

The mind, which is the focal point for all conscious perception, is basically in the driver's seat. The perspective of the eye of mind defines the other two domains of experience (eye of flesh and spirit), whether or not it is always able to correctly perceive and understand those worlds from its own perspective. This is the greater gift of the mind, and also its inherent flaw.

There is also a *holarchical* relationship (or *nested hierarchies of increasing holism*) between these three categories of knowledge. This holarchical relationship is defined in such a manner so that the category of reason is nested within the category of sense, and the category of spirit is nested within the category of reason. However, the category of spirit is a higher order structure of consciousness than reason, which is a higher order structure of consciousness than the sensory and instinctive states. It follows that the eye of flesh cannot wholly comprehend the eye of mind, but the eye of mind can easily comprehend the material world, since it represents a higher order structure. The eye of mind can also easily comprehend the mental domain as a form of self-comprehension. Correspondingly,

---

21   Adapted from Wilber, Ken, *Eye to Eye* (Shambhala Press, 2011) pp. 2–4, 35.
22   Wilber, Ken, *Eye to Eye* (Shambhala Press, 2011) p. 5.

the eye of mind can't comprehend the eye of spirit, and the eye of spirit wholly contains and derives all reason and sense. It is therefore called the metaphysical world perspective, the deep structure of conscious reality, or *transcendelia*, for it paradoxically sees everything from the root of nothing.

Relationship of the Modes of Knowledge

The five relationships that exist between the three modes of knowledge (the three categories of knowledge) clearly define the qualities found at each of the three levels of consciousness of sense, mind, and spirit. The lowest relationship represents the lowest order of consciousness, and the highest relationship represents the highest order of consciousness. As previously stated, when the seeker is continually exposed to the process of transcendental transformation, they experience the world as described by the highest mode of knowledge, gnosis, or *Spirit to Transcendelia*. Ultimately, this can become a permanent mental state, allowing the higher adept to experience the world from a perspective that is wholly transcendental and non-dual. This is also the goal, whether witting or unwittingly undertaken by the spiritual seeker.

The Five Modes of Knowledge, from Lowest to Highest

- **Mode Five:** Sensorial Awareness. Direct perception through the five senses.
- **Mode Four:** Mental Editing of Sensorial Data. The mind examining, processing and distilling input from the five senses.
- **Mode Three:** Abstract Mental Models and Paradigms. The mind examining and analyzing mental constructs and abstract generalizations—thought reflecting on the nature of thought itself.
- **Mode Two:** Mental Perceptions of Spirit or *Transcendelia*. Models and theories are attempted to be applied to higher order spirit, producing paradoxes, riddles, or negative descriptions.
- **Mode One:** Transcendental Awareness. Illumination, or awareness of the domain of Spirit through direct perception. Knowledge of spirit, or gnosis, and intuitive awareness of transcendelia.[23]

---

23   Adapted from Wilber, Ken, *Eye to Eye* (Shambhala Press, 2011) pp. 61–65.

When considering the above modes of knowledge, it can be easily seen that the esoteric sciences include modes one and two as methods of gaining knowledge. The Mind to Transcendelia mode is used both cautiously and with great artifice, since it can never replace the direct perception of Spirit by the Eye of Spirit, but only lead one to it. Through this secondary mode of knowledge all patterns, practices, and techniques of a spiritual discipline are defined to allow one to gain direct access to the spiritual domain of human consciousness. This is why esoteric doctrines and occult systems and models seem so absurd to the rational intellect. They represent in mental formulations what is patently transcendental and paradoxical to the eye of mind, describing through symbols a world that is beyond the symbolic. Wilber eloquently states the nature of spirit and sense, as opposed to mind, and begins to assist in the definition of the spiritual domain of consciousness:

"Neither the sensorimotor realms...nor the spiritual realms...form theories. They can be the object of theories...The one is pre-symbolic, the other, trans-symbolic...There is valid experience, valid knowledge, valid apprehension in the spiritual and sensible realms, but not symbolic or theoretical experience."[24]

The above statement by Wilber and our analysis of the modes of knowledge seem to warn us about getting too fond of models or theories that attempt to exhaustively explain or tightly define both the spiritual domain and the domain of the senses. The mind is ever-fond of its rationalizations and its propensity to make the world conform to simplistic generalizations and biased values. This is to the detriment and expense of all real knowledge, which requires an unfettered mind. The mind can become a great tyrant, forcing its limited perceptions and expectations upon the larger world, which is not so bound or limited as the petty mind perceives it. In order to truly acquire knowledge, all avenues or modes must be explored, particularly modes one and two, since they address the human issues of spirituality and the evolution of consciousness. The student of the occult spends a great deal of time learning to shut off normal internal narratives (speaking to oneself). They may experience the domain of pure sensory perception without built-in editing or bias,

---

24   Wilber, Ken, *Eye to Eye* (Shambhala Press, 2011) p. 62.

and therein realize the domain of Spirit for the first time. Once in this state, they will perceive the whole as well as all the integrated facets of their being. Ken Wilber also states that spiritual experiences are a valid type of knowledge, and that they can be subjected to an objective regimen, similar but not the same as any of the softer forms of science such as psychology, sociology, history, art, literature, and philosophy.[25]

BASIC METHODS OF DATA ACCUMULATION

Verification Procedures

Ken Wilber has defined the method of objectively gaining knowledge from some kind of experience as representing the three basic processes of verification, the same used in all the sciences, hard or soft.[26] This includes the esoteric or occult sciences as well. Nothing is exempt from the test of the three verification procedures if it is to be judged as valid or true in an objective sense. This paradigm also shows that spiritual or transcendental knowledge conforms to these basic rules.

There are, according to Wilber, three methods for verifying subjective knowledge. These three methods are the *instrumental injunction,* the *intuitive apprehension,* and the *communal confirmation.* The instrumental injunction is where the experimenter is required to perform the experiment under the specified conditions and in a very specific manner in order to verify the results. The intuitive apprehension is the experience gained through the experiment: the observations and collection of experiential data, as well as the realization and understanding of the instrumental injunction if the experiment is successful. The communal confirmation is the manner in which results are corroborated by others who have also performed the experiment and completed the instrumental injunction and intuitive apprehension strands.[27]

The above three verification procedures are the means where subjective experiences become objectified so that they can have a more universal application and can be stripped of their personal bias and subjectivity. This is not to say that subjectivity is in any way inferior to objectivity,

---

25 Wilber, Ken, *Eye to Eye* (Shambhala Press, 2011) p. 39.
26 Adapted from Wilber, Ken, *Eye to Eye* (Shambhala Press, 2011) pp. 39–41.
27 Wilber, Ken, *Eye to Eye* (Shambhala Press, 2011) p. 40.

since all experiences of reality, both internal and external, are subjective. The root of all knowledge is subjectivity, but the fruit of all knowledge is objectivity, where that knowledge can apply to more than just the individual who experiences it. These three verification procedures can be applied to transcendental inquiry.

Transcendental Inquiry

Transcendental inquiry requires that one must first master the methodologies in order to perform the experiment. These methodologies are always the means of gaining access to, and a realization of, the subtle and causal levels of consciousness. Without an ability to access these domains of consciousness, the experimenter is unable to verify any of the experiences or related data gained by others who have accessed them. Once these methods are mastered, then the experimenter is able to verify the experiences and transcendental data, and can not only realize them, but also apprehend their own spiritual dimension and personal soul qualities. This experiment doesn't limit itself to cold, objective facts about some exterior phenomenon, but is also very intimate and internal. Of course, data obtained in this manner must be subjected to some kind of peer review (examination by other practitioners) since it's very subjective, but this in no way diminishes its importance or significance.

The acquisition of spiritual knowledge requires specific tools, which are the techniques of one's spiritual discipline. One can't judge any spiritual injunction without first obtaining the perspective of the spiritual domain. Without this ability to perceive through the eye of spirit, all spiritual knowledge appears irrational or paradoxical and doesn't lend itself to being known, since the mind alone is unable to perform the task. Techniques of transcendental inquiry would include all methods of contemplation: Eastern systems of meditation, such as yoga, pranayama (breath control), concentration, and the martial arts; and from the West, there are the techniques of prayer-meditation, theological contemplation, speculation, and ritual and ceremonial magick. Knowledge that's gained through transcendental techniques must be verified communally. This means that occult knowledge should never be taken as a truth without being subjected to some kind of peer review. This is also why it's important for transcendental transformations to be fully acknowledged by the seeker. The fruit of their experiences should be examined and judged by more senior and adept seekers. In this manner, transformations precede initiations, which are used to confer public recognition upon seekers for their spiritual accomplishments.

Transcendental transformation not only assists the seeker in self-discovery and the realization of the spiritual dimension within, but it also causes the seeker to evolve. The transformation of consciousness causes the emergence of a higher order structure of consciousness, which supplants and integrates the lower order structure that it replaces. Wilber calls this the process of *transcendence as self-transformation.*[28] It is a process that occurs when one is continuously exposed to the domain of Spirit.[29]

THE PROCESS OF TRANSCENDENCE AS SELF-TRANSFORMATION[30]

Psychological growth occurs through the process of self-transformation. A certain set of stages of consciousness occur, which allow these kinds of changes to become stable and permanent. It is self-defeating (and probably impossible) to experience higher states of consciousness and then return to one's lower basic level and never learn anything in the process.

The first thing that happens is that a higher order structure surfaces in one's conscious mind. If this emergence doesn't pose any threat but instead is compelling and attractive, then the self will identify with that higher order structure and allow it to completely emerge and merge with the self. The self will then have two conflicting structures within it and will begin to let go of the older lower structure, while fully investing itself with the newer higher order structure. In this manner, the conscious mind adopts higher order structures, which replace the lower order structures. The mind does not discard the lower structure because it is integrated into the higher structure, although it has lost its power and identity in the process. Wilber calls this process *differentiation.* The important consideration is that we don't lose parts of our self; we integrate into higher structures while still retaining the functionality of the lower structures.

---

28   Wilber, Ken, *Eye to Eye* (Shambhala Press, 2011) p. 105.

29   Adapted from Wilber, Ken, *Eye to Eye* (Shambhala Press, 2011) pp. 55–56, 104–105.

30   Adapted from Wilber, Ken, *Eye to Eye* (Shambhala Press, 2011) pp. 91–93.

The means of introducing this higher-order structure is through the techniques of establishing higher states of consciousness. This process of transcendence causes the seeker to become profoundly altered, transformed, and integrated within the domain of Spirit. The method of this kind of growth is also followed throughout one's conscious development, from an infant to an adult, and it operates when one engages with the subtle and causal states of consciousness. As Wilber states:

"Each level of consciousness consists of a deep structure and a surface structure. The deep structure is the defining form of a level, which embodies all of the potentials and limitations of that level. Surface structure is simply a particular manifestation of the deep structure. The surface structure is constrained by the form of the deep structure, but within that form it is free to select various contents."[31]

Within occult circles, the deep structure is referred to as the *archetypal level of being,* which determines the nature of all phenomena that arises to the surface structure. Occultists are concerned with the nature of the deep structure since they operate on the correct assumption that affecting the deep structure will profoundly affect the surface structure. All occult models, practices, and techniques focus exclusively on that deep structure, seeking to know it directly. The model or technique, however irrational, perfectly expresses the nature of what is most intrinsic to one's own being, as well as the spiritual nature of everyone.

Most people experience changes through translation, since surface structures are always in movement, but deep structures are often static or change very slowly. The movement of deep structures within one's conscious mind can cause severe changes in people since they affect both the deep and surface structures simultaneously. This is why people like to avoid anything that causes a movement within the deep structure of their conscious being, since it causes instability and necessitates a re-translation of the self. However, once the transcendental transformative process is started, one's deep structure begins a process of continual movement or change. This can be perceived by the individual as either a process of illumination or madness, depending on whether they retain a certain degree of cohesive self-control or lose all self-control as a prelude to a

---

31   Wilber, Ken, *Eye to Eye* (Shambhala Press, 2011) p. 92.

loss of soul. A spiritual discipline has the methods of self-awareness and self-control as its most essential practices, so the seeker who is adhering to such a discipline is guided through illumination and avoids madness or self-dissolution.

Psychological change has basically two dimensions: one that affects the surface structure and one that affects the deep structure. Changing the surface structure changes its appearance or quality; this is a surface change. Changing the deep structure changes the essence of something; this is always experienced as a transformation. Transcendental transformation always indicates that we are in the process of transition from a lower to a higher order structure of consciousness, and that the deep structure is being altered as part of the transformational process. One could remark that initiation, which does not appear to change much in one's deep and inner nature, is actually a surface change or the modification of a surface structure, and one that translates the self as opposed to transforming it.

When a person experiences a transcendental transformation, such as what might be experienced as the result of a series of pivotal magickal workings leading up to an initiation, they become aware of the teleology of their soul, which causes them to realize their destiny, thus revealing their part in the grand scheme of the cosmos. This revelation isn't straightforward, since Spirit communicates to us in arcane symbols, archetypes, and myths. A person must ultimately objectify a transformational experience in order to translate it into an intelligible medium. An initiation rite may assist this process of translation since it brings this highly subjective and personal experience into the social dimension of a person's life. They share the experience with their peers and receive validation and recognition for it, as well as determine a context for spiritual achievement within that person's spiritual path.

LEVELS OF THE UNCONSCIOUS MIND

The source of all consciousness is, of course, the unconscious mind. The unconscious mind isn't merely the repository of repressed desires, pathological complexes, regressive states of being, and the ever-present mindless beast, whose dangerous nature must be controlled and sub-limated at all times. The unconscious mind contains all that is not conscious, and that includes many diverse structures. It's said that one's soul, spirit, and the highest expression of the self resides in the unconscious mind, as well as the repressed bestial tendencies of a more primitive nature. Since the unconscious mind is the source of all that is conscious, then an understanding of the components of the unconscious mind would assist us in understanding the complex nature of the self and the necessity for certain unconscious mechanisms to become realized in the conscious mind, if one is to accomplish the evolution of consciousness.

Ken Wilber presents a really excellent definition of these various levels of the unconscious and how they interact with each other. I have adapted his words in the following paragraphs, adding my own analysis and comments where I wish to tie this additional knowledge into our accumulated understanding of spiritual processes and self-realization. Wilber has defined six basic structures, and they are as follows.

1. Ground Unconscious
The deep structure of the conscious mind acts as the field of potentiality and is capable of briefly emerging at some point of development, particularly when one is experiencing a crisis in development. The deep structure is a collective, which means that it's common to all humanity, and represents the potential of all aspects of the domain of consciousness (both higher and lower) that is merged into an undifferentiated union. A good analogy is a seed that genetically represents the potential of the plant that it might become but is undifferentiated and self-contained. The ground unconscious represents aspects of the self that have not emerged from out of the unconscious mind, and so have never been repressed.[32]

2. Archaic Unconscious
Elements of the archaic self include the building blocks of consciousness that are inherited from the phylogenetic past, such as instincts and the primitive responses associated with them. The archaic unconscious contains the history of our species and its evolution, from its most primitive expressions of existence (search for food, sex, dominance, and survival by fight or flight), from the fish, amphibian, and reptile

---

32 Wilber, Ken, *Eye to Eye* (Shambhala Press, 2011) p. 95.

mind, and the early mammalian and primate mind. The structures contained at this level are the least developed and seldom emerge into consciousness unless the higher cortical structure of the brain is severely impaired.[33]

3. Submergent Unconscious

These are structures that had once existed in consciousness, but for various reasons have submerged back into unconsciousness. Surface structures can submerge and re-emerge due to forgetfulness or disuse. The mind can also seek to omit any issue or memory that is uncomfortable or painful, or clashes with the current status quo. This is called *repression*.[34]

4. Embedded Unconscious

The negative image of the self or ego acts as the suppressing agent of the conscious ego. This is where reality is interpreted from the perspective of the ego, and where anything that is threatening or antithetical to it is kept within the unconscious through suppression. The embedded unconscious part of the mind contains the darker and least savory aspects of the ego, and, therefore, is necessarily suppressed itself.[35]

5. Emergent Unconscious

These are deep structures that represent aspects of the self that have not yet emerged into consciousness, usually representing higher and more developed aspects of the self. Thus, the levels of conscious awareness that represent the subtle and causal states of consciousness are considered *emergent unconscious* to one who has not developed to the point where they would be experienced consciously. These structures can be part of one's potential or aspects of the self that are repressed, particularly when one has evolved to the point where they should be conscious.[36]

---

33 Wilber, Ken, *Eye to Eye* (Shambhala Press, 2011) p. 96.

34 Wilber, Ken, *Eye to Eye* (Shambhala Press, 2011) p. 98.

35 Wilber, Ken, *Eye to Eye* (Shambhala Press, 2011) p. 99.

36 Wilber, Ken, *Eye to Eye* (Shambhala Press, 2011) p. 102.

6. EMERGENT-REPRESSED UNCONSCIOUS

When the emergent unconscious is repressed by the ego, then it is referred to as the *emergent-repressed unconscious*. There are a number of reasons that the ego will repress potentially higher ordered conscious structures from emerging into consciousness, and these are time-honored defense mechanisms such as over-rationalization, fear of ego-death, disbelief, substituting or mistaking lower pre-self states for higher trans-self states, retrenchment, or contraction. Defense mechanisms such as these cause the self to distort its interpretation of reality rather than allow for a full and profound transformation.[37]

LEVELS OF CONSCIOUS DEVELOPMENT

Most systems of psychology, when considering levels of development from a newborn child to an adult, only consider the normal states of consciousness, ignoring the transcendental states of consciousness. There are further levels of development beyond the normal adult level of development, called the *formal operational* (by Piaget) or *Mental-Egoic* level. Ken Wilber has done a great job of defining these levels of consciousness. Let us examine them.[38]

EARLIER LEVELS OF DEVELOPMENT

The earlier levels of development consist of pleromic self, the alimentary uroboros, the typhonic self (as axial-body and image-body), and finally, the syntactic membership self. These levels are defined below.

PLEROMATIC SELF

"...the self and the material cosmos are undifferentiated. The self is embedded in the materia prima, which is both the primal chaos of physical matter and the maternal matrix when all creation was fashioned."[39]

---

37 Wilber, Ken, *Eye to Eye* (Shambhala Press, 2011) p. 103.

38 Quotations for this section are adapted and taken from Wilber, Ken, *The Atman Project* (Shambhala Press, 1999), chapters 5–9.

39 Wilber, Ken, *The Atman Project* (Shambhala Press, 1999) p. 77.

Alimentary Uroboros

"...pre-personal 'self,' wherein psychical and physical have not yet been differentiated. The Uroboros is collective, archaic, still mostly oceanic; the word 'uroboros' itself is taken from the mythical serpent that, eating its own tail, forms a self-contained, pre-differentiated mass, 'in the round,' ignorant unto itself."[40]

Typhonic Self

"...the emergence and creation of the organic or body-ego self. The bodyself or bodyego is, in a sense, the transition from the serpent stage of the uroboros to the truly human stage of the mental-ego -the realm of the 'typhon'—the typhon, in mythology, is half human, half serpent." Typhonic Self contains two sub-stages: the axial body and the image body.[41]

Axial-body

"...differentiating the perceiving subject from the perceived or felt object."[42]

Image-body

"...ability to create an extended world of objects and an expanded mode of time, both of which contribute greatly to the establishment of 'object constancy.'" Also "concrete image."[43]

Membership Self

"...the acquisition of language brings in its broad wake a complex of interrelated and intermeshed phenomena, not least of which are a new and more unified mode of self, a vastly extended emotional life, elementary forms of reflexive self-control, and the beginnings of membership. He simultaneously learns to construct, and thus perceive, a particular type of descriptive reality, embedded, as it were, in the language structure itself. The structure of his language is the structure of his self and the 'limits of his world' —membership cognition."[44]

---

40 Wilber, Ken, *The Atman Project* (Shambhala Press, 1999) p. 78.

41 Wilber, Ken, *The Atman Project* (Shambhala Press, 1999) p. 82.

42 Wilber, Ken, *The Atman Project* (Shambhala Press, 1999) p. 82.

43 Wilber, Ken, *The Atman Project* (Shambhala Press, 1999) p. 94.

44 Wilber, Ken, *The Atman Project* (Shambhala Press, 1999) p. 94.

Paranormal states of conscious development concern themselves with the Centauric, Subtle, and Causal Levels of Being, in that order. Examining these levels of development, and the base that they operate upon (Mental-Egoic self), will define the characteristics of their corresponding levels of being. It is important to understand these higher states of consciousness, for they are the realms that one encounters during the practice of contemplation, meditation and magick.

Definition of Terms

- **Cognitive Style:** the way of perceiving reality and the world.
- **Affective Elements (habitual self):** influences moving within the existential body. Also: dispositions, tendencies, emotional perspective (stimulus or motive arousing emotions).
- **Conative factors (conation):** the act or faculty of striving or making an effort.

States of consciousness are described using Sanskrit and Buddhistic terminology, since Western languages completely lack this capability. These terms are defined below:

- **Bijamantra:** symbolic vision (lights and audible illuminations).
- **Karuna:** transpersonal love-in-oneness.
- **Savikalpa samadhi (God Consciousness):** merging of higher self and lower self, until individual and self is in fusion.
- **Nirvikalpa samadhi (unmanifest):** subject and object forgotten, realization of the eternal and infinite void.
- **Turiya (ultimate reality as unity):** oneness in nothingness.
- **Lila and Tzujan:** final spontaneity.

Mental-Egoic Self

"**Cognitive Style:** *syntactic-membership; syntactical secondary process; verbal dialog thinking; concrete and formal operational thinking.*

Affective Elements: *concept affects, dialog emotions, especially guilt, desire, pride, love, hatred.*

Motivational & Conative Factors: *will-power, self-control, temporal goals and desires, self-esteem needs.*

Temporal Mode: *linear, historical, extended past and future.*

Mode of Self*: egoic-syntactical, self-concept, dialog-thinking ego states, various personae.*"[45]

The Mental-Egoic self represents the basic level of development that is one's starting point. The power of language and the mental constructs that it fosters represent a powerful static protective force that ensures the survival of the egoic self. All adults, whatever their socioeconomic living conditions (tribal subsistence or postmodern largesse), operate at this level of consciousness. The key to evolving beyond this level requires flexibility, openness, and the ability to transcend these mental constructs, and to realize that they do not exclusively determine the nature and quality of the "self."

Centauric Self

"**Cognitive Style***: transverbal, vision image, high fantasy, synthesis of primary (parataxic) and secondary (syntaxic) processes—vision logic, transconsensual.*

Affective Elements: *prehension, spontaneity, impulse, expression, supersensory, heartfelt.*

Motivational & Conative Factors: *intentionality, creative wish, meaning, spontaneous will, self-actualization needs, autonomy.*

Temporal Mode: *grounded in present moment, aware of linear time as exfoliating from the present.*

Mode of Self: *integrated, autonomous, trans–bio-social, total body-mind being, centauric.*"[46]

---

45   Wilber, Ken, *The Atman Project* (Shambhala Press, 1999) p. 108.

46   Wilber, Ken, *The Atman Project* (Shambhala Press, 1999) p. 138.

The Centauric self represents a stage where the mental and physical body aspects of the "self" fuse together to form a higher order structure: the body-mind. This new state of being doesn't force the mental control of the body, as does the Mental-Egoic self, but allows the body and the mind to freely flow together and transcend rigid verbal and mental self-definitions. The Centauric individual is creative, integral, and autonomous, and does not require self-approbation from others in order to function.

Low Subtle Self

"**Cognitive Style:** *clairvoyant perception and cognition, extra-egoic and extra-sensory; 'cosmic' states.*

Affective Elements: *transpersonally sensitive, suprasensory (the state beyond the supersensory centaur).*

Motivational & Conative Factors: *sidhi, supranormal and para psychological drives.*

Temporal Mode*: transaxial or transphysical; 'point-source' time, able to read world lines with precognition or post cognition.*

Mode of Self*: astral-psychic, transcending and embracing entire gross realm, 'Cosmic Consciousness.'*"[47]

The lower subtle self is the realm that one usually encounters when experiencing spiritual phenomena, often accompanied by various forms of psychic phenomena. In order to transform to this level, the Centauric self must give up its autonomy and its strongly built-up sense of self must be abandoned as too limiting, so the definition of the "self" might transcend the egoic level all together. Once the Centauric level is transcended, there remains little or no obstacle to the process of continual conscious evolution, for the petty ego has been completely subsumed into the greater dimensions of the spiritual "self" and no longer has any power to repress one's natural development.

---

47   Wilber, Ken, *The Atman Project* (Shambhala Press, 1999) p. 144.

High Subtle Self

"**Cognitive Style:** *actual intuition and literal inspiration, archetypal form, audible illuminations, revelations of light and sound.*

Affective Elements: *rapture, bliss, ecstatic release into super consciousness.*

Motivational & Conative Factors: *Karuna, compassion, overwhelming love, and gratefulness.*

Temporal Mode: *trans temporal, moving into eternity.*

Mode of Self: *archetypal-divine, overself, overmind.*"[48]

The higher subtle self represents the highest level that one can attain and still have some kind of recognizable individual traits. The high subtle also represents the highest state that one can encounter without having completely evolved beyond the egoic mental plane. The realms that are higher still are completely incapable of being fathomed with any sense of personal identity since they are so far beyond any kind of individual being-ness.

Low Causal Self

"**Cognitive Style:** *final illumination, essence of audible revelation, root of Bijamantra, Savikalpa samadhi.*

Affective Elements: *radiant bliss, ananda.*

Motivational & Conative Factors: *only karuna, or transpersonal love-in-oneness.*

Temporal Mode: *utterly transtemporal, eternal.*

Mode of Self: *final—God, point Source of All, Archetypal forms.*"[49]

---

48   Wilber, Ken, *The Atman Project* (Shambhala Press, 1999) p. 147.
49   Wilber, Ken, *The Atman Project* (Shambhala Press, 1999) p. 150.

The low causal self can only be expressed as the state of consciousness where the final boundary between self and Deity has finally been erased forever. One loses their individual humanity but gains the pure essence of the being-ness of the Godhead itself. A perfect assumption of the God-within will approximate this mental state, but it's totally beyond any conceptualization or verbalization—it's the constancy of pure being in its highest state.

High Causal Self

"**Cognitive Style**: *unknowing or perfectly divine ignorance in cessation, Nirvikalpa samadhi, boundless consciousness.*

Affective Elements: *primal or formless radiance, perfect Ecstatic.*

Motivational & Conative Factors: *only karuna and transcendent love-in-oneness; final spontaneity, or Lila and Tzujan.*

Temporal Mode: *transtemporal, eternal.*

Mode of Self: *formless Self-Realization, transcendent witness, turiya.*"[50]

The high causal self is beyond even the concept of the One in All and breaks down into the paradoxical states of non-being and complete non-duality. As stated previously, there isn't emptiness in this sublime state, but a form of completed all-potential that contains all things but isn't itself contained within the union of all things.

I have shown the progression or spectrum of consciousness from the lowest order of manifestation, the Pleromatic self, to the highest order of being, the Higher Causal self. In examining these levels, we can see that most people function at a level of consciousness that is midway between the lowest and highest states of being. We have far to go to achieve these higher states, but transcendental transformation will trigger the process that leads one to these higher states of being, provided the

---

50   Wilber, Ken, *The Atman Project* (Shambhala Press, 1999) p. 151.

seeker who undergoes these transformations can meet the challenge of overcoming the Mental-Egoic and Centauric self (which is no small task). Wilber has noted in his books that we must undergo a difficult process to experience a true transformation to these higher realms.

Transformation requires that a person surrenders their current perspective of reality (translation) and learns to adopt a higher order structure that will determine a more unified and complex perspective of reality. The key to higher forms of conscious evolution is the ego, since it's the maturing ego and its integrated-ness, individuality, and autonomy that are the hallmarks of the Mental-Egoic and Centauric self. So, it's the transformation and translation of the ego and the loosening of its exclusive ownership of the perspective of self that must occur to allow the higher orders of selfhood to emerge. In this case, as previously stressed, the ego neither dies nor is it destroyed. It's integrated into a higher order structure itself. In other words, the ego dissolves into a conscious perception that is trans-personal and cosmic in its scope. The mechanism for obtaining this profound transformation is to shatter conceptual and verbally reinforced beliefs about the self and the domain of experience to stop the internal dialogue that translates, defines, and limits a true experience of the world. It's the application of a strict spiritual discipline that fosters this kind of break with old habits and comfortable manners of perceiving and behaving. Meditation, contemplation, rituals, and ceremonies performed within a strict periodicity is the tool used to cause the transformation of the self so that it begins to emerge into the subtle and, later, causal realms of consciousness.

Meditation and magick open up the self so that the egoic mind, which seeks to self-perpetuate itself, is challenged and ultimately dissolved. This allows for a rebirth of the self on a higher plane of conscious being. The symbols of transformation are the myths and archetypes of the process of esoteric initiation. A spiritual discipline consists of the ordeals of ritual magick, laid out in an ever-ascending order of difficulty and accomplishment. If one faithfully adopts this magickal and spiritual discipline, following and successfully resolving these ordeals, then one will attain these higher states or realms of being, wittingly or unwittingly.

Because of the requirements to "think outside of the box," most adherents of the Western Mystery tradition, who are initiated and practicing magick, are either at or beginning to enter the transformation into the Centauric level of conscious development. In looking at the levels of conscious development beyond the normal adult level, we realize how profound these higher levels are. We can also easily see how a person could think that they had achieved a higher state of consciousness when, in fact, they had actually failed to do so. We need to have a means of measuring and verifying that we have achieved these higher states, a method of determining higher levels of spiritual maturity and accomplishment. As stated previously, peer review is very important to determine a person's actual spiritual or magickal accomplishments. But this search that the seeker undertakes must have a fundamental purpose—and so we ask, "what does the seeker seek?"

WHAT THE SEEKER SEEKS

Ken Wilber, in his book *The Atman Project*, outlines the difficulties and the challenges that one must face in order to truly gain these higher states of consciousness in a permanent fashion.[51] Whether one is aware of it or not, we're all seeking enlightenment. It's the fundamental drive that pushes all of us through the vicissitudes of life. However, there are forces within us that disguise our motives or lock us in a static mental state of development, where complacency and comfort are far more important than gaining any kind of new vista or spiritual perspective in life. We all begin our paths with the same objective—union with the All—but very early on we are thwarted by the necessities of life, and at some point we must return to the fundamental quest of all being-ness if we are to find true fulfillment and completion. We should make certain we always question our motives and the nature of our quest in life, so that we have not substituted our goal of perfect at-one-ment of Atman for some kind of imperfect and shallow surrogate—an *Atman Project*.

The ultimate nature of reality, according to Wilber, is an emptiness or voidness, but one that is not a true emptiness that is void of all forms or features. It is also a unified field of holism, where all space and time, and even consciousness itself, is part of one seamless whole. The ultimate reality and the ultimate state of consciousness are one and the same, a kind of "super conscious All."[52] This unity is the only true reality and all else is an illusion, particularly anything that is egoically or independently real.

51 Wilber, Ken, *The Atman Project* (Shambhala Press, 1999) pp.183–185.
52 Wilber, Ken, *The Atman Project* (Shambhala Press, 1999) p. 184.

Even in the nature of Deity itself, there is only the timeless, transcendent one-ness, and so there is no difference between anything, even between humankind and God. We're all part of a greater whole, and magick is a process that has validity and power because of this wholeness and cannot be comprehended outside of this unity of being and its various conscious derivatives, since it operates on and through that wholeness.

To be an individual—even an individual god—is to exist in an illusion, since everything is truly one and indivisible. We exist as separate entities glorifying our uniqueness and individuality, but we are also seemingly always seeking something apart from ourselves; that quest is also an illusion, since everything is whole and subsumed into the oneness. Therefore, to function and survive, living beings have learned to suppress this perception of one-ness, since it would lead to a disintegration of the self at the level of the undeveloped or Typhonic state. At the trans-personal or Centauric level, the boundaries between the oneness and our individuality must be breached and done so in a manner that does not destroy that individual but illuminates them instead. Therefore, we live through the illusion of individual entities existing in space and time in order to function, but the irony is that we must transcend this state because it is a barrier to attaining the highest levels of conscious-ness. What this means is that whether or not we are aware of it, our ultimate quest is for oneness and unity, the rediscovery of this infinite and eternal wholeness.[53]

Before the emanation of spiritual creation, where Spirit was imbedded in matter, there was the wholeness that is oneness, and we seek that wholeness that is oneness within ourselves. That is the nature of the spiritual quest that the seeker seeks: to be one within the wholeness of the All, our perception of Atman, or God/dess Within.

However, the means to obtaining this sublime state necessitates the death or dissolution of the ego. This perception of ego death is frightening to the individual, especially at the Centauric level, since the ego has become invested with autonomy and seemingly drunk on its own empowerment and uniqueness. The irony is that to die, the seeker learns to truly live and perceive reality as it actually is without the limitations of time and space. But getting past that boundary is the most difficult task that the seeker can face, and usually they become trapped into

---

53 Wilber, Ken, *The Atman Project* (Shambhala Press, 1999) p. 184.

accepting their own ego as a surrogate god, thus denying their ability or willingness to evolve to the next higher level. Many occultists have failed this greatest test. Yet the desire for attaining those higher states and the union of All-Being continues its alluring and seductive siren call, and we as seekers always seem to hear and are drawn to it. It is the ultimate approach-avoidance conflict. We are drawn to it, but we are also terrified of the outcome of embracing it.

It's for this reason—because we greatly desire this ultimate achievement and also greatly fear it—that we end up choosing surrogates instead of actual transcendence. Substitutes range greatly in terms of their variety, but they are usually huge distractions that take the seeker far away from true attainment, such as the usual sensual additions of food and drink, drugs, sex, fame, money, power, and knowledge, but also hidden addictions, such as hubris, self-righteousness, prejudice, misplaced or false piety, cynicism, apathy, and a loss of soul. All a seeker truly seeks for is the attainment of oneness, but what they actually get if they fail the test is a substitute gratification that makes them think that they have achieved the great quest. Therefore, we must always carefully examine our motives, and ask ourselves the fatal question: are we truly seeking Atman, or are we engaging in a diversion? That question can't be quickly or easily answered, but we must be aware of what is motivating us, and at what level of our being. At some point in the career of the magician, they must step outside themselves and transcend all of these prior limitations or be faced with living out their life with those same limitations forever haunting them. They must cease working magick, and instead *become* the magick.

Chapter Four

MECHANISMS OF RITUAL MAGICK

We have covered some basic theories about magick and how it works. We've also examined the maps of consciousness itself. Now we need to examine how magick is performed, what its components are, how they are assembled, and what the dynamics that are used to formulate good rituals are. The three primary points that have already been covered include:

- That magick appears to happen when the higher states of consciousness overwhelm our mundane consciousness, and that this state can be deliberately produced by a combination of altered states of consciousness and symbols of transformation.
- The combination of altered states and symbols of transformation are the triggers that cause magickal phenomena to occur, where the higher self and mind, which is normally dormant, becomes temporarily activated and realized.
- This occurrence is found anywhere a magickal process is active, whether it is a simple ritual, a complex working, or the simple use of a divination system—the effects of the higher self are made evident.

The manner in which altered states of consciousness and symbols of transformation are used isn't random but performed in a very structured and sequential manner. Magickal rituals are not a disordered or discordant chain of operations; they are actually an elegant, harmonious, and flowing sequence of operations. They naturally start with self-preparation and proceed to set the environment, generate the power, then imprint that magickal power with the desire and intention and, finally, exteriorize it. Magick proceeds from the inner self to the outer self in stages and cycles, and the magician adopts the correct conscious states and works with the symbolic tools and symbolic constructs in a natural and ordered fashion. This is necessary for the magician who must memorize and establish a ritual discipline. The higher self, with its trans-temporal qualities, sees all sequences as a holistic unified expression, and therefore sequential steps and their order are not necessary, but completing the process is critical. An incomplete magickal process has no effect since its cumulative holistic expression is null within the domain of higher consciousness. So, for the sake of making certain that an operation is performed completely and correctly, we perform it as a strict sequence of operations.

The pattern or sequence of operations that is used most productively to perform successful ritual workings is called the *master pattern* of ritual workings. The master pattern consists of seven categories that progress from the preparations of the self to the release of power and the performing divination exercises; thus, it progresses from inner self to outer self in a series of steps or stages. The master pattern is used as a simple model for performing magickal rituals and certainly does not represent all the possibilities that might occur in a complex magickal working, but it does represent all of the stages necessary to make magick work for the magician. If any steps or stages are completely omitted, then the rite will fail, but some steps can be implicit and not overtly performed and the magick will work. The seven categories of the master pattern are: *self, space, power, alignment, empowering the link, exteriorization* or *objectification*, and *divination* or *insight*. The last stage, divination, is actually used at all stages of the magick to determine the target and nature of the magick before a rite is performed, and afterwards when the magickal power is sent out to determine the efficacy of the magickal rite. Divination is the eyes and ears of the magician and helps them to understand the more subtle nuances of magick and how it works. If a magician performs magick without performing divination both before and after the working, then the magician is functioning blindly and will not be able to really determine if the magick that was worked was valid, whether the target was correct, or the force used was sufficient, and so on. They will know only if it succeeds or fails, and never why it did so. Divination is a crucial part of the magician's repertoire.

Understanding the master pattern is critical to understanding the organization of a magickal working, as well as determining how ritual magick functions. In order to perform magick, we must understand all its components in greater detail, and these seven categories will serve us very well in this task. Let us examine the master pattern in the sequence and manner that a magician would use it to perform a magickal operation.

SELF

The first step is the Self. What this means is that the magician must prepare themselves for a magickal operation. They must be prepared to perform the magickal working, which means knowing what they are about to magically do, why they are doing it, and what they intend to make happen when the operation reaches its successful completion (the goal). The magician must perform techniques and exercises to control their mind and generate meditative states that cause them to become relaxed and detached from their mundane self and allow them to enter into mild states of trance, where they will be able to perform the ritual work. They should put as much effort and detail into their preparations as feasible and should perform their magickal working only when resolved to do so and when fit in both mind and body. They shouldn't be functioning with an overly full stomach or be hungry from fasting, since this would certainly draw their attention away from the operation. In fact, they should not be distracted by anything having to do with their normal bodily functions. For purification purposes, they should be bathed and anointed. They should dress in clothes suitable for the occasion, such as a magick robe or some other loose-fitting comfortable garment that won't distract them. All mundane considerations should be banished from their mind, and only the pending magickal working should occupy their attention. The magician needs to have a certain degree of mental control and be able to exclusively focus on what is required.

Other considerations are represented by the magickal working that's to be done and the necessary preparations, such as creating sigils or assembling various regalia (such as candles, incense, wine, and oils). All of these are covered in the ritual instructions. The magician should be determined and passionate about the magick that they are performing. They should have examined the ethics regarding their objective and made certain that everything is in place for a successful outcome. The magician must realize the feasibility of what they desire and determine the mundane steps necessary to make it work. The magickal working will assist the magician in executing the mundane steps, giving them the confidence and powerful optimism necessary to make their endeavor successful. They have performed divination on their desired outcome and have a deep sense of self knowledge and symbolic confirmation from that divination system, be it Tarot cards, astrology, I-Ching, Runes, or some other method. They can even have another person perform the divination so that it may be as objective as possible. The more knowledge that they have about the outcome and the steps required to make it happen, the more they will feel confident in the results of the magick.

Magickal workings involve making contact with our higher selves, and so our objective, no matter how well thought out, may undergo slight or even dramatic alterations once we perform the corresponding magick. It's an old and wise saying that ritual magick often produces far more results than one expects, and sometimes the realized objective of the magick can be quite different than what one planned in the beginning. This is why divination is so important: it can usually detect if something unusual is surrounding the objective that a magician is seeking to realize.

For instance, a magician may be seeking a specific job, a lover, or to heal someone. There may be far more details involved in accomplishing that goal than the magician thinks, since things are not always as straightforward in life as they outwardly seem. The job may have been promised to a relative of the company president, the magician may have unreasonable expectations in finding a mate, or the sick person may actually want to die.

Divination will usually uncover these kinds of situations, but the magick will produce results far different than what the magician expects. This fact doesn't invalidate magick as a tool for empowering and defining ourselves, but it cannot be expected to change what is deeply entrenched or highly complex overnight. Magick, as a spiritual system, changes the magician far more than it changes the world they live in; this is an important lesson that the magician must completely understand when undertaking a magickal operation. If self-transformation will assist a mundane pursuit, then magick is the right tool to use; otherwise, there are other methods that one can use to gain an edge in this world, such as hard work, dedication, consistency, open-mindedness, education, good social skills, technical prowess, and so on. Magick isn't the answer to all our problems; in fact, it can create more mundane problems than it solves. However, we work magick to gain self-determination and personal meaning in an otherwise meaningless world, and if this aids our quest for material gratification, then we are most fortunate—but magick usually doesn't work that way.

The key method for performing self-preparation techniques is the meditation session. The magician must master their moods and mental states. They do this by adopting the discipline of performing meditation sessions every day at a certain hour or time of day. These sessions must be uninterrupted and must last at least thirty minutes, gradually becoming an hour in duration. They should be performed in the temple or a space where the magician can have complete privacy and relative peacefulness. The magician learns to sit in a state of comfortable repose and adopt that posture or asana for long periods of time. They can sit on the floor in a cross-legged stance, use one of the many yogic asanas (half or full Lotus), or even sit in a chair. The magician can also use movement or a form of repetitive dance as a meditation technique as well, but we will focus on the basic sitting postures for meditation.

The meditation session begins with the simple technique of breath control, such as the four-fold breath technique (which we will cover later in this book). Other methods may be added such as intoning simple mantras (such as *aum*), staring at complex and contrasting colored posters or diagrams (*yantras*), or performing special contemplation sessions, where a single topic is examined and all its qualities and considerations noted but not dwelled upon. They may also practice their concentration skills and exercise them by concentrating on the second hand of a watch as it moves across the watch dial, making certain that no other thought interferes with their attention. They can also practice gaining trance states by doing a combination of these practices. In this state of consciousness, the magician learns to see subtle things, such as lines of magickal force. They also learn how to visualize objects that don't exist in their environment. The meditation session is always performed as part of the self-preparation rite in a magickal working.

We should also consider the concept of the magickal persona, which a magician adopts to assist themselves in gaining the correct mental state and develop a symbol of transformation for their own self-definition. Since the combination of altered states of consciousness and symbols of transformation triggers the ultra-conscious powers of the higher self, making a symbolic expression of the self assists the magician in connecting with their magickal powers whenever they adopt their magickal persona and enter a trance-like meditative mental state. The magickal persona is the primary magickal tool for the magician and, lacking any other tools (or even a temple), simply possessing a magickal persona and adopting the proper altered state of consciousness will enable them to work magick effectively. Building the magickal persona begins with the selection of a name, which usually has some lore and mythology behind it that the magician can use for the magickal persona. If the name isn't derived, then the magician will have to develop the myths and lore associated with it using their creative intuition, since there won't be any of the usual mythical or historical correspondences associated with it. In developing a magickal persona, the magician will also determine the spiritual tradition that they are to be associated with and the definition of the Deity as well. The magician can determine an entire spiritual tradition and alternative magickal persona all together. The mechanism for developing a magickal persona is covered more extensively in my work *MARM;* getting into greater detail here will be out of scope for this work, which is concerned with assisting the beginner in developing a simple persona.

The magickal persona also has an associated personal image. The magician usually has decorated robes of various colors, a pentacle necklace, a magickal ring, and various other jewelry, and perhaps even masks, makeup, or other regalia specific to the persona. The magickal tools are also a part of this alternative personality, since they are either custom made or altered to be the personal property of the magician. Tools and vestments are magically charged and consecrated for use, meaning that they are set aside and used only for magickal purposes. All the magician's equipment and personal regalia are used exclusively for magickal purposes, right down to the candles, scented oils, water, salt, wine, bread, and other sacraments. Anything that is put aside for magickal uses must never be used for mundane purposes. When items are purchased for magickal use, the magician should pay whatever the retailer asks, and never barter for a lower price. Whatever is acquired for magickal use is considered the property of the gods. It is also prudent that other people (whether members of the household, guests, or friends) should be aware of this fact and never handle or use anything that is set aside for magickal use unless they're also going to use it for magickal purposes. It's wise never to handle a charged and consecrated tool anyway, unless requested or required by its owner. This is not only a kind of magickal etiquette, but it is a commonsense consideration as well, since it's all too easy to pick up the influences of a magickal tool when handled.

We'll cover the methods and exercises that a magician uses to adopt and function through a magickal persona later in this book. However, the student should start thinking now about what their magickal persona will be like, and perhaps start things off by thinking about their name and any other related topics that come to mind. The important thing to remember is that the name that is chosen should be one that has some mythic history behind it. It's better if it's a mythic hero or heroine, a legendary person, demigod, or goddess than an actual recent historical personage. A magician who idolizes Merlin the magician, who is more a mythic figure than an historical one, could call themselves Ambrosius (one of Merlin's alternate names), rather than just calling themselves by that magician's known name, which would be pretentious or even silly. Identifying with Merlin would allow a magician to have access to the Celtic Pagan and early Celtic Christian pantheon of gods, goddesses, heroes, heroines, and even the specific Celtic saints, some of whom—like St. Bridget—were actually Pagan goddesses in disguise. The Arthurian romances would be the source material for the building of their magickal tradition, and the Grail would be a particularly important theme, representing the profoundly important but ever-elusive symbol of enlightenment itself. The selection of a magickal name and developing a persona ends up defining the magician's whole magickal tradition as well.

Other preparations involving the self would include the magickal bath, which is, in my opinion, the most enjoyable part of preparing for ritual work. The magician prepares a bath in their adjoining temple bathroom, if they have one, or if not, then a suitable bathroom will do. The water is consecrated and charged using sea salt, other kinds of bath salts, fragrant oils, soaps, and even rose petals. The room is decorated with candlelight and low playing music. Self-preparation is very important, and whatever the magician can do to help set and enhance the mood of the moment is worth the investment of time and materials. Once bathed, anointed, dressed, and adorned with jewelry, the magician performs their meditation session for half an hour, and then is ready to perform a magickal working.

SPACE

The next stage in the magickal working is the magickal space. This is the magickal temple or grove where the magickal working is performed. The optimal arrangement is where the magician has a separate room (with adjoining bathroom) for a temple, but other arrangements can be used, such as having multipurpose rooms that serve different functions. I wouldn't advise that the magician work magick in their bedroom or living room, since these areas are associated with a lot of mundane activities. Also, sleeping in the same space where one works magick can have some very uncomfortable and disturbing effects, unless one is seeking to extend the magick through dream workings. However, if a temporary space is to be used, then it should be decorated and equipped to work ritual magick and appear to be used exclusively for this activity. The space where one works magick should be clean and free of debris and clutter, allowing the magician the optimum working space and freedom of movement. For instance, a room that doesn't allow the magician to circle around the periphery of the magick circle would not be considered a good area to work ritual magick, nor would an area be considered a good candidate if it can't afford the magician's privacy.

The equipment used for ritual purposes is notably sparse, since only an altar and four small tables or stands for the Watchtower candles would be required initially (the four Angles are also used somewhat later in the magician's ritual work, but they would not require much to be accommodated). The temple may be decorated with pictures, banners, or even wall hangings or painted designs applied to the walls themselves. The floor can be carpeted or bare, with a circle outlined and painted on it. The diameter of the circle can be one of the classical dimensions of nine, eleven, or thirteen feet (three to four meters), or it can be a convenient measurement relative to the diameter of the room's floor. There should be two candles on the altar, candles placed at the four quarters (Watchtowers), a chalice and dish for the salt and water, another chalice and a plate for the sacramental wine and bread, and a thurible or incense burner. The magician will need a consecrated dagger (athamé), wand, sword, and staff. The altar can be covered with a cloth or kept bare, and it should be at least as tall as the magician's waist. There should also be a bell or gong, and the room can be equipped with a simple stereo system (or not, depending on the tastes of the magician).

In addition, the magician will need charcoal, incense, pure spring water, sea salt, scented oils, wine, bread or cakes, and extra candles, most of which can be bought at health food, occult, or church supply stores.

The magician prepares the temple for working magick by performing a ritual called the *circle consecration rite*, where the temple space is purified, consecrated, and the circle and four wards or Watchtowers are defined. This rite is used to generate sacred space. It's important to make a distinction between profane space, which is outside of the circle, and the place where spirit may participate in ritual activities, which is sacred space. Once the temple is consecrated, then it can contain and direct the magickal powers and objectives that are the core of the magickal working. However, the creation of sacred space is as critical a function as assuming the magickal persona and performing the meditation session. These operations are never omitted from a working since they represent the foundation for all magickal workings.

An alternative to the temple is the magickal grove, which is a private outdoor location used for working magick. A grove is very different than a temple and should be approached in a very different manner. A temple has to have everything brought into it for magick to be performed there, and it needs to be purified and consecrated; a grove is already in a consecrated state and needs nothing to add to its empowered and sanctified state. The only thing that the magician brings to the grove is fire and the sacraments.[54] Everything else is already there, including the powerful sense of sacredness that merely needs to be adopted by the magician for it to be realized. A grove is neither consecrated nor empowered. All that needs to occur to prepare a grove for ritual is for the magician to attune their sensitivity and perceptions to the sacredness and latent empowerment that is already evident. The grove is built up only once when it is erected. It may contain a delineated circle, markers or torches for the four or eight compass points, a small table to hold the sacraments and tools, and a central marker consisting of a decorated post and two torches.

We will go over the circle consecration rite and the grove preparation rite later in this book, but these two rituals represent what is required to meet the second stage of a magickal working: the creation of sacred space.

---

54 Only if the magick is to be performed during the night. Otherwise, the Sun becomes the source of fire during the day.

The combination of self-preparation and the creation of sacred space are fundamental to any kind of magickal working, and conjoined, they prepare the magician for all that happens within the field of the domain of magick. All ritual acts are performed by the magician as a magickal personality affected by an empowered trance state within a defined symbolic place where Spirit has dominance over mundane consciousness.

POWER

The next stage is the generation of magickal power, which is also called *empowerment*. Once the self is prepared and sacred space is created, then the magician will generate the energies required to power the magickal spells. Magickal power is probably the least understood of all appellations in the practice of ritual magick and is often confused with an actual objective energy. Our earlier discussion on this matter has resolved that magickal power or energy is metaphorical and subjective. It denotes the quality of intensity and meaningfulness rather than some quantifiable EMS energy.[55] The magician performs specific symbolic operations within sacred space and perceives their area in a mild trance state. This causes the subtle atmosphere within the magick circle to be greatly intensified. The magician performs these rites of empowerment as if they were working with energy, even though there is no actual energy involved other than the emotions and perceptions of the magician and whoever else happens to be in the magick circle.

The key concept to magickal power is simply stated: it is a form of ecstasy. Obviously, the most powerful and meaningful experience a person can possibly have is to be transported by ecstasy. It seems that ecstasy is the greatest trigger for awakening the higher self and its domain of Spirit. However, other than having an unplanned religious sexual experience, most people lack the mechanism to deliberately experience this higher state of consciousness. So rather than engaging in some kind of pretentious sexual activity to attempt to achieve this state, the magician can deliberately trigger the same kind of emotional excitation without recourse to sexuality. Through the use of symbolic

---

55 EMS (electromagnetic spectrum): The spectrum of light/energy as defined by science. Magickal power does not seem to be a quantifiable energy, for reasons specified previously.

and ritual artifices, the magician obtains the same profound sense of spiritual meaningfulness. All this is accomplished through cultivated mind states and ritual activity—and these can be performed by the magician alone. This form of trance- and ritual-induced ecstasy is the objective for all magickal workings and represents the foundation for all heightened spiritual experiences. On a symbolic level, magickal power as derived from ecstasy is represented by the concept of union: the joining of the archetypal masculine and feminine qualities within us. It is the fusion of light and darkness, good and evil, life and death, spirit and the body-mind; it's really love in its highest expression. As you can see, this is a very different—and I believe more accurate—interpretation of magickal power and empowerment than the usual discussion of magickal energy as some kind of objective force.

In regard to using sex as the means to trigger the higher self, it represents a far more daunting task than one might think, since a couple would have to use sex and ecstasy to perform magick and could not allow themselves to be distracted or carried away by the sexual pleasure. Only a highly trained couple could do this, and it would require they both be very knowledgeable about magick and sexual techniques. It's simpler to produce a surrogate experience of ecstasy than practice sex magick with all its possible distractions, pitfalls, and complications.

The magickal energies, based as they are on the principle of ecstasy, are found in two opposite but complimentary forces known as the *deosil cone of power* and the *widdershins vortex*. The characteristics of these two forces represent the erotic cycle of the male and female human orgasm; this fact should not be too surprising, since they contribute to the experience of ecstasy.

The cone of power and the vortex symbolically imitate the masculine and feminine cycles of orgasm and can be used separately or together. The cone of power is used to generate an energy that projects itself into the mundane world like a bolt of lightning. There, it travels to its target, irresistibly attracted to the imprinted magickal link like static electricity is to the earth, and blasts the target with the full force of its potency. The cone of power is generated, imprinted, and released, and what remains is banished or cleansed, so the unleashed bolt of power is unable to rebound upon the magician.

The vortex is used to contain energy and to amplify it over time. A vortex is an energy field that's deeply centered and internalized, but when it reaches a climax, it produces waves of energy radiating out in all directions, gradually and completely altering the target through multiple waves of force until it totally complies with the will of the magician. The vortex type of magickal energy is more subtle and deeper than the cone of power, which suffers from the single-mindedness of being able to miss its mark, especially if the targeted objective is not clearly defined. A vortex surrounds its objective with waves of power, which are more instrumental in making a greater and dynamic change more possible. A cone of power is raised and used in a single magickal working, while a vortex is used over a series of workings. The cone of power must be banished when the magickal working is completed, while a vortex is sealed at its highest point of power so it can be used later. On subsequent evenings, the vortex is unsealed and realized at its previous apex of power. Then the magician can add more levels of power and symbolic meaningfulness until it eventually achieves the highest level of power needed to effect the transformation, and only then is it unleashed. The vortex can contain any magickal pattern or energy field, including a cone of power (or many cones of power), generated over a period of weeks. The vortex is a simple energy field, but it represents a greater articulation and manipulation of magickal energy than what a simple cone of power by itself is able to produce. A magician who seeks to work the most effective and potent magick makes use of both of these methods of magickal power generation.

Resonance is also a factor with raising and sending magickal energy, and it's used as a means of controlling the intensity and exteriorizing magickal power. The online Merriam-Webster dictionary defines the term resonance as "a vibration of large amplitude in a mechanical or electrical system caused by a relatively small periodic stimulus of the same or nearly the same period as the natural vibration period of the system."[56] Another word is *reverberate*, and in the terminology of magick, it represents both the mechanism that produces magickal energy and the mechanism that increases and "discharges" its intensity. Magickal energy is generated by an iterative process—a stimulus such as chanting, dancing in a ring, spinning in place, or any kind of repetitive activity or movement—and as the amplitude or rate of acceleration is increased, the level of magickal energy is also increased. When the magickal energy

56 "Resonance." *Merriam-Webster.com.* Merriam-Webster, 2024. Web.

reaches a climax, an increased amplitude or acceleration causes a spike of energy or power to be realized, producing euphoric and even ecstatic states of consciousness.

Producing magickal energy in this manner requires two techniques: first, the energy must be generated and brought to a plateau level of stimulation. Second, the energy is given a final intense stimulus to cause it to reach a climax. Between the generation of the field of energy and its release, the magician imprints the magickal power with their will and desired objective. This is done by projecting a symbol of that desire, called the *magickal link,* into the energetic field. An energy field impacted by the will of the magician is released into the outer world to seed it with an empowered potential, causing an objectified link to be realized. Such a realization occurs both inwardly, as in the unconscious mind of the magician, and outwardly, as the super symbolic world that the magician dwells in. Full realization of the magickal working requires the magician to also perform the necessary mundane steps, but these steps would seem charmed and fool-proof when the magick is properly projected out into the world. When the magick works effectively, the goal or objective seems not only attainable, but almost a certainty. This is the nature of the magickal working of acquisition, which the master pattern clearly defines.

MAGICKAL RITUALS OF EMPOWERMENT

Rituals that cause altered states of consciousness use symbolic devices (such as a pentagram), physical techniques (such as breath control), and symbolic patterns of ritual expression to impact the physical awareness of the practitioner. These rituals are simple in structure, yet very capable of manifesting results. The process of generating magickal power is joined with the expression of symbolic meaning to produce a magickal effect. Considering what has already been discussed about magickal power, the necessary driver for this type of ritual is a strong and implacable desire for a certain objective to be realized. The greater passion a magician feels for a specific desire, the greater magickal power they will direct to it in a ritual. Yet the desire for a given thing isn't enough to realize it. As in life, the magician must follow a pattern and successfully execute a series of simple ritual actions in order to accomplish their goal.

The easiest method of self-empowerment is the realization and accomplishment of a goal. We can dream and scheme forever, but when we act to make our dream a reality, we are engaging in a process in which we're objectively tested and measured. This process of accomplishment begins with a need or a desire that becomes almost obsessive and therefore must be acted out so that it will be fulfilled. The dynamic interaction of desire and action is the core of all magickal work.

The magician begins with a potent desire called the *objective,* and then derives a method of symbolizing it. The objective is analyzed and compared with various categories of symbolic correspondences until one is selected that best represents the nature of the desire, and then it's prepared for use in a ritual format.

The magician must consider the ethics and justification for taking action to fulfill the objective. It should be subjected to an internal inquiry to determine if it's indeed necessary and important. The magician must also understand the nature and source of the need to exact its expression in symbolic form. If the desire is important and necessary and the actions taken are deemed ethical, then the magician proceeds to develop a ritual to fulfill that desire.

The ritual base is always a consecrated and purified environment. There, the magician performs ritual actions that generate magickal power. The activated desire drives the empowerment process. The ritual technique consists of the symbolic polarization of the archetypal masculine and feminine and their subsequent union within the mind of the practitioner. The fusion of polarities is conceptualized as a personification of the archetypal male and female in sexual union, with assistance differentiating and defining this polarity from the magick circle. The consummation of this polarity is achieved through the manipulation of devices and tools, symbolically enacted in a ritual format, causing a profound alteration of consciousness. The mind of the magician is polarized between light and darkness, consciousness and unconsciousness, and their fusion causes a unified state to occur, thus releasing a great potential of psychic energy. This is the process that fills the magick temple with a field of magickal power and represents the *prima materia* out of which the magician shall forge the magickal effect.

The second part of this process of empowerment is one in which the magician imprints the raised energy field with symbols of meaning and intent that represent what the magician desires. This process is critical to the effective conclusion of the ritual because the empowerment needs to be defined and then projected to cause any outer manifestation. There are four specific elements for this manipulation of magickal meaning: the purpose, intention, link, and objective. The magician develops each of these elements to impart the greatest meaning and significance to the combined ritual expression.

The first element is the *purpose* of the ritual. The magician may begin the ritual with a statement of purpose after performing the circle purification ritual. The statement of purpose is a ritual action that grounds the rite within the stated importance of the objective and the ethicality of the ritual actions (a settled determination). All other actions in the ritual will support and build upon the stated purpose. This is because the purpose has determined the objective of the rite and the authority of the magician who seeks its fulfillment. However, the magician may also begin the ritual without stating its purpose. It may be implied within the expressed intention of the ritual, but it will always exist in some form and act as the foundation of the ritual. Without a strong sense of purpose, the efforts of the magician are groundless and weak.

The second element is the *intention* of the ritual. The intention is actually the underlying pattern of the ritual, containing the design or plan through which the ritual will be successful as the product of attention directed to an object of knowledge. The intention also contains the outer and non-ritual actions that the magician will perform to affect the outcome. It's the artful combination of ritual and mundane actions that cause a ritual working to be successful. The ritual actions give boldness and single-mindedness to the mundane actions, and as these actions are reinforced by mundane actions, they increase the odds for a successful outcome. The dual nature of the intention is important to a ritual's success; ritual actions without mundane actions are full of potential but empty of physical effectiveness. The reinforcing quality of ritual actions followed by mundane actions is not to be scorned as a crutch or an artificial deviation from the simple act of just doing it. There are many books and articles attesting to the efficacy of positive thinking, yet the art of ritual magick has a greater effect and impact. It's as if the Deity willed the outcome of the desired objective.

The *magickal link* is the third element of the ritual's manipulation of symbolic meaning. A magickal link symbolizes the expressed desire or goal of the ritual. It is a ritual process where the goal or desire (objective) is reformulated and deployed in a symbolic format. A magickal link causes the merging of the Macrocosm (archetypal world) with the Microcosm (physical world). This fusion between the archetypal and physical worlds causes the target of the ritual to be perceived at the highest level of consciousness. Once identified, manipulating the magickal link also transforms entities and events existing on the archetypal plane. This transformation of the archetypal plane will then charge and empower analogous factors and processes on the physical plane, causing them to be realized as a profound potential. Therefore, when the magician performs the corresponding mundane actions that assist them in acquiring the ritual actions' objective, the material world is already predisposed towards its successful realization.

The *objective* is the source of all ritual actions and the fourth element of the ritual. The objective is the primary cause, and it precipitates the ritual's events and gives them significance. Desire is the primary stimulus of all magickal ritual, and the ethical pursuit of one's desires, using the coincidence of the two worlds, ultimately causes empowerment and a profound inner knowledge within the magician. The objective must be symbolized as a spiritual concept, transforming it from an association with the physical plane to the spiritual plane. The magician is actually pursuing a spiritual objective rather than a mundane one in ritual, but its successful resolution impacts the physical world and fulfills a desire in that domain. The accomplishment of the spiritualized objective empowers, reinforces, and further spiritualizes the self at both levels, emboldening the magician to pursue ever-greater spiritual objectives.

If a magician seeks money, love, employment, security, friendship, peace, positive aspirations, insight, knowledge, or the psychic healing of themselves or another, then they must translate that need into a symbolic quality that is justifiable to their spiritual process. The desire for money or love becomes the spiritual requirement for having an adequate material basis for the practice of ritual magick and personal satisfaction. The love of another can bring the magician closer to the Deity if that love is universalized, especially if it represents the indirect love of the Deity. Money is a useful tool, and if the need can be eminently justified as an important part of the magician's spiritual process, then it will be forthcoming without a single obstacle. The magician seeks all things required for their existence from the universal source and justifies it as the inherent human need for survival. An impoverished magician cannot focus on anything but fulfilling their basic needs. Therefore, to evolve, the magician must first fulfill the basic needs for material security. When these needs are met, then a more spiritual perspective can be developed.

The magician must also learn what is truly necessary for their survival, as this factor is different for everyone. It is also an implied rule in ritual magick that the magician always receives what is needed through the labor of ritual and mundane actions, but not necessarily what is desired. Therefore, it's fruitless to seek great wealth and an easy life through ritual magick unless it can be justified accordingly. Through successive workings, the magician accumulates what is needed for them to complete the Great Work and determine their individual destiny. All else is under the influences of chance and dictated by the socioeconomic matrix into which we were born. If magick were an easy means to become rich and powerful, our economic base would be radically different than it is, and magick would be taught as an important course in business colleges around the world.

Magick is the bridge between material and spiritual existence, and as another value system that incorporates both worlds, it must be understood and put to use. Magicians are seldom wealthy, but they are also seldom without the means to fulfill their needs as they (hopefully) serve the spiritual needs of humanity.

Once the field of magickal power has been set with these four elements of symbolic magickal meaning, then the imprinted field is exteriorized through the process of resonance. Exteriorization is a ritual action in which the magician simultaneously projects the imprinted field of energy outwardly and increases its level of intensity to ecstatic levels. This increase of intensity is called *resonance,* and it causes the imprinted energy field to reach a critical mass where it explodes and is hurled toward its objective. When the imprinted field is released, it impregnates the symbolic potential of the objective within the archetypal plane and allows for the corresponding mundane actions to be imbued with encouragement and accessibility. The process of resonance is ritually enacted through chanting rounds, ecstatic dance, and breathing techniques that use hyperventilation, repeated at a greater velocity, frequency, and intensity. The climax is executed at the moment of maximum resonance, during which the magician is nearing total exhaustion, producing one final and momentous action before complete cessation.

The above processes of empowerment, setting the symbolic field, and exteriorization represent the three steps of a simple ritual of empowerment. This is the ritual pattern of acquisition, the most basic of all ritual working patterns. It is found in all the systems of ritual magick throughout the world; therefore, it is the most essential structure of a ritual working. If a ritual is performed and is missing any of the above basic elements or processes, it is guaranteed to fail. A working that fails is always indicative of a poor ritual structure. Failure is also symptomatic of poor planning or insufficient insight into the nature of the desire; a working always includes both ritual actions and mundane actions or it may fail to realize complete manifestation. (There are also other mitigating circumstances that may thwart the success of a ritual working.) The success of a ritual hinges not only on the harmonious integration of the above structures, elements, and actions, but also on the preparations, meditations, divinatory insights, and clarity of purpose and intention. If all these items are successfully practiced and included in a ritual working, then nature itself will present no obstacles to the successful realization of the objective.

A magickal working answers the following questions in logical sequence: What is the reason for the magick to be done (the purpose)? What are the actions that will cause it to be successfully accomplished (the intention)? What is the spiritual definition of the desire (the link)? What is the desire (the objective)? A ritual must seek to fully incorporate all these elements for the ritual working to be complete and intelligible.

In the Alexandrian tradition of Witchcraft, the above pattern is used in its most simplistic and effective manner. The coven raises a cone of power through the performance of the Witches' circle dance. This dance consists of a ritual structure characterized by a clockwise or deosil circumambulation of the magick circle and the focusing of energy to the center of the circle in its zenith. The resonance of the dance tempo causes the polarity of creative (archetypal masculine) and receptive (archetypal feminine) energies of the dancers to fuse into a single force, drawing from the periphery of the circle to the center and then up to the zenith. The Cone of Power ritual is analogous to the act of creation from an archetypal masculine perspective, completed after the climactic action and release of energy.

The Witches' circle dance is a means of harnessing the magically creative energy because of its emphasis on the polarity of archetypal female to archetypal male. The power is focused by the High Priestess wielding a sword in the center of the circle, and therein she embodies the ritual intention. Then, the coven chooses one of the ten Sephiroth God names of the Qabalah that best suits the working, using it in a chant, and the resultant spell would act as the symbolic link. The member(s) to whom the intention of the rite was to be dedicated sit in the center of the circle around the High Priestess and act as the focus and embodiment of the link, holding the objective of the rite in their minds. The final action is one in which the coven chanted the God name in an accelerated mantric round, and the member(s) in the center collected the power. At the climax of the ritual, they sent the power through the High Priestess to fulfill its objective, thus activating the intention. The magickal power was generated and accelerated through the process of resonance; the coven members increased the intensity of the energy by increasing the associated ritual movement (the tempo of the dance or chanting).

The symbology surrounding the generation of power appears to be in the form of a symbolic enactment of sex because every ritual ends with a climax. The principal effect of such an emotional and spiritual climax is that it causes the individual to become tangibly aware of the state of the Union of All Being, which is also called *super-consciousness.* The sexual imagery isn't as much a means to sexual gratification as it is a means of imitating the super-conscious state of spiritual union. In this state of mind, one becomes aware of the connection between all things and experiences the ecstatic bliss of wholeness and perfection. The emotional impact of such a state is very empowering! The feelings of solidity and empowerment are essentially the whole of the experience of magickal power, and they transform all who share in it.

The use of magickal power in ritual causes the participants to experience a psychic transformation. It produces a revelation of meaningfulness that alters their lives and a corresponding expansion of their personal awareness. They are liberated by their own ecstasy. However, this state is not the goal of magick, but the means by which magick affects the outer world. Also, this state is not permanent, making magick a process that must be continually re-experienced. Therefore, magickal power is the medium through which the individual is opened to the symbolic reality of super-consciousness and made ready to integrate with the spiritual dimension of existence.

Another method of power generation, the vortex, is less known and rarely practiced. While the cone of power has an upright vertex, the vortex has an inverted one; the Witches' circle dance proceeds in a deosil circuit, whereas the vortex uses a circuit that is widdershins or counterclockwise. The four Quarters or Angles of the magick circle are drawn together into the center of the circle instead of being polarized along its periphery. This process, therefore, causes a fusion of the polarities and gently implodes, becoming like a psychic black-hole vortex with its central singularity. This ritual structure is built upon an already consecrated and charged magick circle, for otherwise the circle would collapse and nothing would remain. Unlike the cone of power, the vortex cannot be banished and remains intact (usually in a sealed state) after its use. The vortex contains and preserves what is established in it. When its powers are focused on a specific object, it emanates a wave-like force that is both subtle and effective at surrounding and permeating the target of the magic. In this fashion, the energy field of the vortex resembles the waves of ecstasy of the feminine erotic cycle. It is the opposite polarity of the cone of power, which resembles the masculine erotic cycle. Therefore, these two methods together represent the polarity of magickal power itself and are more effective when worked together.

FOUR LEVELS OF MAGICKAL EMPOWERMENT

The ritual magician can employ power through many possible variations. We have examined not only the basis and the definition of this phenomenon, but also discussed a direct methodology for the assumption of these powers through partaking of sacraments. However, there is a means of generating magickal power through the interplay of ritual structure and the use of symbolic archetypes without having to resort to any substances. First, it's necessary to classify the techniques of empowerment as they digress from the principal method of symbolizing magickal power; this is the joining of the archetypal male with the archetypal female.

There are four levels to the technique of the generation of magickal power. As already stated above, all methods of generating power emulate the joining of the archetypal male and female in various manners. The resultant fusion causes the mind of the magician to directly experience the source of all consciousness, known as the Union of Being. The conscious state of union is the most absolute state that one can possibly achieve.

The Absolute Spirit, the Union of Being, and the Spiritual Process (various terms for the Deity) are words that represent the same quality, which is this conscious state of union.

The first level of empowerment is the symbolic union of polarities, represented physically in the act of love between consenting individuals. This union isn't common or profane; rather, it's exalted through the glorifying and building up of each person through the assumption of the godhead for each participant, and their subsequent physical and spiritual union. Such a union, when emphasized through magic, becomes an emblem for the union of the One, where all being is united into a single expression.

This process of polarization and fusion represents the primary model for ritual empowerment, and all subsequent ritual techniques replicate its essential pattern. Ritual methods of self-empowerment could be said to represent the state of ecstasy as experienced through the union of opposites performed within a spiritual context. When the magician performs a ritual act of empowerment, they share in the experience of the superconscious state on some level of awareness. This experience of magickal power may be the pinnacle of one's life experience, or the barely noticed phase of an entire array of experiences; but the symbolism always causes some level of spiritualization to occur.

The symbolic archetype for union is modeled on the fusion of opposites, and the stages that one undergoes to achieve this sublime state are the archetypal patterns of ritual empowerment. The very actions of ritual empowerment evoke the images of the God and Goddess in divine union, and this powerful archetypal image causes one to psychically experience a corresponding ecstatic union and liberation through the oneness of all. The very expression of magickal power is then the symbolic source of orgasmic passion. Magickal power can become polarized to orient itself to a masculine or feminine expression, and these polarities may be joined in various combinations to form ever more subtle hybridizations. The ritual pattern of empowerment may also be used to represent the ritual steps for the practice of sex magick. However, the technique of ritual magick allows the magician to symbolize this process of sacred sexuality and still produce the same magickal empowerment with all its original potency using a symbolic analogue. The actual practice of sex magick, then, represents the first level of empowerment. The participants of such a work may actually perform a ritual enactment of sexual union, or they may symbolize that primary ritual action (plunging the dagger or wand into the chalice) but still use their bodies as the triggers for their latent desire, thus giving the empowerment its potency and analogous ecstasy.

The second level of empowerment is represented by the symbolic substances of sexual union. Salt water (holy water or lustral water) represents sweat or semen. The wine is the blood or menstruum. The cakes are the flesh itself, which in some ancient forms of magick was the actual flesh and blood of a sacrificial victim. In the same fashion, the scented oils are the hormonal bodily secretions and the lubricating mucus of the sexual organs. All these substances are the symbolized sacraments from the bodies of the God and Goddess in union. To partake of them is to become one with the Deity, as is demonstrated daily in the performance of the Catholic Mass. However, a sacrament represents the symbolizing of substances that could only have a nonphysical existence. Sacraments are still quite physical and have their own qualities apart from what they represent. However, sacraments are only one step removed from that which they symbolize and so impart a profound source of magickal empowerment. Therefore, they are used as an analogue to the ecstatic union of all being.

Another type of sacrament is known as a *magickal object*, an item that has been charged through one of the four levels of empowerment. In some traditions, the athamé (magick dagger) and the wand are charged between the naked embrace of a male and female practitioner;[57] thus, the tools receive a charge associated with a first-level empowerment. Other tools can be consecrated by being purified with a sacrament (salt water) and charged by the already charged athamé or wand, or by being dedicated exclusively to the workings of ritual magick, thus accumulating a charge through constant use and association. These items are imbued with magickal power because of their association with a particular symbolic magickal concept and their manipulation in a ritual context. Some tools are charged just by being used. This is a highly symbolic level of empowerment produced by association, transference, or both. In this fashion, the tools of magick are also sacraments, including the furniture and the temple or grove itself.

The third level of empowerment is represented by the expression of a purely abstract symbol that has no physical basis in space and time except in the mind of the magician. This is the level of empowerment

---

57 The practitioners may also be robed as a more cautious but no less effective symbolic analogue of the naked embrace.

of the pure intellect, symbolized by the Universal Mind that exists as consciousness without physical form. The polarization of power is therefore reflected on an abstract level, and it is the relationship of pure form to structure and linear space to curved space. The linear form of a cross could be construed as being masculine, and the nonlinear curves of the spiral as feminine. When these forms are drawn together, as, for instance, in the diagram of the Rose Cross (two bisecting lines with a spiral in its center), the polarities are brought into union, temporarily generating magickal power.

Another important concept is that magickal power is realized through movement, so the magician draws the abstract patterns and devices in the air with their wand or dagger. Where the structure of line or curve determines the polarity of the potential power, the movement of drawing determines the level of intensity or resonance that is expressed from the action. Projecting the masculine power through linear devices consists of the magician drawing straight lines of force between two or more points, creating structures that are joined into a linear matrix. Linear matrices occupy the standard three spatial dimensions, and their movement within that field (the drawing of the devices) is the fourth.

The feminine component (as the nonlinear curve) has no true linear vector; it evolves or dissolves, expands or contracts, and waxes or wanes, always returning to its source. However, all abstract mental structures (linear space) have a subtle curving formulation by which all points eventually lead back to themselves, thus demonstrating the recursiveness of all mental creations. The masculine and feminine polarities blend into each other and are therefore only relatively polarized within their idealized form. Ultimately, they represent the polarities in their most fundamental expression.

The symbolic devices, such as pentagrams, hexagrams, crosses, triangles, sigils, and the occult symbols (gestures or mudras) used in ritual performance, can be divided into two categories. There are devices that are purely symbolic and therefore must be drawn in the air or illustrated on talismans, and there are other devices that are represented as bodily movement or ritual choreography. The former type of devices usually involves a joining of the archetypal feminine and masculine polarities. In the merging of the two forms, a new form is created, and their synthesis is the basis for the symbolic shape of a magickal device. The hexagram is an excellent example of this type of composite as the union of two opposing triangles. Sigils and angular forms that are charged by having a spiral drawn over them are another type of this form of empowerment. The magician can also draw lines of force (vectors) between objects or locations in the magick circle (such as the four Quarters), thus expressing this level of empowerment.

The other type of device consists of direct forms of movements, such as circling the magick circle, performing chanting rounds, expressing dramatically verbalized concepts or incantations, and performing complex ritual dances and movements. These techniques are all resonance-triggered, meaning that they are repetitiously performed in ever-greater cycles of rapidity and intensity until an expression of climax releases the generated power.

Another technique of this type involves the visualization of a kind of metaphorical light energy in a specific color and attribute that represents the type of power that the magician chooses to use. The action of the visualization merges with the symbolic image to become something projected from one's mind directly into the physical world, where it is observed as a superimposed image. This is the way in which a magician looks into a crystal ball or a magick mirror; the technique can be expanded until all the tools, sacraments, ritual environment, and even the temple itself become projected images of empowerment residing wholly in the mind of the magician.

The fourth and final level of empowerment includes the methods of transference and association. The magickal process of transference is the power of associating objects and places with a special spiritual and magickal value, causing them to become imbued with meaning so that they resonate with the symbolic analogues of the archetypal plane. Magickal objects gain their independent value by association, becoming metaphors for the symbolic archetype that exists in the mind. For instance, the mental concept of a chair that we associate with all physical chairs in our minds is the archetypal chair. When we use the word "chair" without any modifying adjectives, it can pertain to all the classes, shapes, and colors of objects that fit the semantic concept of the word chair. Magickal objects, which exist on the physical plane, symbolize the corresponding mental representations existing on the archetypal or super symbolic plane, just like the analogy of the archetypal chair.

In this fashion, the temple or grove of the magician and all it contains becomes the Microcosmic representation of that archetypal or

Macrocosmic analogue that exists on the absolute plane. The will of the magician combined with their established altered state of consciousness causes the two levels of being to become congruent, and in that union is found the joining of opposites wherein the Union of Being is experienced. The fourth level can also be experienced as the realization of mythical places that are produced by the perceived superimposition of the spiritual world upon the physical world. This level is experienced through adventure, upon a mystical search through the inner and outer worlds. It is what a magician might experience when embarking upon a magickal quest trekking through the wilderness (such as a vision quest). This certainly answers the age-old question of why mystics and magicians like to hike to inaccessible places.

Magicians often talk of geographic locations that are reputed to have magickal powers, such as power zones, ley-lines (both overland and underground streams), and other topographical formations. This could also be considered an example of the application of association when an archetypal grid or matrix is superimposed upon physical reality. Through self-empowerment, the magician projecting the symbolic world upon the physical realizes that, combined, they are the true reality. This is the realization of the principal occult mystery: the world of magick is all around for those who can perceive it. Through this process of association, the individual not only receives that potent sense of personal significance, but they also discover the revelation of the spiritual world existing upon and within the physical plane.

ALIGNMENT

The next stage is called *alignment* and represents the alignment of the magician to their operational concept of Deity. Where some magicians work magick strictly through the personality and imago of their Deity by assuming it as their own magickal persona, other magicians seem to have little to do with any concept of Deity, and yet their magick still works. One could point out this discrepancy, and that might make this stage invalid (or at least optional), but to omit it entirely is to omit the power of the mysteries, including the most important Mystery of the Self. When a magician works magick without including the alignment of Deity within their working, they perform the working as if alone and in isolation, and indeed they are alone and isolated. The kind of magick performed without the intervention of Deity or some kind of spiritual immersion is the mere acquisition of personal power and success, which does indeed happen but in a far less meaningful and profound manner than would occur if the magician were in deep and intimate alignment with the Deity or other equally profound spiritual elements. In addition, other types of ritual workings, such as the Solar and Lunar Mysteries, would be nearly useless; the magician would certainly not progress as they might if they were engaged in the Mystery of Self, which is called *transformative initiation*. A magician who lacks such a spiritual dimension to their magick would also seem to lack in any real personal growth and would represent a potentially static process of self-gratification, or a kind of spiritual materialism. However, even the most stubborn, materialistic atheist practicing magick would eventually develop a spiritual rapport with their own inner self and, out of such hubris, even enlightenment might ultimately occur.

I propose that the magician extensively define their notions about the nature of their Deity and then practice them as the magickal discipline of alignment. This is succinctly achieved through the four methods of devotion, communion, invocation, and assumption, and there are rituals that assist the magician in each of these operations. The easiest of these four operations is devotion, since we're all exposed to some kind of religious devotion to Deity in our religious experiences as children, as adults, or through global cultures at large. However, the devotion that a magician gives to their chosen aspect of Deity is also a form of self-devotion and self-love since the magician aspires to behold their concept of Deity and seeks to emulate and unify with it. Some would call this narcissism. However, since it has the spiritual objective of transforming the magician and it forces them to admit a greater power and wisdom in the world than what they possess, it would not really be narcissism, nor would it be regressive. This practice actually causes the magician to internally develop a personal symbol of transformation (themselves as Deity), and when it is exposed to altered states of consciousness, it causes them to literally transcend themselves. Through the artifice of devotion, the magician builds a shrine to their God and performs rites and ceremonies to celebrate all the great qualities of that Deity, making offerings, performing devotional meditations, and inculcating themselves with the morals, teachings, mysteries, and charisma of that Deity, ultimately readying themselves for union with that Godhead.

Rites of communion are when the magician generates sacraments (sacramentation), imbuing material things with the spiritual essence of the Deity, and then consumes them (food and drink), applies them to their body (oils, medicines, and ointments) or wears them (vestments, masks, makeup, jewelry, and so on). These rites of sacramentation forge an intimate relationship with the Deity, and the magician practices them on a continual and periodic basis, which ultimately allows for complete identification with (assumption of) the Deity. *Invocation* is the magickal rite where the Godhead is summoned to materialize to the magician in a tangible form.

The Deity is given an image through descriptive metaphors and annotative qualities, mixing the spiritual aspect with human characteristics. This makes the trans-personal and trans-rational qualities of the Deity approachable by a human being, who is burdened with all the limitations of a rational ego. All these rites and ceremonies prepare the magician for full immersion into the Godhead, called the Rite of Assumption (or *drawing down*), where the magician becomes, for a moment, the transcendent Deity associated with the domain of Spirit. It seems almost obvious that these rites and ceremonies, if practiced diligently and continually over time, will cause the complete transformation of the magician, and with all due and deliberate effort, indeed, this is exactly what happens. It is the ultimate objective for the magickal practitioner.

It is patently obvious that developing the magickal discipline of alignment is crucial to any kind of spiritual development, which makes the practice of magick greater than the mere mechanism of material acquisition and self-mastery. Certainly, it is important for the magician to be equally successful in their material and spiritual endeavors, but if one or the other dominates, then the magician's development will be skewed as well. They will either succumb to mystical hubris and lose all ability to affect the world around them, or they will lose all sight of spirituality and forget the very thing that makes magick possible, which is their higher self enveloped in super-consciousness. I propose a middle path in this book, so the student can find a balanced way between materialism and mysticism.

THE LINK:
EMPOWERING THE INTENTION

From the perspective of the magician, everything—whether animate or inanimate—is connected to everything else. What determines the nature of that connectivity is the symbolic essence of all things. There is a level of conscious being that is called the *super-symbolic*. In it resides the symbolic essence of all things as a kind of deep structure within the subtle and causal levels of consciousness. All material things (and even processes) can be reduced to a symbolic essence at the super-symbolic level, and it is that symbolic essence which the magician uses to represent their goal or objective. The symbol can be abstract (such as those derived from creating a sigil, a magickal signature, a magickal formula, or found in Qabalistic correspondences), or it can be quite concrete (such as a poppet, manikin, or a fith-fath that has the hair, nail trimmings, clothes, or other associated materials of the target upon or within it). The latter kind of link is referred to as a *gross link* and has other analogues, such as the spirit bottle, spirit bag, or magick container that is used to assemble several material links together, like herbs, dried fruits or vegetables, stones, and various animal parts or secretions (particularly body parts, blood, or parchment made from the skin). The gross link is quite effective, but it is also archaic, cumbersome, and requires a great deal of careful preparation before it can be used in a magick rite. Modern magick has already passed over the gross link for the purely symbolic one, since it requires very little preparation and, in some instances, can be reused for other magickal operations. Substitutes for the gross link could even be sacramental wine and bread, in place of the flesh and blood of an animal, if the sacraments are consecrated to the specific use of the spell. The other surrogate for a gross link is a ritual formula, using the Qabalistic technique of *Nortariqon* (formula acronyms). One example of using a magickal formula for a ritual link is found in the Analysis of the Keyword (LUX-INRI) in the rituals of the Golden Dawn.[58]

Magickal links can be elaborate or quite simple. A magickal link is used to imprint the energy field raised by the performance of a ritual of

---

58 See the Ritual of the Rose Cross in Israel Regardies' book *The Golden Dawn*, vol. 4.

empowerment, and it can be simply a mechanism to qualify that magickal power, such as a Qabalistic Godname. Magickal power is essentially neutral and requires some kind of imprint and the establishment of a magickal link to give it a direction and a purpose when it is released. If the magickal link is omitted, then the resultant magick will not be imbued with the desire or objective of the magician. It will just dissipate without having any effect on the outcome whatsoever. In fact, directionless power can easily rebound on the magician or invade their mind and produce all sorts of obsessions, restlessness, and irritability. So, this is one stage that must not be omitted from any magickal working, unless the working is purely ceremonial and celebratory and does not require any kind of objective. There are very few such rites in the repertoire of the beginning magician, since even the mysteries have an objective or purpose interwoven with their theme.

OBJECTIFICATION: EXTERIORIZATION

Exteriorization can be a simple matter of producing one more intense, stimulating action to the power already raised and imprinted so that it reaches a powerful climax, is released, and is sent out on its objective. Resonance is the key to exteriorization, and it can be accomplished with a chant, dance, or any kind of iterative movement that brings the level of intensity as high as can be supported. Breath control can also be used for exteriorization and the magician can perform a kind of hyperventilation, holding and locking the breath before then explosively letting it out all at once. This technique is called the lotus seven-breath, since it is usually accompanied with a vigorous infusion of scented oils (classically lotus scented oil), passed across both nostrils while the magician breathes in the fumes deeply. A sword dance is also used to exteriorize the power in a classic magickal action, made famous by Aleister Crowley in his book *Moon Child*. Whatever method is used, the simple rule is that the imprinted energy is brought to a climax through resonance, then released, where the magician wills the power out of the circle and sends it to its destination. Whether the power structure is a vortex or a cone of power, the manner of exteriorizing the power is the same. The difference is in the outcome and how the power is sent to its intended target.

INSIGHT: DIVINATION

Divination is the most important stage in this series of seven stages of the master pattern. Divination is used both before and after a magickal working to shape it, sharpen its definition, and examine its results. All divination systems use a rich variety of occult symbolism, which, as we have determined, are symbols of transformation. When any of these systems are used with the proper altered states of consciousness, then the higher self is awakened, aiding the reader by enveloping them in a field of psychism that unlocks the oracular powers of that divination system. Randomness also plays a part in all divination systems, which demonstrates that in life there is no true random factor, that all possibilities are reduced to one fate and one destiny, whatever the mitigating factors. This might be difficult to understand, particularly since the concept of fate has always been assumed to represent a fixed outcome in a kind of hardened determinism or fatalism that goes against the openness and fluidic creativity associated with the practice of magick. While it's true that the future is not determined, it's also not wide open either. Future choices and life pathway decisions are determined by imbedded factors that may not be readily known, since all things have predispositions and tendencies and some possibilities may be extremely improbable. Therefore, the random selection of cards or tokens that represents the backbone of most systems of divination determines a vast pattern of possibilities—one that the divination system, aided by the clairvoyant and psychically attuned reader, can reveal before it becomes a fact.

The astonishing accuracy of these divination systems is because they are loaded with symbols of transformation. When delineated by the reader in a mild trance state associated with the higher self, the resultant oracle can see through all the variations to the very core of the issue. This isn't to say that the reader reads the future as if it were already written. In fact, they read it as a road map to a number of possible futures. The divination session (such as the laying out cards or tossing of coins) and the reader's fate are both determined by the same combination of random factors and occult symbols, and they become realized through the agency of the higher self and its potent psychic capabilities. Divination is a system that is highly irrational and therefore paradoxical. It shouldn't be possible except by chance to either predict the future or accurately examine one's possibilities, but it is possible on a consistent basis. What is operating in the systems of divination is not irrational or illogical, but trans-rational and trans-temporal; it's the very paradoxical and psychic nature of the domain of Spirit itself. It represents one of the ways that our higher self attempts to communicate to us through dreams, symbols, strange poetry, fantastic scenes, and visionary artwork. Divination captures the very essence of that spiritual creativity called fate, which moves the human soul and determines our destinies.

We've covered all seven stages of the master pattern for the performing of the ritual working of acquisition, and we should now understand the basic components for the practice of ritual magick. However, the ritual working of acquisition is only one of four important types of workings. The other workings are the mysteries of the Moon, Sun, and the Self. The mystery working is similar to acquisition, except that the vortex power structure is used (sometimes exclusively), and the stages of alignment and exteriorization are emphasized over the establishment of a link.

Mysteries are important because they regulate and define the magickal discipline. The Lunar Mystery can be used as a backdrop to perform specific magical workings of acquisition that are performed within the cycle of the Moon, giving them a deep psychological quality. The Lunar Mystery is an excellent working whenever the magician needs to plumb their own psyche for the root source of issues and if they wish to use the power of the unconscious higher self—symbolized by the waxing and waning moon. The Solar Mystery is used to perform seasonal celebrations, acknowledge milestones in the magician's progress, and give offerings and orisons to their Deity for the bounty of life. The Solar Mystery also represents the entire life cycle of the planet, played out year after year in a Microcosmic expression of the magician's stages in the life, which will allow them to tap into those aspects of life for renewal (birth), insights (youth), blessings (maturity), and wisdom (old age).

The Mystery of the Self is performed at increments representing milestones in the magician's spiritual achievement. The magician may perform their own initiation, witnessed by credible and qualified individuals, but they must be able to function at the level of that initiation, or else performing it will be meaningless. Magickal initiations are always transformational, meaning that they precipitate or establish a powerful change in the consciousness of the magician. For our purposes, we will focus on the first level initiatory achievement, which is dedicated to the element of Earth, since higher degrees would require a mastery of magickal lore far beyond the scope of this book. Merely being able to perform a self-initiation, and to achieve the desired transformation attested to by qualified witnesses, is the greater objective of this book and the final major step for the beginning magician.

The Mysteries use another structure that hasn't been discussed yet: the Gate or Gateway, which could qualify as an eighth stage or step in the master pattern, if it weren't for the fact that the magickal gate is a unique and peculiar magickal ritual structure always used in conjunction with the mystery rites. The Gateway is usually depicted as being double, representing the doorway or lintel crossing that leads into the archetypal Underworld and out of that place. The Underworld symbolizes the dark place deep within the self (the unconscious potential) where all the mysteries are presented, particularly the Mystery of the Self. The Gateway or entrance to the Underworld is aligned to the West, since that is the archetypal place of death, where the Sun sets when the day is ended. Conversely, the Gate or exit out of the Underworld is aligned to the East, since that is the archetypal place of rebirth, where the Sun rises when the day begins. In many ancient myths, the Sun does not revolve around the globe of the earth; it actually enters a passageway, makes its way through the darkness under the earth, and exits from a gateway in the East, where the Sun rises in the morning. The passage into darkness and the subsequent ordeals that follow ultimately lead to a rebirth and an exit into the light, renewed and revitalized. This was the religious belief about the Sun as practiced in ancient Egypt, and it produced an interesting mythic system of the cycle of light and darkness, death and resurrection, associated with the diurnal cycle of the great Solar Boat of Ra. This cycle of light and darkness is found not only in the diurnal cycle of the Sun, but also in the monthly cycle of the Moon and the annual cycle of the seasons. The initiation cycle also uses this double gateway as the primary symbols of transformation, since the stages of initiation represent the transformation of the human soul in the guise of the hero or heroine. There is a great deal of mythology about heroes and heroines undergoing the ordeal of entering and returning from the Underworld, renewed, and profoundly changed. In fact, there is a global cycle of hero myths throughout all cultures and spanning the entire period of history, perhaps representing the most primitive of all source myths for the human race, since the very first hero was the archetypal Shaman.

In summary, there are five basic magickal workings that the practicing magician uses. The first is the linear pattern of acquisition that causes magickal power to be generated and projected for the fulfillment of a material desire or goal. Then there are the workings of the mysteries of the Moon, Sun, and the Self. Through the agency of the Gate ritual, which is the fifth type of magickal working, the mystery workings are extended, and their energies can be projected through a transformative gateway to a personal working using the basic linear pattern. The mastery of the three mysteries represents the basis of a true magickal discipline wherein is found continuous inner growth and spiritual evolution. The grimoire that has these working patterns included with other more basic rituals can be considered as encompassing a complete magickal system.

CHAPTER FIVE

REQUIREMENTS AND REGALIA OF RITUAL MAGICK

THE FOUR ELEMENTS

The most basic symbolism that's used to represent the qualities of magick, repeated throughout all the symbolism of magick (whether it be the tools, sacraments, colors, energies, or other correspondences), are the four Elements. The four Elements represent the domain of Earth and all that it contains and, in occult perspectives, represents the earth and all that grows upon or lies hidden within it: the water of rivers, lakes, seas and oceans (as well as rain); the air, as the sky, the clouds, the winds; fire, as the Sun, lightning bolts, and also, at times, the fire of the infernal regions that erupts from the mantle below the Earth as volcanoes.

However, the four Elements, aside from representing the basic philosophic state of the material world that we live on, are also symbolic representations of metaphysical qualities, which are far more abstract and inclusive. By the power of analogy, we can extend the more temporal definition of the four Elements to include things that have a more spiritual value, taking us from the material world and its philosophic components to the components of consciousness itself.

Thus, the four Elements would be generally defined as the occult qualities of knowledge, will or volition, compassion or empathy, and the vital force, representing Fire, Air, Water, and Earth, respectively.

The fourfold division of the qualities defining our world represent the product of manifestation, which, as the symbolic meaning of the number four, is the occult perspective or definition of the material world, much as the number three represents the essence of Deity in its holistic expression. The four Elements and their quintessence, Spirit, imbue the manifested world with the qualities of consciousness. It could be debated from either point whether nature would be so invested with meaning and spirit without human beings interacting with it, but from an occult perspective, we enter a world of consciousness and spirit that pervades everything, including inanimate physical objects, since they represent the power points, ley lines, landmarks, and topology of a sacred geometry that exists both within the mind and outside of it. An examination of each of the four Elements is important to understanding the first divisions of the emanation of Spirit into matter, beginning with the most subtle and ending with the densest Element. Keep in mind that from the standpoint of the highest reality, everything is indivisible and one.

FIRE

The Element of Fire symbolizes the first Element in the act of creation, representing the first light that appeared in the darkness of nothingness. It was the first light of conscious self-awareness, and is represented by knowledge, insight, and illumination, as well as inspiration and aspiration. Fire is action, but it is action precipitated and guided by knowledge, so it is more like wisdom. Fire is also that which excites and inspires us, so we are set on fire, as it were; thus, it is representative of the archetypal masculine. It is also a kind of realization and a spiritual awakening. Fire is closer in its qualities to Spirit, since it is less defined and concrete than the other Elements, but it requires more effort to realize than the other Elements as well, just as physical fire requires effort to be harnessed and used by mankind. Fire is the light from the Sun and the stars, from the thunderbolts that hit the earth, and the heat and flames from the core of the earth. Physical fire is both healing and damaging and must be controlled. Philosophical fire is always empowered and controlled by knowledge, so it is the most benign of the four Elements and less likely to become imbalanced.

Water

The Element of Water represents the complete domain of the emotions, feelings, and sentiments; thus, it charges all things with an emotional value and represents the archetypal feminine. Where Fire is aloof and abstract, Water is intimate, engaged, and fully immersed. The highest expression of the element of Water is the emotion of love, but it's usually a biased sentiment (love is blind), and it contains a selfish desire to possess and control the loved one. It isn't to be confused with the platonic love associated with Fire. Water receives the enlightenment of Fire and nurtures it within, giving birth to pure happiness and exalted joy, but water can also have negative emotional qualities based on the antithesis of love, which is fear. When fear is conquered, then love dominates, and the converse is also true since fear obscures all positive feelings and, if allowed, can mask and pervert them. Physical water has the qualities of mixing with the other Elements of Air and Earth, and usually finds the lowest places to fill up and reside. Water is represented by all its sources, whether fresh water—as in streams, rivers, and lakes—or as the briny salt water of the seas and oceans. Water can be calm and placid and also brew storms and tempests, much like the range of emotions found in human nature. However, Water by itself is usually at rest, but depends on Earth (gravity) and wind to move it and make it volatile, since it lacks that quality within itself.

Air

The Element of Air represents the domain of the will and volition: Air is movement. Sometimes it is restless and moves just for the sake of movement. Unlike Fire, which is action guided by wisdom, Air is pure action, often without any guidance or any goal. Air can be knowledge, but it requires input from Fire in order to generate meaning and order. By itself, Air is simply disparate ideas and miscellaneous information—a kind of meaningless trivia. Air is lightweight, capricious, flighty, sneaky, but also the driver of all ambition when wedded with the discipline of Fire and the emotional clarity of Water. Air is neither masculine nor feminine, but it shares qualities from both since it was created from the marriage of Fire and Water. Air is the stirrer up of things, and so it is responsible for storms and tempests, having infused itself with Water to cause rain, or stirred the waters of rivers, lakes, seas, and oceans, to cause great waves, storms, and hurricanes. Air can also fan the flames of a conflagration and make it far more damaging and dangerous than it would be in a dead calm. Air can express itself in a myriad of manners, but it is seldom consistent, and its direction can easily change at a moment's notice. Dust devils, windstorms, and tornados represent how Air can work itself into a destruction force, fueled by incessant habit and fury; it can spin around an issue destructively without ever finding resolution until all is destroyed or lost. Constructive ambition and a powerful will that is undeterred by obstacles are the positive effects of the Element of Air.

EARTH

The Element of Earth represents the combination or consolidation of all the previous three Elements, but produces an Element that is essentially inert, except for the dynamism of life (the vital force of the biosphere) and the effects of tectonic plate movements that produce earthquakes and tsunami. The Element of Earth changes slowly but inexorably, crafting itself through evolution and adaptation, even though the results can produce massive extinctions at the end of a geological or biological epoch. The Earth represents all that is good about life, and as abundance, it produces wealth, health, and material happiness. The darker side of this Element illustrates that individual happiness is merely happenstance; it could change in an instant and not even be a factor or concern to life as a whole. Therefore, Earth symbolizes the fortunes of life—both the ascendancy and the fall—and the wheel of life; the seasons turn remorselessly without joy, pity, or sympathy to either the victors or the fallen. The Element of Earth, like Air, embodies both masculine and feminine, but is usually perceived as being feminine due to its fruitfulness and sedentary qualities. The Element Earth represents all that is being born, growing, and waxing, and then failing and dying—it is both the womb and the tomb. It also represents the four seasons and their constant variation, and the fact that nothing is immortal nor eternal within its domain. From dust we were made, and to ashes we return again to the earth. Earth by itself is quite inert but is easily moved by the other three Elements and requires their intervention in order for the material world to change (and perhaps even evolve to a higher order). Life and the vital force is the exception, since it operates against the earthly forces of entropy to produce synergy, the very essence of life and conscious sentience itself.

THE FOUR MAGICK TOOLS

The four Elements are reflected in several different magickal corre-spondences, most notably the four magickal tools and the four cardinal directions, which represent the Element's qualities as magickal instru-ments and the definition of the magicians' domain, the magick circle. The four principal tools of the magician represent the occurrence of the four Elements as they are perceived in symbolic and dynamic form. There is also a fifth tool, which represents the quality of Spirit as the synthesis of the four Elements. The concept of a magickal tool also symbolizes the ability to alter and manipulate the associated powers of the Element. Thus, the magician, wielding the four tools, also manipulates the four Elements. This is the primary concept in applied magick: the Elemental powers are to be controlled by the genius of humanity. Yet, this concept of control should not be exercised upon other beings in a negative fashion but used instead to further the overall good. Therefore, through an internalized discipline, the magician attains all things that are possible. Only the individual who controls the mind, emotions, and body can hope to become a master of the spiritual arts, and thus channel their Higher Self (God/dess Within).

The first tool of the magician is the magick dagger, also called the *athamé*, a black-hilted, double-edged knife that represents the element of Air. Usually, the blade of this magick weapon has been dulled so that it cannot cut or injure flesh, being a spirit knife. Whatever requires cutting can be done with a plain knife (the white-hilted boline), kept for that purpose. The magick dagger is used only to draw the lines of force that establish the magick circle and its various devices, thus establishing the lines of inter-connectivity. The blade of the magick dagger creates divisions between spaces and objects and creates a union between them through connective lines drawn with etheric fire. The magician visualizes the energy that the dagger appears to project just as they would peer at the silhouette of people, animals, or plants to see their aura. It is a phenomenon that is neither imagined nor objectively observed, for it lies upon the periphery of reality, both symbolic and real. The dagger can be a small tool (palm to middle of the forearm in length), or it can be fashioned as a sword. The qualities of Air are represented by the steel metal of the blade, and as it becomes ever larger, it also becomes capable of drawing greater forces together or driving unwanted energies away.

The sword is used as a large dagger, but its effect is more dramatic and empowering. The sword can also symbolize war, as well as justice and the enforcement of order.

The second tool is the wand. The wand is usually the same size as the dagger but represents a far more refined application of force. The wand is symbolized by the Element of Fire, and thus it can even be a torch, a symbol of illumination. The wand is not used to divide or join; it is used instead to invoke, call, or summon the intercession of the Absolute Spirit into the symbolic world of the magick circle. Thus, the wand represents the drawing of the symbolic world of ideals into union with the open and receptive mind of the magician. Trance and meditation cause the perception of this tool (and all other tools) to resonate and increase its expression of power, so that it becomes that which it represents. When the magician uses the magickal wand to draw the form of the symbolic spiral in the air, spirits are summoned. The spiral symbolizes the ascent of matter transformed into Spirit and the descent of Spirit into matter. The descent of Spirit imbues physical substances with its essence, and the ascent quickens the transformation of consciousness begun by the descent. Thus, the wand causes the symbolic spiritualization of matter and the materialization of spirit. The wand is the agent of transformation itself.

The wand is a tool for summoning the Gods and Goddesses because one would never raise an iron blade before the countenance of the Deities. That would be construed as a threatening gesture and considered an insult. An act such as that would cause catastrophic alienation and disconnection from that Deity, a most disastrous occurrence for the ritual magician who is attempting to channel its power and authority. The wand is the symbolic channel or pipeline of the Absolute Spirit, and through it occurs all sanctification. The staff is nothing more than a wand enlarged, and it then becomes analogous to the Cosmic Pole or the World Tree, symbolic of the perpetually centered state of being. The magickal wand is considered only a branch of this World Tree, and therefore it is an analogous force of lesser scale but of equal potency. The staff signifies the power of authority as the medium of spiritual manifestation and the means of ascension and spiritual evolution. When the staff and the dagger are joined to form a hybrid, then the magick spear is created. The magick spear has the qualities of both the dagger and the staff, and it can serve as a replacement for either. Another kind of staff or pole is the Stang, the staff with bifurcated horns at its summit.

It is a place-marker for the manifestation of the Deity within a certain area, like a consecrated grove.

The third tool is the chalice. The chalice symbolizes the container of all things, the empty space of the cosmos, the element of Water, and the power of creation. It's also the container of the spirit and is the symbolic analogue of the body. As the matrix of spiritual life, it represents the archetypal feminine. The chalice is the container for the lustral water, where pure water and sea salt are charged and joined in harmonious fusion. The joining of water and salt is a metaphor for the fruitful joining of the archetypal male and female. The lustral water is the Holy Water of the Catholic Church and is thus able to transform or imbue all that it touches with Spirit, causing a sanctification to occur. The magician uses the lustral water to asperge the premises of the magick circle, thereby making it spiritual and sanctified.

The chalice can also be enlarged, changing it from the magickal cup into the alchemical pot, or *ambelic,* the mixing matrix that produces the stew of spiritualized matter (which is the Elixir of Life). This pot is called the cauldron, the symbolic tool of creation. From within its depths can be found the Elixir of Enlightenment: the power of spiritual nurturing, healing, and emotional harmony. The cauldron symbolically restores the dead, causing them to be awakened, melded into a new form, and reborn as a new life. Thus, the cauldron is the womb of creation, the more ancient and earthier embodiment of the chalice.

However, as the Grail, the chalice also contains the wine that is the Blood of the Spirit, the Sangreal that gives the partaker immediate spiritual rapport with the Absolute. The Grail was also the love cup of ancient magick; it was used to bond two souls in deathless love, joined when they had partaken of the sacral wine contained therein. It was later adapted to become the Grail Chalice, whose elixir was used to bond humanity with the Deity, thus harnessing the potency of the sacring of the individual though the love of that Deity.

The fourth tool is the pentacle, paten, or dish. This tool represents the power of the element of Earth, the manifestation of the beautiful and ideal form as the marriage of Spirit and body. The pentacle is depicted as a disk inscribed with the symbol of a pentagram or a rose, usually made of silver, copper, or gold. The pentacle is also the base upon which the chalice rests. In the performance of the Holy Eucharist (magickal sacrifice), the pentacle becomes the paten or dish that sits atop the chalice, protected by the chalice veil. The pentacle or paten is usually made of the same substance as the chalice, but this is not always strictly followed. The *ciborium* is a chalice with a tight-fitting cover, representing the complete union of the two receptive magickal tools (the pentacle and chalice).[59] The dish or pentacle is used to ground the spiritual activities of ritual magick upon the most idealized of physical forms.

The dish is the symbol of the life of the Spirit to which all initiates aspire. The dish can bestow the blessings of good fortune and good health, sanctifying physical substances so that they may embody the power and light of the Spirit. As the chalice contains the Spirit as wine (the sacred blood or Sangreal), the dish holds the Spirit as bread (the flesh of the Gods). The dish or pentacle can also be enlarged to become the magick shield, and therein embody the powers that guard and protect. This weapon of defense sends out a radiation of beneficial forces that thwarts the action of all evil intent and ill-chance. It creates a barrier that protects its wielder from the contagion of the world of the profane. The pentacle or shield can also symbolize the magician's magick by depicting an engraving or illustration called the *lamen*. The lamen is the magickal representation of the magician's universe, depicted as an inscribed pentagram with letters and words of magickal power carefully integrated into its design. The lamen can assume many designs and configurations other than just the pentagram, since it is like the magician's coat of arms and subject to personal tastes and variations, but that's another topic beyond the scope of this book.

The pentagram is an apt choice for the magician's lamen because it illustrates the Great Work of the magician as the achievement of spiritual unity. The pentagram represents the dual processes of channeling the Spirit and seeking union with the Deity that activate the path of the ritual magician. When this star is positioned with its point up, it represents the ascendancy of the magician through the mastery of the Four Powers or Elements of the spiritual universe; thus, the individual has become the synthesis and quintessence of the Four Powers. The magician is the mediator of the World of the Spirit and therefore represents the supreme channel and arbiter of its source, the Absolute Spirit. The magician becomes Deity by assumption and imitation, which causes the activation of the spiritual symbolic analogue (the Godhead, or mask of God) that

---

59 *Ciborium:* A chalice-shaped container for hosts found in Catholic churches.

arrives from deep within and is superimposed over the self. By wearing the mask of God, the magician has assumed the state of mind in which they are become Deity.

The inverted pentagram represents the emanation of the four worlds' (Elements') spiritual powers becoming manifested into a physical substance or physical being. This is the process of *sacramentation*. The descent of spirit into physical manifestation represents the process that produces the *avatar,* known as the Deity with a human face. The avatar is the mediator of the Deity in its most brilliant expression. Thus, the descent of the Spirit into being is a necessary complement of the ascent of the individual.

The fifth tool is the sacred space used for the performance of ritual, namely the temple (indoors) and the grove (outdoors). It can also be symbolized by a crystal, which acts as the ground base for the spiritual work of the magician, distilling everything that is encountered in the field of magick. All ritual actions are acted out within or through it, and it contains the power and meaning generated therein. The temple or grove is the magician's spiritual container, and so is the crystal. Both are the model of the world as perceived by the magician. The feminine archetype is expressed in the chalice, the pentacle, and the temple or the grove, leaving the dagger, the wand, and crystal to represent the masculine archetype.

The symbol of Spirit is represented by the quality of synergy and manifests as the Unified Field of Consciousness. Spirit has a powerful effect upon life, causing it to become highly significant and meaningful; therefore, the magician wields the power of Spirit to transform the mundane world into the realm of the sacred. Human nature symbolizes the joining of spirit, mind, and matter. The mind is the bridge between the worlds of matter and spirit. Humanity creates words for thoughts that initiate actions, imprinting the pattern of magickal creation upon the super-symbolic field of conscious reality. The magician as spiritual engineer, through the artifice of ritual, creates a domain in which the symbols of language and thought are physically identified and manipulated, thus dynamically changing their psychological and physical reality. The magician becomes the mediator of meaningfulness and is able to alter events before they occur.

The place where this divine mediation is performed is in the sanctified space of ritual magick called *the magick temple*. The temple is a model of the inner self mirrored in all its beauties and imperfections. When many rituals are performed in that space by one or many individuals, the layers of occult meaning produced by those rituals join to form a unified expression like a magically animate being, known as an *Egregore*, or group-mind, which characterizes the space. This Egregore becomes the embodiment of successful groups and organizations, being born, living, and even dying when the group completely disbands. Corporate identities, national images, and the mythical ghost in the machine are actual entities or beings that live within the collective mind of humanity. The magician uses this law (synergy) to produce their personal Egregore, seeking to perfect their spiritual alignment through it.

The temple contains only a few necessary structures, the first being the magick circle. In a grove, the circle can be engraved upon the soft earth, but in a temple, it must be conceptualized or illustrated upon the floor. The classical magick circle consists of three concentric circles, with the outermost circle usually having a diameter of eleven feet. The dimensions of these concentric circles may vary in either direction as long as they consist of odd numbered measurements.[60] Magick circles represent the symbolic ritual structure of containment, the definition of a miniature world, and a barrier that separates the world of the sacred from the world of the profane. The interior of the magick circle is blessed and purified with incense, candlelight, and lustral water, and then the circle is drawn with a sword, establishing the perimeter of the working. The circle is then quartered through the invocation of the Four Wards, aligning the circle to the four cardinal directions. This last action truly causes the sacred space of the temple to become the magician's miniature world with its own alignment and boundaries.

A practical necessity when working magick is to illuminate the area (but not too brightly) with candlelight or lamplight so that a soft warm glow is created. Candles symbolize the quality of light within the darkness, as the mind seeks to know the mysteries of the Spirit. This is why most magick rituals are performed at night: to represent the quest for self-revelation within the darkness of unknowing.

Candles used in the temple can be of any variety or color but should be dedicated to magickal use so that they are sanctified for

---

60 Odd numbers hold a special quality in magick: they can't be divided by two (duality) and are thought to be subversive and indicative of the left-hand path.

only spiritual operations. The magician anoints the altar candles with oil to consecrate them for ritual magick. This rule is applied to all the magician's tools. Therefore, all magickal tools are used exclusively for magickal purposes so that their consistent usage in ritual will forge a powerful association with magick. When one picks up a wand or dagger, the surrounding atmosphere should resonate with the anticipation of some magickal action.

Another useful tool is the incense burner, also called the *thurible*. The best type of thurible resembles the censer used in the Catholic Church; it is an enclosed vessel attached to a chain that also secures its top. This type of thurible can be swung back and forth, quickly dispensing the incense smoke. A censer can be replaced outdoors with a brazier, which is actually a large censer mounted upon a long metal stake and implanted into the earth. The smoke produced from burning incense symbolizes the burnt offerings that once consisted of the fat of animals (an unspoiled ram in some ancient religious traditions) but has presently become the resins of trees and bushes. As an offering, the incense smoke causes the atmosphere of the temple or grove to be sanctified through the giving and the acceptance of this offering. Incense smoke also assists in generating that warm golden glow of energy evident in superior temples or groves.

Usually, a temple or grove will have some furniture, such as an altar, a chair, or pillows. The altar may occupy any of the four Quarters (the Watchtowers), Cross Quarters (the Angles), or even the center of the magick circle. The altar should be at least three feet high, or about up to one's waist. The structure of the altar should be a rectangle (a double cube sitting on its side) so that it can be used to hold the various tools of the magician. Two pillars can be found on both sides of the altar: the one on the right is painted white and gold, and the left one is black and silver. The pillars represent the polarities of mercy and severity, with the magician and their altar being the middle pillar of mediation. The pillars also act as magickal transmitters and receivers, drawing down and sending up the energies of light and darkness into the higher planes. The two pillars may also be represented by a simple obelisk set in the center of the magick circle, symbolizing the powers of light and darkness in union.

Another magickal weapon that can also symbolize Spirit (or at least the concept of change and its obligatory suffering) is the scourge or flail. Despite some people's beliefs that the scourge is only a new (albeit perverted) addition to the tools of a magician introduced through Gardnerian Witchcraft, the scourge is actually an ancient tool and a very reputable one. Because its use as a magickal tool was pervasive in the ancient mysteries, the scourge represented a common feature in human existence. It represented the essence of the spiritual discipline of magick and the fact that the initiate must inevitably suffer in order to learn the mastery of life. Along with the scourge are the cords that are used to bind, join, focus, and release through the art of *ligature,* the magick of knots. While we have no need for these tools in the magickal rituals represented in this book, they are legitimate tools, nonetheless.

The bell or gong is also a necessary tool, in that it punctuates important ritual events with a loud musical tone. The sound of the bell or gong gets one's attention and makes the participants aware of the moment's significance. The drum is also used, especially outdoors, where it establishes the pulse or tempo of the ecstatic dance used to empower a working. The magician should always consider the use of musical accompaniment, which functions as a very effective background to the performance of ritual, making it more dramatic and profound. This can be accomplished through drums, bells, and flutes, but also through sophisticated sound systems with prerecorded music timed for the various ritual actions. When individuals are speaking, though, it's better to have silence, or perhaps the music played quietly so as not to interfere with the reception of the speech. At other times, during periods of ritual action without speech, the music may occupy the foreground, giving a dimension of beauty and drama to the actions it's accompanying.

The final items for consideration in the practice of magick consist of the sacraments: substances that are transformed and imbued with the power of the spirit. They are salt, water, cakes, wine, and scented oils. The salt should be something more exotic than table salt. Nongranulated ocean salt or non-iodized kosher salt flakes are recommended for ritual work. The water should also be something other than tap water; natural spring water is recommended. The cakes should be homemade out of barley or unbleached whole wheat flour, mixed with salt, honey, olive oil, and a bit of wine. However, one may also use hosts of unleavened bread, such as those that Catholics use for the recitation of Mass. It depends on the tastes of the operator and the appropriateness of their use. A magician who performs a magickal Mass may use hosts, but a gathering of co-workers to celebrate a Lunar or Solar Mystery rite would use barley or wheat cakes because of their heavier, earthier, and more nutritious substance.

The wine may be domestic, imported, or even homemade of any color or quality. Once again, it's a matter of individual taste, but the magician ever strives for quality over quantity. The wine may also be replaced by a nonalcoholic fruit juice for those who can't or simply don't wish to partake in alcoholic beverages.

Scented oil is useful to anoint the body and thus consecrate it for magickal work. Where the magickal bath is used to purify and charge the body of the magician, the oil is used to seal in and perfect that state of purification. The scent of the oil is a signature of the magickal identity of the magician, having a similar identifying effect reputed to the various designer perfumes that are commercially available.

The use of incense also plays a major part in ritual because it is the primary herbal offering to the various Gods and Spirits whose beneficial intervention is ardently sought. The choice of incense is important because of the effect it has on the atmosphere of the grove or temple, giving it an aura of sacredness. The very smell of church incense (frankincense and myrrh) still affects some people, causing them to enter a trance state preparatory to worship (the working of ceremony). The incense that's used should have a pleasant and agreeable aroma to the magician, and it shouldn't be distracting or so thick that it interferes with breathing. Eventually, the magician will select a specific incense for most ritual work, and sometimes its presence alone will cause an alteration of consciousness.

THE MAGICK TEMPLE

While the grove is situated in an open but secluded natural site that is built up and prepared exclusively for its sacred purpose, the temple is an enclosed chamber that can be either above or below ground without altering its mysterious containing quality. In either case, the grove and the temple are Microcosmic models of the Macrocosm, and such a model is a definition of the *Mesocosm*.

The temple and all it contains is a symbolic analogue of the cosmos, representing the greater forces inherent in the Absolute Plane. Each piece of furniture, its placement, the decorations covering the walls, the illumination: all these things have a symbolic quality that becomes realized through the visionary experiences and altered states of consciousness of the magician. When the magician manipulates various symbolic objects that are imbued with spiritual power and performs mythic actions within the symbolic environment of the temple, various analogic effects are manifested. The magickal environment, in conjunction with the magician's deeply altered mind, allows for the direct manipulation of the facets of the Absolute Plane, causing profound changes to occur not only in the conscious existence of the magician, but ultimately within the whole of the Universe of Consciousness. All things of consciousness are connected, thus the alteration of one sentient being causes the alteration of all beings and the One.

The temple simulates the network of consciousness of the magician, for beyond the social web of individuals (our culture) exists the super-symbolic level of reality—the Absolute Plane. The temple symbolizes the spiritual reality of the magician who is preoccupied with the performance of specific ritual actions and magickal devices or tools. Through the artifice of ritual magick, the magician creates a material representation of the symbolic plane of the Absolute.

The archetypal model of the temple consists of some specific topographical features, but the material representation and arrangement or use of these features will vary considerably between practitioners. But each item has a symbolic counterpart in the analogous World of the Spirit. As its base, the archetypal temple has a decorated floor that traditionally consists of a tessellated or checkered motif of alternating black and white tiles. The circle, whether physically represented or not, occupies the center of the temple. The magick circle can be elaborately designed and represented, or it may be assumed and not be depicted at all. The circle defines the perimeter of sacred space, and the circle within the square (the walls of the temple) represents the primary fusion of polar opposites, thus generating the confluence of magickal forces. The checkered tile of the floor represents the condition of physical manifestation, that spirit (white) is integrated into matter (black).

Above the temple is a skylight that allows an unobstructed view of the heavens, the Sun shining during the day, and the Moon and stars at night. The four walls are decorated with four banners, representing the four cardinal directions and their associated symbolic correspondences, the four Elements. The four walls of the temple represent the four dimensions of the Mesocosm, wherein heaven and earth converge to form the fifth.

Although temples are sparsely furnished for ease of movement, each item takes on a special significance. The principal furnishing is the altar, which represents the sacred mountain, the holy place where one may commune with the super-symbolic reality of the Absolute. The symbolic image of the altar consists of a solid paneled table placed at the summit of seven steps or seven tiers of a stepped *dais,* representing the place of mediation for the confluence of the Seven Planes.

The placement of the altar varies considerably from temple to temple but, whether it occupies one of the four quarters or the center, its placement will have a subtle effect on the quality of the magick produced. The placement of the altar distinguishes the orientation of the temple and directs the lines of force that it resonates.

The shape of the altar can vary, but usually it is two cubes joined together. This structure is either stood on its end so that it produces a tall and narrow structure (a pulpit) or it's placed on its side so that it produces a long and low altar structure. The high altar should be around 1.2 meters tall (50 inches), and the low altar should be around one meter in height (39 inches). Thus, the low altar is around waist-high, and the high altar is roughly chest-high.

The altar is usually made of wood but may also be made of stone (marble) or a combination thereof. The wood the altar is made from may be from a particular sacred tree, painted and decorated with symbolic diagrams, glyphs, or sigils upon a selected corresponding background color. A temple must have at least one altar, but isn't limited to only one. The temple that I use has five different altars: one for each cardinal direction and one in the center of the circle.

The temple will also have two pillars that do not support the ceiling and are terminated with lamps or candles. These two pillars are placed on opposite sides of the altar and represent the principal polarity of magickal forces. One of the pillars is painted black, and the other is white, and they occupy the right (dexterous, white) and left (sinister, black) sides of the altar area. The area behind the altar defined by the arch created by the two pillars is known as the shrine and can be decorated with an icon or statue of the Deity, symbolizing its place behind and slightly above the altar.

The twin pillars represent the polarized channels of the ascending and descending spiritual forces of the Deity. But they can be united, as befits a unified Deity, and represented as a pylon (a pole) or an obelisk. Such a device would occupy the center position of the area just behind the altar, thus becoming the point of mediation between the twin pillars.

The pillars, pylon, or obelisk also represent the spinal column of the archetypal human being as the principal mediator between the Cosmic Body and the Universal Mind. The pillars also represent the dual forces of Kundalini that encircle each other as they ascend to the crown of the head. The pylon and obelisk represent the dual forces unified, causing a pulsing of an upward and downward flow of energy that is representative of the dynamic and recursive nature of consciousness.

The chair or pillow is placed where the magician will sit, occupying their place of centering and self-empowerment. Similar to the altar, the place where the magician will reside (their home base) will vary from temple to temple, and its placement also has a subtle significance. The magician's center will determine where the energy will find its end and its beginning, for all magickal phenomena begins and ends with the actions of the magician.

The magician's home base can be decorated. The chair can be a throne, equipped with a lectern or a table and a lamp. A personal banner representing the lineage of the magician may adorn either the chair or the area of the home base. This space is the personal point of the magician, their home and symbolic body within the cosmic analogue of the temple. It's the place where the magician establishes the symbolic lever and fulcrum that moves the world according to the power applied.

The lectern or table has the magick book or grimoire placed upon it, which contains all the ritual notes, incantations, invocations, the diagrams of magickal power and the sigils of spiritual intelligences. The book also is a diary that contains the visions and experiences of the magician. There may also be a crystal ball sitting on a mount and occupying the center of the table. The location of the magician is the place of meditation and visions, the place where the spirit world is observed through scrying or astral projection.

The temple may contain many other furnishings and can be quite elaborate, perhaps even seemingly cluttered, but there must be room for the magician to move about the floor. However, all temples should contain the basic items specified above.

THE MAGICK GROVE

The magick grove is an outdoor environment, so it isn't as static as a temple. While the environment of a temple is strictly controlled by the magician, the environment of a grove is subject to the variations of nature, which become part of its distinctly unique features. The floor of the grove is the ground itself, and the ceiling is the sky. The circle may be identified by rocks, chalk, or by an engraved trough in the earth itself. The circle is always deliberately marked because there are no walls to limit its perimeter and establish a circle. A pentagram is also constructed within the circle and is done in the same manner as the circle. For instance, if rocks are used to delineate the circle, then the pentagram should be outlined with rocks, too.

The area of the grove is usually enclosed by hedges or bushes and encircled by trees to give it the highest degree of privacy. Four markers should be erected denoting the exact coordinates of the four cardinal directions, and these should be placed outside the circle area. The magician may also choose to denote the four Cross Quarters in the same manner, thus establishing the traditional eight-position circle structure. Natural occurrences are aligned by these coordinates and belong to their associated correspondences. The four to eight markers may consist of color-coded demarcations on trees situated in close proximity or on mounds of earth or piles of rock illuminated by torches at night. The markers may also consist of erected wood or stone structures as pylons, cairns, or henges, similar to magickal sites in Northern Europe.

The area of the grove is usually decorated with magickal earth features, such as etched ley-lines, which may reinforce the naturally occurring ley-lines, strategically placed rocks, and boulders, buried talismans, wind chimes hanging in the trees and other enhanced natural features. These embellishments assist in directing and qualifying the natural powers inherent in the site, deliberately forming a sacred space and artistically emphasizing it. The central area of the grove is where the circle is inscribed, the fire-pit is dug, the altar built, and the tabernacle erected. The altar and tabernacle are typically placed in the center of the circle. The fire-pit should be placed a safe distance from the tabernacle and altar, perhaps located at the farthest point away from it within the circle or even outside the circle proper. The altar can be a portable table, or a permanent wood or stone edifice.

The tabernacle is a small high-peaked tent that protects the area of the altar from the elements and keeps the magician dry and comfortable when the weather becomes intemperate. When it's used, the tabernacle occupies the same site as the altar. The tabernacle consists of four poles supporting the periphery and a central support pole that is taller than the four outer poles, determining the height of the tent. A decorated canvas is secured to the four outer poles and supported by the central pole. Inside the tabernacle are one or two braziers for burning incense, oil lamps, and the altar. The tabernacle should have fine white sand for its floor, and there can also be a small carpet for kneeling. The tabernacle tent should have flaps on all four sides that can be opened and secured or lowered as needed.

The magician may be required to sit in meditation for long periods of time in the tabernacle; thus, a chair or pillow is provided to assist them in assuming an asana without distraction. The chair that is in the temple usually assumes a symbolic stature, becoming an analogue for the massive throne of the Deity, carved with symbols, and decorated accordingly. However, the chair in the tabernacle of a grove should be smaller and more portable than one used in a temple. The chair or pillow should be off to the side of the centrally located altar where it will be out of the way.

The magick circle for the grove, as stated earlier, may be etched into the ground and marked with different colors of chalk. The magician may also etch specific ley-lines into the area of land surrounding the grove, with the ley-lines converging at the magick circle in the center of the grove. Within the circle, a pentagram should be engraved and chalked with symbols sparingly placed within it. When using chalk, the magician should take care to leave specific trails that will allow them to traverse the grove without crossing and smudging any of the lines. This will assist in maintaining the integrity of the lines of power, even though there will be gaps in the overall design for the magician to walk or dance.

The area of the grove should be decorated and maintained as befits a holy site. The operation of magick as performed in a natural setting should be made to seem as inspiring and as aesthetically pleasing as possible. In this manner, it represents the incarnation of a spiritual world. The devotion applied through the site's maintenance will add to the potency and significance of the magick performed therein.

THE MAGICK CIRCLE

The magick circle represents the boundary between the world of humanity and the World of the Spirit. By erecting a magick circle, the magician is symbolically recapitulating the creation of the cosmos by the Deity. The magick circle is an instrument designed to focus the energies generated within it and contain those energies, lest they dissipate. The magick circle is also a gateway and a symbol of the separate world of the magician. The magick circle can be of any length, but traditional lengths include seven, nine, eleven, thirteen, and twenty-one feet, and there can be a symbolic justification for using any of those lengths based upon the magickal symbology of that number. This is a topic that would fill a whole volume, so we won't go deeper into it in this book.

The four Elements are represented by the magickal device of the Cross, and the four Elements and Spirit are represented by the magickal device of the pentagram. The pentagram is used to summon and project the symbolic powers of the four Elements and Spirit, and it is used by the magician as a talismanic symbol of magickal power. The four Elements are also represented by the four cardinal directions, which defines and symbolically qualifies the four powers and sacred intelligence of the domain of the magick circle. Thus, the pentagram is used to set a symbolic expression for each of the four Elements to the four cardinal points, and these are called the four Wards of the magick circle.

The magick circle that's used in earth-based magickal traditions consists of the four Wards set to the four cardinal directions and a circle that's set or drawn as a circular boundary that the four Wards protect and empower. These four Wards are also called the four Watchtowers, and the points between the four Watchtowers are the four Angles. The Ultrapoint, Infrapoint, and the Mesopoint occupy the place in the center of the circle along the axis of the central energy pylon. The four Wards are symbolic definitions superimposed upon the traditional four cardinal directions. The correspondences of the quaternary, which have been already discussed in their most basic form as the four Elements, are used to define the world of magick. These qualify the traditional correspondences of the four winds and the four seasons, and compose a model that establishes the spiritual world within the material, neither touching nor separate from the other.

The four Wards have the basic function of protecting the circle, maintaining its integrity, and connecting the World of the Spirit to the magician's specific space and time. The four Wards also represent the sources of the four Powers (i.e., the Elements) and, once established, they continuously emit their energies into the magick circle, converging at the center and forming the mythic crossroads. The center is the place where the magician stands and directs the four Powers in the guise of the Deity.

The inner part of the circle is blessed with lustral water, candle or fire light, and incense, as well as the summoning of powerful Spirits of the four directions to occupy the four Wards and the Deity to occupy the center of the circle. The lustral water—consisting of water and salt—is the Elements of Water and Earth, candlelight or a circle fire is the Element of Fire, and incense is Air; thus, all four Elements are represented.[61] The Ward of the Element and the Spirit of the Cardinal Direction, when charged and combined together, represent the activated Watchtower, which acts as both a device of protection and method of empowerment. When all four Watchtowers, four Angles, and the Ultrapoint, Infrapoint, and Mesopoint are thus empowered and the inner part of the circle is consecrated by the sacraments representing the four Elements and blessed with the invocation of the Deity, the magick circle is said to be charged and purified and ready for the work of magick.

The concept of a magickal Watchtower was first presented in the writings of John Dee, the Elizabethan magus, and although these writings were intended to be the private workings and writings of Dee (to be destroyed after his death), they survived to the modern times and became the focus of Enochian magick as practiced by the Golden Dawn. The Watchtowers are actually derived from Dee's Great Table, a collection of square grids or tablets consisting of forty-nine by forty-nine squares, each containing a letter of the Enochian alphabet and representing the keys to the gateways of the inner magickal worlds of Enochian magick. The Watchtowers are the four quadrants in the central equal arm cross that divides the four Elemental tablets. The four Watchtowers and the

---

61 In some traditions, the incense smoke represents both Fire and Air, so there is a precedence where Water, Earth, Fire, and Air are joined to produce sacraments that bless the magick circle.

Great Table are surrounded by a circle. This is why some individuals have seen the circle as the magickal structure for working ritual and ceremonial magick, although Enochian magick doesn't propose such a structure. This system was incorporated into modern magick by the Golden Dawn, who creatively assembled magickal lore from various sources into a single discipline. Masonic forms of ceremony had a place attributed to three of the cardinal directions (East, South, and West), but avoided the North as a place of darkness. The Golden Dawn restored the North to work with the four cardinal directions as part of their astrological and planetary magickal workings.

The Watchtower is also represented by a high place where the spirit watchers guard and protect their domain from interference. In Masonic temples, a single doorway is guarded by the Tyler, who holds a sword and bars all from entry unless they can demonstrate that they possess the secret password, grip, and sign that identifies them as initiated members. The Watcher is considered an emissary of the gods and is imbued with the power and authority of Deity, and like the Tyler, allows only those persons and entities who belong to that sacred place both entry and exit. The word "watcher" is analogous to the concept of angels, who were the eyes and hands of the Hebrew and Christian God. But it is truly an old concept, and it has its origin with Semitic Pagans in Mesopotamia, who were the authors of the lists of demons, angels, and other spirits appropriated by the Hebrew people living in captivity in ancient Babylon. For this reason, modern practitioners have little problem using the entire hierarchy of angels and demons, since it represents a more Pagan and polytheistic approach to theology (the original concept of the Elohim being the various gods) and does not actually fit into the context of a pure monotheistic theological tradition. As magicians, we see these angelic and demonic beings as Deities in their own right and not merely as appendages of the one God. Therefore, to each Watchtower belongs a suitable watcher, and the four Archangels (or arch-gods) function very well as guardians and emissaries of the magickal perspective of Deity (a form of applied polytheism).

The basic concept behind the magick circle and its cardinal markings was to facilitate a spatial orientation so that the world defined by the magick circle would be in alignment with the greater world of spirit, therefore acting as its analogue. The cardinal points are set or charged with a warding sign, perhaps originally a rune or character carved on a tree or rock that was situated on the line of the compass point of the magick circle, but later became an impermanent sign, such as drawing a sigil or symbol in the air, which left no trace to the uninitiated eye. The act of marking the four cardinal points creates what is called the *compass round*, and these points are not only marked but also warded with protective magick, and even guarded by a Totemic spirit who protects the secret rites from being violated from without (non-initiates) or invaded from within (by unwanted spirits). The warding sign has eventually become the pentagram, and this symbol is used to invoke and banish each of the four Elements as well as two forms of Spirit, one that is superior (dexterous, right hand) and inferior (sinister, left hand), also known as the masculine and feminine archetypes of the Spiritual powers, which always exist in perfect union.

The Watchtower is also known as an emblem of ancient Pagan British fire worship that took place in round towers or mounds like at Glastonbury, representing the threshold borders of the world of the Faery. In the center of the circle is placed a representative of the World Tree, which is the Stang (horned pole), for it unites heaven and earth, and allows the powers of both worlds to merge and mingle. A fire is also kindled near the center before the Stang, known as the *cunning fire*, since a sacramental fire is particularly important to earth magick, representing the core of the spiritual powers of a grove, valley, or hill. The mystery of fire is also an ancient tradition, connecting the past with the present. The cunning fire marks the center of the compass round, and a circle can be either engraved on the earth (drawn with a central stake and nine-foot cord) or assumed by placement of the four wards. The cardinal points are warded and protected as Watchtowers, and perhaps even illuminated by lanterns or smaller fires representing the archetypal magickal space, fortified and sanctified within and without. In Witchcraft and the traditions of magick, the magick circle is perceived as an in-between place that borders the world of humanity and the world of Deities.

An indoor magick temple is a space where the magician would use candles for the ancient cunning fire and the markers for the four wards, and the circle could be painted on the floor or visualized. An altar can be placed at any one of the four wards, or in the center of the circle. The room is decorated, adorned, and kept in a state of readiness, representing the readiness of the congregants to practice their magickal arts. Certain tools would be required, and four of these tools would be considered archetypal, representing the four elements and the four original treasures of humanity. The primary working tool is the athamé, a consecrated black handled dagger inscribed with magickal characters. A sword is also used (for high ritual magick, or to denote an initiate), as well as the wand, a staff, chalices, dishes to hold the sacraments, cords, a scourge, salt and water, wine or ale, bread and cakes, scented oils, incense, charcoal, and an incense burner. The magician has robes when needed and can be sky-clad when required or desired, too. The magician is fully vested with the accouterments of their magickal persona, bathed, anointed, and purified for the work.

The magician performs the rite that purifies, charges, and establishes the sacred space where they worship the Deity and practices magick. The rite that performs this operation is called the *circle consecration ritual,* and it is a simple rite but no less profound, for it marks the transformation of the world into that of the sacred domain of magick and the Deity. This is accomplished first through the generation of lustral water, which is used to create sacred space. The temple space is blessed with the four elements. The magick circle is drawn with the sword, the four wards or Watchtowers are erected, and their guardians are summoned.

The central mystery of this ritual is the blessing and mingling of the salt and water, representing the union of the archetypal male (salt) with the archetypal female (water). The fusion of spiritual and physical polarities creates the basic magickal charge as a sacrament to be used to hallow the ground or floor of the sacred space. The lustral water also represents the combination of Water and Earth (salt), so when it is dispensed around the circle area through the technique of asperging (lightly sprinkling), it is both hallowing and giving forth the blessing of those two Elements. The asperging is followed with the procession of the Elements of Air (as incense used to purify the atmosphere) and Fire (as a lantern or candle directing the light to the four cardinal directions). Once the space is hallowed with the lustral water and blessed by the four Elements, the magick circle is drawn in a clockwise (deosil) direction to define the boundaries of the sacred space.

The final act is where the four wards or invoking pentagrams are set to the four cardinal directions. The Watchers are summoned, and they become the spiritual guardians of the temple and emissaries of the God and Goddess. The attributes of Elements and spiritual personifications of the four cardinal directions have many variations, and each represents a different manner of generating the powers of the Witch's magick circle. We shall cover several of these and also describe the system most commonly used in the tradition of ritual magick.

There are essentially three different methods for determining the four cardinal directions or Watchtowers. These three methods are the Elemental configuration, the Alchemical configuration, and the Astrological configuration, and there are a number of variations for each of these three methods. The method most commonly used is the Elemental configuration, which is used in most magickal systems in the various traditions of Neo-Paganism. This system can be summarized by showing the correspondences of the four directions with the four Elements, and various magickal creatures, Archangels, and totemic emissaries. Included is a correspondence for a fifth element, which is Spirit.

Cardinal Directions	East	South	West	North	Center
Elements	Air	Fire	Water	Earth	Spirit
Winds	Eurius	Notus	Zephyrus	Boreas	N/A
Elementals	Sylphs	Salamanders	Undines	Gnomes	N/A
Totemic Animals	Raven, Owl	Serpent	Cat	Goat	Godhead
Archangels	Raphael	Michael	Gabriel	Uriel	Ratziel
Colors	Yellow	Red	Blue	Green	White

The totemic animals (which can vary from temple to temple) are usually given names and further qualifications. They represent divine powers and authorities of the God and Goddess, and, as such, are gods and goddesses in their own right, thus being the Dread Lords of the cardinal directions. The Godhead is represented by the specific aspect of Deity associated with the religious cult of the magician, so these would vary from magician to magician (of course).

The second method is more obscure but is based on the technique of polarizing the four Elements within the magick circle. In the method above, the Elements are polarized along the periphery of the magick circle, in a deosil manner—thus Fire in the South polarizes Water in the West, and Earth in the North polarizes Air in the East. The second method places the Elements of the magick circle in opposition to each other: Fire is placed in the East and polarizes Water, which is placed in the West and Air, which is placed in the North, polarizes Earth, which is placed in the South. Thus, the four Elements are polarized across the magick circle, allowing the energies of the circle to be drawn into union in the center. This configuration is further qualified by Alchemical qualities, where the typical three base Alchemical elements (salt, mercury, and sulfur) are broken into four elements.[62] This is the configuration used by the practitioner of sacral magick, usually involving the higher forms of the art called *Theurgy*. It is also a configuration used in alchemical workings, including sex magick.

The third method was developed by the Golden Dawn and is based upon the Elemental associations of the four cardinal or fixed signs of the zodiac. The configuration based upon the cardinal signs and the four fixed signs are shown in a table below.

EAST	SOUTH	WEST	NORTH
Aries	Cancer	Libra	Capricorn
(Fire)	(Water)	(Air)	(Earth)
Leo	Taurus	Aquarius	Scorpio
(Fire)	(Earth)	(Air)	(Water)

In these two variations, only Water and Earth are switched, while Fire and Air retain the same cardinal directions. In addition, the characteristics of the four Cherubim can be used to qualify the fixed signs:

- **Leo:** Lion
- **Taurus:** Bull
- **Aquarius:** Man
- **Scorpio:** Eagle

The Golden Dawn made good use of this configuration, and it also serves the magick of a more astral (planetary) or stellar orientation.

62　The three Alchemical elements, plus the addition of the base matter: the Black Dragon.

The magick circle is used to assist in the generation of magickal power by the projection of the four Elements and their analogical tools and representatives. However, magical power is also created through the process of resonance, as expressed in the magickal dance. Movement is the essence of magickal power and the medium of its expression. Once formed, the magick circle suggests a pattern of continuous movement. The four Wards create a convergence of forces: a focusing and transformation of consciousness. The miniature world of the magick circle is the ritual expression of the Microcosm, wherein all is created and manipulated by the magician in a similar manner as the absolute scale of the Macrocosm. Thus, the magician is transported to another world—another dimension—where the archetypal expressions of ritual magick become the embodiment of conscious reality.

All things have their opposites in the symbology of magick; thus the four Wards or Quarters have the four Angles or Cross Quarters. Where the four Wards establish the confluence of emanations, the four Angles establish the polarization and fusion of those energies, generating the phenomenon of the vortex. The Angles represent the "in-betweenness" of the cardinal directions and symbolize the result of the joining of Spirit and matter through synthesis. When the Angles and the Wards are joined together, an eight-fold vortex symbolized by the octagon is created, and the center of the circle takes on the symbolic significance of the Union of Being, representing the essential expression of the Deity. This state is referred to as the *Mesocosm,* the point of transition between the Microcosm and Macrocosm, and the combined world of individual humanity and the Unified Deity. The fusion of polarities, then, defines the world of the Magician.

In the center of the circle is the pylon. Although it's usually a metaphor for the primary polarities of light and darkness, in some traditions it's represented by an actual physical pole: the Stang or "Poteau-mitan." The pylon consists of the three points that occupy the center of the circle.

The place of the center of the circle is divided into the two points of the zenith (Ultrapoint) and the nadir (Infrapoint). The highest point in the center of the circle represents the absolute polarity from its opposite dimension, which is the lowest point in the center. These positions symbolize the Yang, the archetypal masculine, and the Yin, the archetypal feminine. The midpoint between these polarities is occupied by the magician, and they represent the synthesis between the polarities, the directive agency that is the focus of the magickal work. The center of the circle is also the place called the still-point, the primary power spot, or zone of power and the *Axis Mundi*. It's the convergence point for all the forces unleashed in the magick circle and functions as a black hole, which is the core of the vortex and the nether gate of the transformation of nonbeing into being.

A final point of consideration is that the grove or temple will be illuminated with torches, lanterns, and candles appropriately chosen for the type of space. There will also be incense burners or braziers, which produce a very light mist of incense smoke pervading the sacred area. There should also be music played at various times to add to the drama of the working. These last items assist in developing the atmosphere of the temple or grove and are an integral part of the magickal working. A proper atmosphere will greatly assist the senses in establishing the proper state of consciousness.

THE MAGICK SPIRAL

The magick spiral represents the progression of consciousness through three dimensions, suggesting a fourth. This device has dual flow of energy that moves both in a clockwise and a counterclockwise direction. Since the spiral also has an inward or outward trajectory, there's the additional dimension of expansion and contraction.

INVOKING   SEALING

INWARD
MAGICKAL SPIRALS

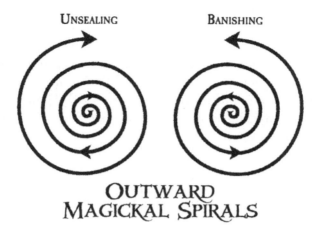

UNSEALING   BANISHING

OUTWARD
MAGICKAL SPIRALS

There are a total of four possible permutations: the combination of the direction of the spinning movement (clockwise or counterclockwise) and the movement toward or away from the center (inward and outward). The resultant four spirals represent the energies of the ritual actions of invocation, banishment, sealing, and unsealing.

A spiral may be drawn around another device, or it may be used by itself to generate a specific type of energy. The spiral always has a target or specific object that is centered in its midpoint, thus establishing the place where that energy is to converge or diverge.

When drawing a spiral, the magician usually uses a wand. It has the quality of summoning, and the gentle and magnetic nature of its energy is more conducive to drawing a spiral's lines of force. This is because the energies associated with the spiral are feminine in nature and best projected with the tool that has the same corresponding magnetic quality. The primary exception is when the magician draws an invoking spiral around a pentagram that they have just completed drawing with the dagger or athamé.

A magical dagger is principally used to draw straight lines in the air or on the ground within the magick circle, and in the form of the sword, it is used to draw the magick circle itself. Where wand draws the various spirals of magnetic potential, the dagger draws the electric and creative straight lines of force.

The spiral, as a symbol of movement, represents the expression of magickal power, where the energy field defined by the magick circle is wound up and intensified or released and projected outward. Winding up or intensifying of power is accomplished with the clockwise circuit, and the unleashing is accomplished with the counterclockwise circuit. Inward or outward directions cause the energy to be either solidified or dispersed. The combination of direction and orientation represents the energies in their various expressions of resonating, fusing, reactivating, or being released, establishing the quality of the magickal power generated.

Spirals are a dynamic part of the magick circle, representing the energies of the domain of the magician. Curved movements of the circular spiral also represent the essence of the vital energies as found in all living things. By definition, the spiral represents the domain of the animate world. Energies that are contained within the magick circle could be considered analogous to the ever-changing process of life, particularly just after the circle is cast.

Additionally, qualities of the spiral have a mysterious element to them. A spiral is symbolic of life itself, from the ever-turning bodies of the cosmos to the twisting strands of DNA. It is the natural process associated with the progression of life, signifying evolution and extinction, the expansion of infinite consciousness, and the coalescence of the individual. Spirals represent the magickal powers of invocation and banishment, internalization, and projection. As one of the few magickal devices that symbolizes the natural flow of physical and spiritual phenomena, it is one of the few magickal devices that governs both. The spiral is also the pattern by which consciousness is determined. Therefore, it governs the process of the individual's spiritual ascension and the incarnation of Spirit.

Ritual actions of invoking, banishing, sealing, and unsealing represent four different magickal energy states that use the device of the spiral. Invocation is very magnetic and draws things into its center. It is the power that summons and calls, establishing a center for its attracting force. A spiral of invocation turns clockwise and inward to the center. The action of banishing is the opposite of invoking, generating an energy that is releasing and exteriorizing. The spiral of banishment turns counterclockwise and outward to its periphery.

Spirals that denote the action of sealing hold and close the energy that has been already generated. Thus, the action of sealing creates a stasis that holds its target in a perpetual embrace. Its energy preserves and fixes magickal structures simply by being superimposed over them. The sealing spiral turns counterclockwise and inward to the center. Perhaps obviously, the action of unsealing is the opposite of sealing; thus, unsealing is a ritual action that releases a ritual device or structure that was sealed. The unsealing spiral turns clockwise and outward to its periphery.

THE MAGICK PENTAGRAM

Perhaps, the most widely recognized magickal device is the pentagram. Although some currently believe that it is a device of Satanic origin, the pentagram has been found in many different guises, spanning numerous centuries and many cultures globally; until recently it was always treated with veneration and respect. The Pentagram was documented as a magickal diagram of great power in the medieval European grimoire *The Key of Solomon*, where it was embellished with sigils and sacred words of power. However, the place of origin of the pentagram may have been in the Middle East and so far in the remote past as to be undeterminable.

A pentagram symbolizes the eternal cycle of life and its ultimate perfection. As a lamen (the magician's personal cosmic diagram), it is a symbolic model of the universe. The two arms and legs represent the four Elements, and the head represents the *quintessence*, the fusion of the four Elements as Spirit.

Five-pointed stars have always been an emblem of humanity, representing the erect human form or even the spread fingers of the human hand. The Pentagram also symbolizes the spiritual ascent of humanity and the descent and incarnation of the Deity. As a symbol of the cycle of spiritual powers, the pentagram was used throughout the ages as a ward against evil and a focus for healing and protection.

Pentagrams were believed to be a generator of spiritual power, and magicians employ it in that capacity today. It is for this reason that the pentagram has come to symbolize the powers of magick itself. As a device, however, the pentagram allows for eight different linear transcriptions along its outline, each with a different starting and finishing point. Each of these eight different tracings of the pentagram represent a different type of symbolic power, and six of these tracings have an invoking and a banishing direction pair.

A method of establishing the nature of each of these eight powers is through the placement and determination of the five points of the pentagram. The top point has always been associated with the element of Spirit. But the other points are defined usually by tradition and without any explanation. The five points are analogous to the divine tetrad already examined, plus the addition of another letter. The traditional YHVH is modified to become YHShVH, which is a variant of the Hebrew word for "deliverer." The addition of the Hebrew letter Shin symbolizes the Elements of Spirit and Fire (the Hebrews originally believed in the existence of only three Elements). Because the Hebrew alphabet was written from right to left, as were all Semitic languages, the placement of these five letters on the pentagram would begin at the bottom right point and proceed around the periphery of the pentagram counterclockwise to the bottom left point. This placement establishes the letter Shin at the top point where the element of Spirit is placed. The other points take on the attributes of their associated Elements.

There is a method of testing the above placement of the five points, and it focuses on the relative polarities of the Elements. The Element of Spirit is considered neutral, but both Fire and Air are considered creative, and Water and Earth are considered receptive. If one examines these polarities and their placement on the pentagram, it becomes evident that there is a natural polarity of masculine and feminine forces either directly across or on either side of each point, but not diagonally. Because of this polarization, the pentagram is a natural generator of magickal elemental powers.

The pentagram is usually drawn by the magician with a dagger or athamé. The basic rule of drawing a pentagram is that the magician begins by pointing at the position that is the diagonal opposite from the target point, then draws a line towards the target, and continues drawing the rest of the linear outline of the pentagram in a continuous and unbroken line with a final thrust from the opposite point to the target. This pattern is recursive in that the beginning stroke is repeated in the last stroke. To invoke one of the four Elements associated with a point on the pentagram, the magician draws the beginning stroke towards that point. To banish the Element, the magician draws the beginning stroke away from that point. In this manner, using all the five points of the pentagram and the lines that make up its outline, the magician can manifest eight different elemental qualities. Illustrative examples and the directions for drawing them are below.

1. **Fire:** Bottom right point.

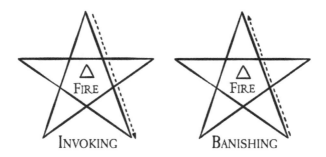

Invoking: Start at the point of Spirit and draw diagonally down the right side of the pentagram to the point of Fire and then continue the circuit, ending in the same manner. The invoking circuit is clockwise.

Banishing: Start at the point of Fire and draw diagonally up the right side of the pentagram to the point of Spirit, continuing the circuit, and ending in the same manner. The circuit for banishing Fire is counterclockwise.

2. **Water:** Middle right point.

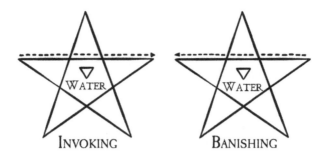

Invoking | Banishing

Invoking: Start at the point of Air and draw straight across the middle of the pentagram to the point of Water and then continue the circuit, ending in the same manner. The invoking circuit is clockwise.

Banishing: Start at the point of Water and draw straight across the middle of the pentagram to the point of Air, continuing the circuit, and ending in the same manner. The circuit for banishing Water is counterclockwise.

3. **Air:** Middle left point.

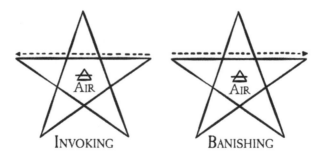

Invoking | Banishing

Invoking: Start at the point of Water and draw straight across the middle of the pentagram to the point of Air and then continue the circuit, ending in the same manner. The invoking circuit is counterclockwise.

Banishing: Start at the point of Air and draw straight across the middle of the pentagram to the point of Water, continuing the circuit, and ending in the same manner. The circuit for banishing Air is clockwise.

4. **Earth:** Bottom left point.

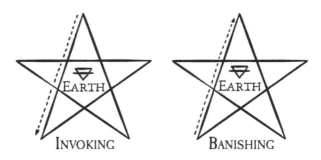

Invoking: Start at the point of Spirit and draw diagonally down the left side of the pentagram to the point of Earth and then continue the circuit, ending in the same manner. The invoking circuit is counterclockwise.

Banishing: Start at the point of Earth and draw diagonally up the left side of the pentagram to the point of Spirit, continuing the circuit and ending in the same manner. The circuit for banishing Earth is clockwise.

5. **Masculine Spirit:** Top point (right side).

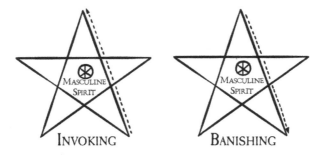

Invoking: Start at the point of Fire and draw diagonally up the right side of the pentagram to the point of Spirit and then continue the circuit, ending in the same manner. The invoking circuit is counterclockwise.

Banishing: Start at the point of Spirit and draw diagonally down the right side of the pentagram to the point of Fire, continuing the circuit and ending in the same manner. The circuit for banishing Masculine Spirit is clockwise.

6. **Feminine Spirit:** Top point (left side).

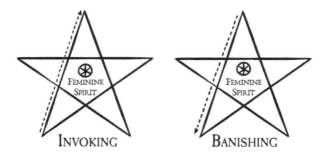

Invoking: Start at the point of Earth and draw diagonally up the left side of the pentagram to the point of Spirit and then continue the circuit, ending in the same manner. The invoking circuit is clockwise.

Banishing: Start at the point of Spirit and draw diagonally down the left side of the pentagram to the point of Earth, continuing the circuit and ending in the same manner. The circuit for banishing Feminine Spirit is counterclockwise.

7. **Lesser Invoking***:* Bottom right point. Start at the point of Fire and draw diagonally up the left side of the pentagram to the point of Air, and then continue the circuit, ending in the same manner. The invoking circuit is clockwise.

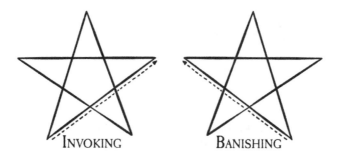

8. **Lesser Banishing:** Bottom left point. Start at the point of Earth and draw diagonally up the right side of the pentagram to the point of Water and then continue the circuit, ending in the same manner. The banishing circuit is counterclockwise.

The magician uses these eight qualities of the pentagram to invoke and banish the four Elements and the feminine and masculine qualities of Spirit, and to establish an invoking or banishing force of the Element in the magick circle. The magician would invoke an Element to generate its power in the place where it is drawn and, conversely, banish the Element to release its power.

The lesser invoking and banishing pentagrams create an energy field that is either attracting (invoking) or repelling (banishing). The qualities of the lesser invoking and banishing pentagrams are used to set the atmosphere of a circle and, therefore, function as a preparation for other magickal actions. The lesser banishing pentagram is used for purifying a circle of all other influences, and the lesser invoking pentagram is used to establish the primary spiritual alignment prior to a working. I would refer the student to the Golden Dawn teachings for the Lesser Banishing and Invoking rituals of the Pentagram, as these are shown for documentation purposes but not used in this book. The Lesser Banishing Ritual of the Pentagram (LBRP) and the Lesser Invoking Ritual of the Pentagram (LIRP), as these rituals are called, are replaced with the circle consecration rite.

The advanced student will notice that this book uses a slightly modified method for drawing the invoking and banishing active and passive Spirit pentagrams and the lesser invoking and banishing pentagrams.[63] The Golden Dawn method uses the inside lines that connect Fire with Air and Earth with Water for active and passive Spirit. The lesser invoking and banishing pentagrams use the point of Spirit and proceed clockwise or counterclockwise, respectively. These variations aren't contradictory but represent different approaches to accomplish the same end. This book bases the patterns of drawing the pentagrams on the representation of polarized Elements, so that the magician must invoke with a stroke towards the Element and banish with a stroke away from the Element. The actions of invoking and banishing the masculine and feminine Spirit are best served with a stroke directly towards and away from either side of the point of Spirit.[64] But what's important is that the magician chooses a model and remains consistent with it. I place no greater merit in the

---

63   The Golden Dawn active and passive Spirit pentagrams are the same as the masculine and feminine Spirit pentagrams used in this book.

64   See pages 139-140 for instructions on how to do the strokes.

way I do things than in any other method. They all work based upon their relative merits, or they all fail for the same reasons.

As a final note, this section will present the relative symbolic qualities of the upright versus the inverted pentagram. Because the drawing of the pentagram is always followed with an invoking spiral drawn over it, the device of the pentagram spins with the spiral device. Thus, the pentagram is at one moment upright, and at another inverted. There are two levels of polarities at work here—the polarity of straight lines and curves, and the polarity of the pentagram spinning—thereby showing its two aspects of magickal power. Many accept the opinion that the inverted pentagram represents the forces of evil and that the upright pentagram symbolizes the powers of good, but it is inaccurate. Although there is a polarity between these two structures, it's neither good nor evil. The upright pentagram represents the human goal of mastery over the four Elements, and the inverted pentagram represents the incarnation of the Deity, not the subversion of the individual by the four Elements as a symbol of chaos or evil. These two structures represent two sides of the same coin, different perspectives of the same process. In magick, the question of good and evil is never inherent in a symbol, but always in the intention of the magician.

THE ROSE CROSS AND ROSE ANKH

The symbol of the cross represents the joining of spirit and matter to forge a mediation point where they converge, which is the focus of greatest significance for the cross. The cross is also symbolic of the joining of the four Elements to form a fifth, the synthesis being the form of the cross itself. This makes the cross analogous to the pentagram. However, the cross represents the hidden or intrinsic (immanent) expression of Spirit, while the pentagram represents the objective (transcendental) or revealed expression of Spirit.

The cross is the oldest symbol of transformation, and its origin profoundly predates its use by Christians. It symbolizes the state of self-conscious humanity, the place wherein spirit and matter converge to create the mind, the mediator of spirit and matter. The cross represents the transformation of eternal change. The interaction of the four Elements converges upon the still-point, which is the hidden spiritual source of immutable being. The spiritual nature of all things is central and unchanging, but the physical exterior is dynamic and peripheral. Although all things are physically changing, the spiritual center is poised and unchanged, for it is the model, essence, or archetype of physical manifestation. However, the mind is able to bridge this dichotomy, linking the eternal ideal with its physical form and causing all things to be unified in a web of relativity. In this fashion, all things are in union with the One Eternal Being at the highest and most abstract level of existence.

There are many different styles of the cross, but the above definition serves to cover all the variations. In the grimoire, there are three different styles of cross used (even though human creativity has produced hundreds of variations). For this reason, we will focus only on these three variations.

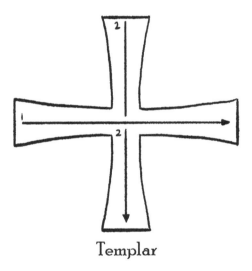

Templar

The first and simplest cross is the Equal Arm Cross, which consists of four arms of equal length joined at the center. Another variation is the Tau Cross, which is like the Equal Arm Cross, except that it is missing the top arm. The Tau Cross is likened to the Greek letter of the same name. The Tau Cross can specifically symbolize the spiritual powers of the archetypal masculine, representing the creative powers. These two crosses share the same concept of the symbolic union of the creative and receptive powers, with the creative attribute at the base of the cross. Thus, this type of cross represents the transformation of consciousness through the manifestation of Spirit, and as such, it denotes the evocative quality of mind within spirit and matter.

When the magician stands in the center of the magick circle with their arms held parallel to the ground, then they have become the physical representation of the cross. The structure of the cross seems to represent the human body in its complete state of openness and vulnerability; it is the analogy of the human condition seeking spiritual communion with the Deity.

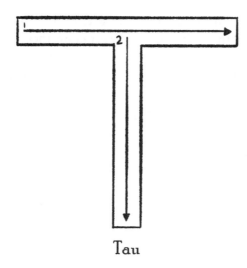

Tau

The strategic points of the body, called chakras or power zones, may also be joined to form a Cross superimposed upon the torso of the magician. This form of crossing (i.e., the Qabalistic Cross) is called the Mantle of Glory and represents the joining of the spiritual and physical qualities of the body of the magician into a unified whole. The resultant activation of this magickal body of light protects the magician from harm and assists in fortifying the integrity of their magickal will or ambition.

The second cross is the Crux Ansata, also known as the Egyptian Ankh. This device is thought to depict a common sandal strap and represents the fundamental structural basis to all existence: birth, death, and the continuum of life. The structure of this cross is similar to the Tau cross with the addition of a loop at the top. The loop represents the pregnant womb; thus, the Ankh symbolizes the spiritual lifeforce that mysteriously pervades all incarnated beings. This symbolic form represents the joining of phallus and yoni, producing life and incarnating the spirit through the agency of the conscious mind.

The Equal Arm cross represents the infertile action of union. Instead of the generation of life that the Ankh represents, the Equal Arm Cross depicts the ecstatic nature that transcends all life. The Ankh is the feminine counterpart to the masculine Equal Arm Cross.

The third cross is called the Latin Cross. It's distinguished from the Equal Arm Cross by the doubling in length of the bottom arm. Therefore, instead of four arms of equal length, there are five arms of equal length, but the fifth is grafted to the bottom arm. The Latin Cross differs from the other three in that the fifth quality is no longer hidden in the center of the Cross, but becomes an active part of the other four, integrating the bottom arm of Earth in the synthesis of Spirit.

The Latin Cross symbolizes the action of the mind that has split off from the spirit and now actively participates in the integration of the self in a higher form of life. The Latin Cross, with its five parts, represents the fate of humanity differentiated from nature by the action of the mind and reintegrated by the same process. The Latin Cross symbolizes redemption: the process by which an individual, divided from their spiritual nature, can be reintegrated, and thus become a whole being.

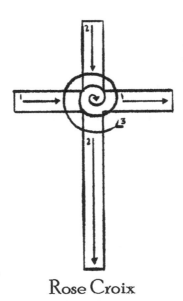

Rose Croix

145

The Rose is the invoking spiral device that is drawn over the already drawn cross, used to charge its center. The Latin Cross and the Ankh are the beneficiaries of the Rose, and the combination of cross and spiral rose alters their significance. The Rose as a symbol represents the passionate expression of spirituality. The lush, sensual beauty of the flower and the potential pain symbolized by the thorns represent the pleasure and pain of spiritual love. The Rose Cross symbolizes the passion of the incarnated Deity's transformation in the release of ecstasy or death. The Rose Ankh symbolizes the passion of the incarnation of Deity through the joining of the polarities (archetypal male and female) and, therefore, the joyous communion of humanity and Deity.

The Rose has its analogous opposite in the symbol of the Lily, which represents the transmutation of physical life into spiritual life through personal ascension and evolution. The Lily symbolizes the redemptive forces that are active in human nature and expressed as the desire to embrace and become one with the Deity. The way of the Lily renounces the material world; therefore, it represents the path of the Mystic. When the Lily and the Rose are intertwined, as they are in certain variations of the Tarot Trump of the Magician, they represent the complete cycle of initiation—the transformation of the individual and the incarnation of the Deity.

The magician uses the cross to invoke the powers of light and applies the transformational qualities that it generates to ward, protect, and heal. The magician draws the cross in the air with the hand or wand (but not the dagger) and therein establishes a magickal field of transformation.

This field directly alters and affects the psychic environment of the magick circle, and when this device is set to the four Wards or the four Angles, the resultant effect is intensified. The psychic effect of such a construct causes the superimposition of the Absolute or Archetypal World over the mundane world, transforming it. The magician standing within such a construct experiences a transformation of consciousness that causes all things perceived or imagined to be of enhanced significance. The cross is, therefore, a potent generator of the transformative field of magickal power.

The Tau Cross and the Equal Arm Cross are used to represent the unification of the four Elements. They are primary symbols of spiritual union, and their use causes a transformation of all previous energies within the magick circle into a unified whole. This simple cross device requires no invoking spiral; thus, it functions as a pure symbol. The Equal Arm Cross is drawn with two motions, from the top down to the base and from the left arm through the right. The Tau cross is drawn in the same manner, but the horizontal arm is drawn through the top of the vertical arm and not through its center.

The Latin Cross is used in conjunction with the invoking spiral, forming the Rose Cross device. This combination produces a transformation of consciousness received by the heart, causing the magician to be open to the positive and benevolent influences of the Deity. Thus, the Rose Cross can easily nullify any negative energies and allow for a harmonious and protective force to be installed.[65] The symbolic qualities of the Rose Cross are compassion, mercy, spiritual love, protection against evil, and good fortune. When drawing the Rose Cross, the device of the cross is drawn before the invoking spiral.

The Latin Cross is drawn in the same manner as the Equal Arm cross, except the base is extended further down. After the cross is drawn, the magician draws an invoking spiral over its center, terminating the spiral in the very heart of the cross.

The Ankh is also used in conjunction with the invoking spiral, forming the Rose Ankh device. The combination of the Ankh and Rose represents the passion of the eternal renewal of all life, or Eternal Life. This combination signifies the activated lifeforce as a symbol of the feminine Spirit, the Goddess of Creation.

The Rose Ankh is a symbol of passionate love, fertility, and fulfillment in life. It can generate a powerful field of magickal force that can heal sickness and regenerate injury. The Rose Ankh also protects the home and those who live within it from all harmful effects and corrupting influences. The Rose Ankh represents the heart of the Goddess and expresses its power as spiritual love. Where the Rose Cross represents the ascension of the individual spirit as spiritual evolution, the Rose Ankh represents the incarnation of Spirit into matter, the manifestation of spiritual grace and blessings.

---

65 The Rose Cross is used in conjunction with the invoking pentagram in the Pyramidal Pentagram ritual to negate any possibility for that rite to be used to project a negative intention.

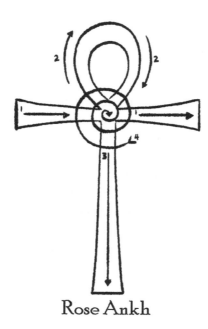

Rose Ankh

The Rose Ankh consists of two devices. The Ankh is drawn by starting at the left arm of the cross, proceeding past the center, then drawing the loop counterclockwise and continuing to the right arm. The base is drawn starting at the middle of the cross at the point of the loop and drawing down to finish at the foot. The invoking spiral, the Rose, is drawn around the center of the cross, terminating at the point where the base, the two arms and the loop meet.

RITUAL STRUCTURES AND TECHNIQUES

Ritual structures owe their formulation to the topology of the magick temple or grove where they are performed. A ritual used to set a magick circle in a temple will be quite different than one that is performed to set a grove. However, if we are to consider the magick temple as the most abstract ritual environment and examine its symbolic topology, we'll understand all of the nodes that can be used in such an environment—or any other environment.

The magick temple has four Watchtowers, four Angles, and, in the center of the circle, a nadir or Infrapoint, a zenith or Ultrapoint, and a middle or Mesopoint. Thus, there are a total of eleven nodes in the circle of the magick temple. The circle can really be cut and sliced in many other divisions than four or eight (one could even use the twelve points of the nautical wind compass), but these eight are customary, and all the basic ritual structures are derived from them; a lot of very complex ritual structures use them as well. The circle itself is a structure, and it can contain movement along its periphery (circumambulation), as well as imploding and exploding spirals (spiral ambulation), traveling in either deosil or widdershins direction around the circle.

There are, then, the eleven circle nodes, and four methods of ambulation or movement within and along the magick circle. These are the focus points used to create the most basic ritual structures, including the Circle Consecration rite, the Cone of Power or Pyramidal Pentagram rites, the simple Vortex rite, the rites of Alignment, the Western and Eastern Gateways, and the three mysteries that use them. There are also rites to consecrate the magickal tools and perform divination.[66] For the beginner in the art of magick, these are the only patterns needed to work a basic—but most effective—set of ritual magickal workings.

Each of these eight rituals contain various components that are ritualized versions of the symbols of transformation. As was stated above, there are six basic symbols of transformation: the point, line, circle, triangle, cross, and star. For each of these symbols of transformation, there is a ritual technique to express them.[67] For the point, there's the magickal declaration, which is usually given as a spoken oration, such as an orison or invocation. The line is represented by the pylon, which is where two magickal devices are united through a drawn line of force and an invoking spiral. The circle is the magick circle, the four spirals, as well as the two types of circumambulations (deosil and widdershins). The triangle is represented by the Western and Eastern Gateways, and the cross is symbolized by the Rose Cross and the Rose Ankh. The cross is also the crossroads associated with the four Watchtowers or Angles leading to the center of the circle, as well as the magick square. The star

---

66 The eight rituals are the Circle Consecration; Pyramidal Pentagram; Rose-Ankh Vortex; Assumption of the Godhead and Communion; the Mysteries of the Moon, Sun, and Self; and the consecration of the five tools.

67 Each of these techniques are further defined in the ritual directions for the eight rituals, and one only needs to examine the rituals later in this book to understand how these structures are actually performed.

symbolizes all the star patterns, but the one that we will focus on will be the pentagram, and this is the device that we will use to generate magickal power within a powerfully defined field of energy.

There are a few other structures, which are three-dimensional extensions of a couple of the six symbols of transformation. Thus, the circle becomes a sphere, the cross produces the cube, and the triangle is used to construct the tetrahedron. If the Watchtowers and Angles are set with devices and drawn together, then the octagon is also produced. The square based pyramid is a hybrid of the cross, triangle, and pylon, since it uses all these structures in its construction. All these ritual structures are used in the basic set of rituals written in this book. There are other structures as well, but these will suffice for a beginner's set of rituals.

As mentioned previously, there are a set of rituals that are used as part of a repertoire for the beginning magician. The first is the Circle Consecration ritual, which is used to prepare the self and the temple space for a magickal working. This rite is always performed as the first step to any ritual working.

The second ritual is the Pyramidal Pentagram rite, which is a more advanced and hybrid version of the Cone of Power. This rite uses the pentagram to generate a specific Element power, then imprint and exteriorize it. The combination of the Circle Consecration ritual and the Pyramidal Pentagram rite represents the ritual working called the Rite of Acquisition, as discussed above.

The third ritual in this set is the vortex, and we will use the Rose Ankh to fashion a simple and succinct version of this rite. The vortex is used to house more complex workings and to assist the magician in working with the receptive forces in combination with the creative (the Pyramidal Pentagram). The vortex is the required base for the more advanced workings of the mysteries.

The fourth ritual is the Gateway rite, which can be used in its Western or Eastern alignment (or both). The two gateway structures are included as features of the mysteries and are not used as a distinct rite in this collection.[68]

---

68 In Mastering the Art of Ritual Magick, the Gateway is written as a separate ritual since it is used with other rituals to form more complex workings.

There is also the ritual of Alignment, which is the fifth ritual, and this satisfies the four components of alignment, which are devotion, communion, invocation, and assumption.

The six, seventh, and eighth rituals are the mysteries, which are the Lunar Mystery rite, Solar Mystery rite, and an Initiation Mystery rite.

There are also some auxiliary practices, such as the meditation session, self-crossing (Mantle of Glory, which is included in the rite of Alignment), centering and grounding exercises, the divination session, and the rite that consecrates the four or five basic magickal tools.[69] The meditation session is performed before any working (and other times as well).[70] Self-crossing is used in the alignment rite, and the divination session can be included as a part of the Lunar Mystery rite. Centering and grounding exercises, similar to the meditation session, are used whenever they are required. These eight rituals are used to form the four basic workings that are required to practice a very powerful and successful ritual magick.

THE MAGICKAL DISCIPLINE

We've covered the various components for ritual construction and named the four basic workings that an entry level magician would need, but now we must concern ourselves with when these workings should be done. This involves the magickal discipline of the magician, for it's just as important to know how and when the magician performs their magick as to know what they actually do. A magickal discipline is based on the cycles of the Sun and the Moon, having an astronomical basis. There is the diurnal cycle of night and day for daily practices. Then there's the cycle of the Moon that determines when the Lunar mysteries would be performed, and there are specific workings for acquisition that can occur any time during the lunar cycle. There is also the cycle of the seasons that determines when the Solar mysteries are to be performed. It's the cycle of the Sun and Moon that determines when specific operations are performed, and these operations make up the more natural cycles of the magickal discipline.

---

69 The consecration of the five ritual tools is the eighth ritual in this book.

70 The meditation session is a staple of the daily exercises.

The magickal discipline eventually becomes the place of greatest solace and regeneration from a world hostile to the individual seeker. The world is filled with a multitude of false teachers, self-proclaimed masters, and other various soothsayers who would exploit those who have sincerely chosen to seek an alternative spiritual path. To the magician, there are no other teachers than the teachings of life itself, and there are no other masters other than self-mastery. The discipline that the magician establishes is the principal tool by which they grow and evolve; it is the teacher, guide, and final consoler. The magician has chosen the solitary path of magick because they are a loner (a true individual) and not a follower or a leader of others. The magician breaks with tradition and embarks upon a dangerous path to independently discover the source of all spirituality, signifying that mainstream religions and mainstream alternatives are insufficient for the aspiring magician. The discipline of the magician ultimately becomes their own personal lineage and tradition of magick that can be taught and given to only a select few as a legacy. But it is up to all aspiring magicians to create their own magickal system so that they may control the process of generating meaning and insight within their self-determined path of spiritual evolution.

The magician uses a high degree of creativity and insight to establish a magickal discipline that is both flexible and capable of being molded around the mundane schedules of life. There are examples of what a discipline should contain, and despite the most complex schedules, certain items should always be included. The following is an outline for a discipline that the student can review and apply as necessary. All the items in this list are important and should be used in the construction of a discipline. What's left to the discretion of the student is the time these exercises are performed and their relative frequency. Therefore, this outline is divided into daily, weekly, monthly, and seasonal exercises, and includes a section for initiation.

Daily

The magician should practice meditation and breathing exercises at least once a day; this would be most effective early in the morning upon awakening and in the evening before retiring. Evening meditations should serve as a method of eliminating the stress accumulated during the day. Meditations should consist of the fourfold breath, trance techniques, and a controlled meditation on a specific subject. The meditation period should not be less than thirty minutes and is most beneficial when performed for over an hour. Certain days should also have some time set aside for reading and studying.

WEEKLY

The magician needs to set aside one day a week for the practice of ritual. A couple of hours during the evening will be used to consecrate a magick circle and practice some of the other more complex rituals in this book. The session begins with a period of meditation similar to that practiced on a daily basis. Then the consecration ritual is performed, as well as a corresponding working. The usual working would probably involve Tarot readings or some other divination method after having raised some sort of energy field through circumambulation. The magician must regularly perform divination to determine the direction of their growth, as well as increase their self-knowledge.

It is also a convenient time for the magician to work specific rituals when emergencies occur or to acquire things for special needs. At such a working, the magician will use the Lunar Mystery rite, performing it during the full moon. They will perform the Pyramidal Pentagram ritual within the core of the Lunar Mystery, charging and exteriorizing the symbols of their desires. The magician can also perform the Pyramidal Pentagram rite alone if there is no full moon, particularly if they aspire to set a magickal working in motion.

MONTHLY

The advent of the full moon represents the symbolic call to the practice of magick by the ritual magician. It is almost as if a call to prayer was shouted from the psychic towers, bringing the magicians to celebrate the Full Moon Mystery and to perform a specific, planned working of magick. The full moon does not represent the most auspicious time for the beginning of magickal endeavors (the new moon phase has this distinction), but it does represent the time when these endeavors are fulfilled. The magician plans the stages of a working so that it culminates during the full moon, wherein they empower the last major piece of ritual action, the Lunar Mystery. The magician is always aware of the phases of the Moon and the status of specific magickal projects in relation to them. The beginning or formation of a working is begun during the new moon phase, when the Moon is waxing. The culmination of the working is given its climax at the advent of the full moon. During the period when the Moon is waning towards the new moon phase (the last quarter), the magician is preoccupied with performing divination to observe the results of the working and guide it to its final objective. The magician can manage these multiple workings over the course of the month by working through the artifice of the vortex.

Seasonal

The magician is also aware of the changing of the seasons and celebrates the occurrence of the four magickal quarter festivals—the solstices and equinoxes. The agricultural significance of this calendric cycle is less evident today than in ancient times, so now it suffices to tap into the energies of the season and add a boost to one's ongoing spiritual progress. The Solar Mysteries also serve to establish annual goals and supply the intervals (changing of the seasons) to renew or change them. The magician can also celebrate their accomplishments, joining with other like-minded individuals to share in the rich diversity of seasonal myths and traditions and commune with the greater spiritual processes at work in the world. The Solar Mysteries allow for the ability to review one's progress and apply a change in direction for greater future success.

INITIATORY

The most important task that a magician undertakes is the training and practice that leads to initiation. Until one is initiated, there can be no true understanding or mastery of the spiritual path of magick. The magickal discipline is adhered to so that the goal of initiation can be realized. After the magician is initiated, then they can begin the work of developing an individual lineage and path of magick. The initiate has the ability to receive direction from the Deity, and this assistance ensures that they traverse a more efficient path to self-fulfillment. Until the magician is initiated, the maze of possible directions seems to yield no certain way and no assured direction. It is through initiation that the magician discovers their spiritual path and receives the protection, guidance, and care of the Deity with whom they have established an alignment. An initiation is best planned as the climax to the end of the first year of practice and study, after the magician has carefully followed the cycles of the Moon and Sun from the first full moon working to the final Solar Mystery. The initiation ritual should be performed with an orientation to the Element of Earth, setting the four Angles with the invoking pentagram of that Element. When this is completed, the magician will have the tools to produce their own system of magick and upgrade and rewrite all the rituals that they have used for a year—including the Self-Initiation rite—so as to continue their spiritual and magickal process.

SOME ETHICAL CONSIDERATIONS AND THE REQUIREMENTS FOR SUCCESS

One of the main considerations in the working of magick is, of course, the ethical considerations and the requirements for a successful outcome. It's said that a wise man always knows how to pick his battles, and that it is better to avoid long shots and impossible odds unless there is no other way and nothing to lose in the attempt. In other words, unless you're desperate, keep your options open and use magick sparingly and wisely. The magician uses magick to cause change in the world when it's strategically optimal for doing so, and they also never rely wholly on it and nothing else. They have the ability to plan for the long term as well as the short term and must be very meticulous in their use of magick, making certain that it is both justified and completely on target. If the magick that is being done will only affect the magician, then ethical considerations are less important, especially if the magician seeks all spiritual and material things needed from the greater source. If they seek to manipulate events to benefit themselves at the expense of others, or to work magick on someone to assist them in some fashion, they better consult their conscience and at least two forms of divination before following through with the magickal working. It is also said that the road to hell is paved with good intentions, meaning that helping someone could actually do more harm than good. A magician must know in advance what they are getting into by taking on a magickal working that is of questionable ethical value.

How do we know if we are going to become ethically compromised by performing a magickal operation? That's a good question, and certainly one that can't be answered easily, since it must be judged on a case-by-case basis, of course. There is a simple rule of thumb, though, when examining the ethics of a planned magickal operation. First, the magician would be wise never to violate the true will of another person or persons, unless it is to defend themselves, their property, or their friends and family. This means that the magician should not attempt to use magick to bend, coerce, seduce, blackmail, delude, or mentally or physically harm another person for their own personal gain, or for the gain of another person (such as a client). If the magician works magick to right a wrong, then they become the judge, jury, and executioner and take upon themselves the ill fate of such a position, especially if they judge the situation incorrectly. Magick is a double-edged sword, as the old magicians say, and it can be worked to both the magician's advantage and disadvantage. No one who works magick is immune to experiencing a backlash from sowing negative magick, no matter how justified it seems. This isn't to say that there is an absolute good and evil, since we have already dealt with that piece of misinformation. However, there are always consequences for our actions, no matter how good our intentions.

If we use magick to help others, then we must do so only if the situation merits the use of magick, and only if we have that person's express permission to do so. Even then, it's wise to perform divination to make certain that our assumptions are correct, and our intentions fully justified before working magick for another person. For the beginner magician, it would be very wise indeed to avoid the whole pitfall of magickal ethics by focusing only on themselves, and only pursuing what is needed, and then, only from the greater source. If the magician is seeking a new job, then they should seek it from the general source of possible jobs instead of attempting to make certain through magick that they get hired for a specific job, which would certainly cause them to violate someone else's true will. The same thing is true for any other need, whether it be for money, love, healing, or justice; the magician should seek generally and then allow for all possibilities. That is the most ethical path that a beginner magician can take, and one that I recommend.

The magician should also question their motives for choosing to perform a specific magickal operation very carefully. Is the magick they intend to perform motivated by altruism, a sense of justice, for the greater good, or is it really just petty greed, lust, anger, or revenge? Our motivations are not always transparent to us, so we need to know and understand those motivations in a very deep manner. The golden rule, which is a bit of common-sense Christian theology, can be applied to the ethical considerations when examining the justification for working magick. We need to ask the question, putting ourselves into the place of the target of the magick. If it were done to us, would we like it, would it profit us or harm us, and would we want justice or revenge? Sometimes, a magickal working can cause quite a series of unexpected and unpleasant—or even disastrous—events. Not everyone is a disbeliever who will be neutralized, and not everyone will wilt away when magick is used to force an unwanted event. Some people can show an amazing degree of fortitude, self-belief, and willpower when confronted with a magician's spell craft. So, it would be prudent for a magician to know what they are about to unleash, and to have considered it from all ethical angles. Of course, this is for magick that will help the magician gain something in the material world.

If a magician is attacked by another person or persons, their property threatened, or their family and friends endangered, then they can act to protect themselves and their associates, but they must be careful not use extreme prejudice in their magickal operations, avoiding excessive force. They must always perform the associated mundane tasks, as well as an extensive amount of divination. If their enemies declare peace, then they should allow a surcease to their magickal activities and use divination to determine their true intentions. A magickal war is one that uses stealth, insight, cleverness, and a powerful clairvoyance to defeat an enemy. An adept magician would quickly determine the nature of any kind of threat and find a path where there would not be any confrontation. They would seem to disappear to their enemies, and they would quickly lose all interest, perhaps forgetting that they even existed in the first place. This is the ideal; we should avoid trouble before it materializes or discretely remove ourselves when it does. It is said that heroes and fools are the same people; yet to be wise is to be shrewd. A wise person judges when a situation requires force, when a situation requires diplomacy, and when it's smart to just be invisible.

A successful magickal working is usually noteworthy for its esthetic value, elegance, simplicity, and profound meaningfulness. When a magickal working seems to hit all the levels of consciousness at once and generates a euphoric sense of rightness and goodness, then it is likely that the magick will produce the outcome that the magician is seeking. It is possible that the magician may be simply deluding themselves, but if others are present, or if they share the experience by showing others the rite and their accompanying magickal journal and they concur with their assessment, then they are likely on the right track. This does not mean that merely performing great ritual workings guarantees results, since nothing is ever guaranteed. The magician must still perform the mundane steps necessary to ensure that all phases of the ritual are completed so the rite will be successful on all levels. Conversely, a ritual working that is executed weakly, so that it seems to have little significance or drama in the magick circle, will have no effect in the mundane sphere. A badly executed ritual that still manages to produce magickal power will cause a dire, negative impact in the magician's world; it may produce results that are the exact opposite of the magician's intention, or it could even produce a purely chaotic and destructive occurrence.

The essential ingredients to a good ritual performance are found in the words *continuity, focus, ritual flow, drama,* and *climax.*

- **Continuity** in ritual ensures that the performance doesn't have any significant breaks in its various actions and expressions, whether it is dialogue or ritual actions.
- The **focus** of a ritual represents the stated and implied purpose of the rite, and how it's communicated throughout the sequence of ritualized actions.
- The **purpose** of the ritual working should be communicated clearly in the various ritual dialogues and the sequence of events should build upon each other to an ultimate conclusion.
- The **ideal** is that all the parts of the ritual must build an effective whole.
- **Flow** is the manner in which the ritual actions are executed, and that when they are performed, a steady accumulation of energy is experienced.
- A ritual should have a certain amount of **drama** expressed in it, and it should be performed with passion and intensity by the magician.
- All ritual workings should be **performed** like a series of acts in a play, with the last act representing the climax of the ritual—where the energy reaches its peak and is exteriorized.

A ritual working that is performed with all these elements functioning as they might will be successful in producing a powerful and profound result. Mistakes occur and ritual workings fail when the above rules are violated.

The difference between a poor ritual performance and a good ritual performance is actually slight, but it's also significant. The magician should follow the simple rules stated above to ensure a more successful outcome. However, I should also cover the things that make a ritual fail, since they seem to be more common and occur more frequently in ritual execution, particularly for a beginner, than the qualities that make them succeed. These are the kind of mistakes that all magicians make, but beginners seem to make them to such a degree that they are fatal to the magickal outcome. I state them so they can be avoided.

When performing a ritual, the magician should avoid prolonged periods of dead space, or places in the rite where there is no movement or dialogue. Movement is the whole basis of resonance, and resonance generates magickal power. If the rite encounters a lot of dead space, then whatever energy has been accumulated will be quickly dissipated. Also, if the magician stumbles over dialogue, clumsily performs dramatic magickal gestures, knocks over ritual equipment, or draws devices in the air in an imprecise manner, then the ritual will suffer from poor continuity, distractions, and a lack of drama; these will certainly become anticlimactic. The magician shouldn't be disabled by coughing fits, dizziness, intoxication, or other maladies, since this will certainly hurt the focus and flow of the magick. It will also cause the ritual continuity to suffer horribly and likely make it completely unintelligible.

The magician should practice their rituals so that they are memorized and should perform all the ritual actions with complete confidence so that they seem to flow effortlessly. They should be able to either adhere exactly to the formulation of the rite or extemporize seamlessly when necessary. They should speak loudly and clearly, enunciating their words so that they have both conviction and power behind them. Mental discipline is essential, so they should perform their rituals with optimism, confidence, and inspiration. A timid, fatigued, or confused presentation of a rite is a hopeless effort that will not produce any successful outcome. As previously stated, it's a good idea to have music playing lightly in the background while a rite is being performed to fill up any dead spaces that occur with soft but inspired mystic rhapsody. The magician should perceive their rites as a theatrical presentation between themselves and the gods and should practice and perfect their delivery and execution of all the ritual actions in order to produce the optimal theatrical presentation. It's an old saying that the gods hate bad ritual and bad theatre, and it's a terrible curse to offend the gods when performing magickal operations for a given end (their twisted sense of humor will no doubt cause the ritual working to go terribly awry).

The most important factor in the success of a magickal working is the magician's familiarity and understanding of the rituals that underlie it. This means that each of the rituals in the magician's repertoire should be thoroughly studied and understood. If a magician learns to execute a ritual flawlessly but doesn't understand how it works, then the results of their working will be flawed, since they won't be able to realize the ritual process as it's happening. A trained and experienced magician can read a ritual and completely visualize its performance in their mind, noting its flaws and imperfections and correcting them before it's performed. This level of knowledge and experience is more readily appreciated when it is demonstrated in the world of classical music, where a musician can look over a musical score and hear the music in their head, noting difficulties and problems before even attempting to perform it. Such a musician would be something of a world class master performer, and such a magician would be a full adept, a master at performing and composing rituals.

SPELLS, RITUALS, AND CEREMONIES

We now turn our attention to the nomenclature for the working of ritual magick. We should define the terms that are typically confused, which are *spells*, *rituals*, and *ceremonies*. These terms are often used interchangeably, and we should address the fact that they are indeed representative of three very different qualities within the practice of ritual magick. First of all, a magick spell is classically defined as an incantation consisting of magickal words of power, often unintelligible (*verba ignota*), that will have a certain reputed magickal effect. I would like to extend that definition to include all ritual actions and declamations used to formulate a ritual. A spell is the underlying part of a ritual, and spells are carefully grouped together to form a ritual. The circle consecration rite is a good example, since it consists of the spells for creating the lustral water, processing the Elements, drawing the magick circle, and setting the four Wards. Any of these ritual actions by itself would be a spell that could be performed in isolation. However, together, they formulate the rite that creates sacred space. Also, an experienced magician can use a simple incantation or ritual action to cause some magickal effect to occur, and this would be a good application of magickal spell work, but it's something that needs an experienced hand to make it actually work. Spells are aggregated to form rituals, and rituals are assembled to form a ritual working.

A ritual is a rite that has a specific purpose or function, and all its parts work together to accomplish that function. Ceremonies, simply put, are *celebratory* and do not require a specific goal or intention to be performed. By default, rituals always have a specific goal and intention. A ritual working consists of a series of rituals that aid the magician in realizing or achieving a specific goal. Rituals are goal-orientated and function-based and are used to make something happen or affect a specific target or objective. A ceremony, however, is used to celebrate an event or milestone, usually a seasonal event or a commemoration. A ceremony is celebratory or instructive and does not need to have a specific function or purpose. An example of such a ceremony would be a celebration of one of the Solar Mysteries, where the rite was written in such a fashion that would allow a large group to perform it together. Ceremonies usually are performed by groups of celebrants, and rituals are usually performed by one or a few practitioners for a very specific purpose. For the lone magician, the Solar Mysteries are usually coupled with an individual working (rite of alignment), so it becomes more of a ritual working than a celebration. A ceremony consists of ritual actions, but these don't have to have any specific magickal effect, so it's more liturgical than magickal. Ceremonies can be mutated to be theatrical events where a select group of individuals play parts for larger groups, and they can be performed as a mystery rite.

Whenever magicians convene in large gatherings, they must decide whether to plan and perform a main rite as a theatrical ceremony (for the group as an audience), a ritual with a specific intention (performed by experienced practitioners on behalf of the group), or a mystery rite (where each person in the group is a participant). Rituals or ceremonies that work well in small groups seldom work in large groups for obvious logistical reasons. However, confusion about the size of the group and whether to use ceremony or ritual will guarantee that the resultant production will be a dismal failure. Also, when performing rituals within a small group, maintaining certain structures and performing an orderly execution of ritual actions are required if the magick produced is to be more than window dressing. The most important thing to remember when writing a ceremony for a large group that when an action is done to one person within that group (as a recipient of some blessing or magickal effect), then that action—and the time it takes to be done—will have to be multiplied by the number of people who are participating. If there is a large group, then a simple action done for each participant, which may take only a few minutes of time, may become a long, drawn-out affair if it is done to fifty or even a hundred participants.

These are the kinds of logistics that one must consider when creating ceremonies for large groups. For instance, the rite of administrating communion for a large congregation in a Catholic Church can actually take almost as long as the Mass itself. A rule of thumb for the performance of ceremonies for large groups is to keep the rite simple, distribute the actions amongst a group of celebrants who can do them simultaneously, and keep the action and the participants engaged in the rite the whole time (avoid dead spaces). Of course, the larger the group, the more difficult it becomes to maneuver them and perform actions on each participant's behalf, so a ceremony performed for a large group ends up being a theatrical presentation.

RITUAL MAGICK VERSUS CEREMONIAL MAGICK

Often in books and articles about the practice of magick, the use of the terms of *ritual magick* and *ceremonial magick* are intertwined. However, these two terms are actually very different and represent distinct traditions and practices. I stumbled unknowingly over this differing nomenclature for many years. I was corrected one day by a very astute friend, and a period of several months was highlighted by heated debate, discussion, and clarification. I then concluded that my friend had been correct, and there is indeed a difference between these two types of magickal practices. A definition of ritual magick began to form in my mind, ultimately producing the following considerations.

The ritual magician practices magick as the Deity, and the ceremonialist practices magick as a means of directing the supernatural forces of the Deity without the presumption of direct assumption since monotheists cannot become God unless they are either delusional or an apostate. The ceremonialist seeks to borrow the powers and authority of the Deity without incurring the liability of either heresy or schism. The ceremonialist can be an authorized and trained cleric (hopefully), but usually they are a layperson of some mainstream faith. When a layperson who has no training or authorization practices ceremonial magick, it allows for the worst of all possibilities. It's in this situation that the ceremonialist is liable to become a pathetic dilettante of no particular faith or persuasion, such as the New Age presently produces in great abundance. Being an accredited cleric in one of the mainstream religions is a requisite to being a creditable ceremonialist.

The ritual magician is the true pioneer of the World of the Spirit since they boldly go outside the religious mainstream to touch and experience the world as it exists through the sensorial and psychic personal experiences of the spiritual seeker. However, the ritualist has excesses, and the many self-proclaimed demigods in our business attest to this fact. We can be an egocentric cast of individuals, being both socially rejecting and rejected, and therein exposed to dark moods of self-pity, despair, and alienation. The world of the ceremonialist is far safer than the world of the ritual magician. The ritual magician is in constant danger of losing their balance and must always exercise caution and prudence in the evaluation and esteem of the experiences of magickal phenomena. It's important for the ritualist to be strongly and personally aligned to the Deity, allowing the vast differences between the scales of Deity and human consciousness to be both humbling and inspiring. The ritualist, functioning as an agent of the Deity, is a creator of new paradigms of theosophical thought and metaphysical insights that give birth to new myths, techniques, and rituals.

Because the ceremonialist lacks the authority to boldly act on their own spiritual initiative, there is a strong tendency to be overly concerned with the correct execution of traditional ritual structures, words of power, and various gestures and expressions. A ceremonialist is more concerned with the letter of the law than with its spirit (form versus intent), and they will attempt to perform ritual in the most painstakingly precise manner possible. A single mistake in execution or a mispronounced magickal word will destroy the efficacy of the ritual. To individuals who practice rituals in this manner, tradition is all-important, and innovation is absolutely forbidden. What is verifiable through countless centuries is deemed of greater value than a profound personal insight; therefore, the ceremonialist collects various fragments of ritual lore from hoary tomes and antiquated grimoires and seeks to string them together into some semblance of sanctimoniousness. This type of magician is easily recognizable by the fact that they will use the word *Tetragrammaton,* which is Greek for "a four-letter word," as a magickal word of power in and of itself, as opposed to using the very secret names of the Deity as determined by personal experience.

In the history of Western magick, the practice of ceremonial magick was the only appropriate medium for the expression of magick until the advent of the twentieth century. The grimoires of Medieval and Renaissance-era Europe were the products of a ceremonial magickal tradition and were performed within the domains of the Christian or Jewish religions. All systems of magick in the Western tradition during that period were part of the ceremonial tradition of magick.

A change occurred in the practice of magick with the advent of the order of the Golden Dawn. Within that order, the creative minds of MacGregor Mathers, Alan Bennett, and Aleister Crowley forged a new paradigm. These individuals (and many others) assisted in the creation of a new form of magickal practice. Magicians of the late nineteenth century had rediscovered the long-forgotten practice of folk magick and spell craft and rehabilitated it with an infusion of the drama and intellectual excellence of the ceremonial magickal tradition. The hybridization of spell craft and ceremonial magick produced a practice that accommodated the esthetic values and existential beliefs of the twentieth century. One could say that out of the ceremonial magickal tradition was born its successor and replacement, ritual magick.

Now that we are poised on the threshold of the New Age, the magick of the individual will become ever-more important for personal spiritual evolution rather than the liturgy of the group. Therefore, the modern practice of magick must also evolve with the times or perish. It is for this reason that we must leave the ceremonial tradition of magick behind to embark on the path of the ritualist so that we may better deal with this "brave new world."

A magician is an artist (not a scientist!), and all their scholarly pursuits are focused on perfecting that art of ritual as a dynamic expression of the Deity manifesting in the physical world. In nature there is no perfection; everything exists as a balance of form and functionality. In the ritual artifice of the magician, there's a tenuous balance between spontaneity and formalism. If a mistake in ritual execution occurs, it isn't really a mistake, but a new creative intrusion that must be examined later. Some mistakes become the discoveries of new techniques; others are variations or aberrations in form. However, sloppy ritual execution (like bad theatre) has no merit, other than reminding the magician to practice their ritual forms more carefully.

The practice of ceremonial magick has seen its day; therefore, we must respect its venerable contribution to the practice of modern ritual magick. We need not perpetuate it nor pretend that it is of any relevancy today. We may lionize magicians and scholars such as Cornelius Agrippa, Abramelin, Honorius, John Dee, Francis Bacon, Francis Barrett, and Frederick Hockley. However, we needn't practice the art of magick as they did, nor should we accept the whole of their philosophies and metaphysics. We must interpret magick as modern people with modern lives and predilections. We are no longer the same people as those who lived centuries ago; thus, magick is very different for us today than it was for our predecessors.

Ceremonial magick has its place as the religious magick in the various denominations of mainstream religions. This is particularly true for orthodox religions, where a trained cleric can also function as a liturgical expert or an exorcist. The rituals of orthodoxy demand a high degree of accuracy from their celebrants, and the prevailing consensus of conservatism assists in the preservation of ritual practices. This is the perfect environment for ceremonial magick, especially today where churches seem to lack a dramatic appeal or require a more direct inspiration for their congregation. But ceremonial magick, as it's defined here, has no place in modern occultism except as the proclivity of the misguided or the charlatan.

SPIRITUAL HIERARCHY
AND THE INNER PLANES

The first thing required to work the higher forms of ritual magick or theurgy would be a spiritual context, and this is important for the beginner as well. What is meant by the word *context* here is simply the World of Spirit and the symbolic qualities and entities that populate it. All models of the World of Spirit fall short of actually describing it because it is paradoxical. It's a world that is numinous and abstract; it can be determined in a symbolic manner as well as by direct experience.

Information from past ages indicates that there was much speculation about both the celestial and infernal realms and the beings that populated them; there were also theories about the kind of entities found in the terrestrial domains of the four Elements. Magicians of the Middle Ages would have had a great deal of oral lore and rich traditions about these worlds based on the theological speculations and literature of the time. This world view was established by the classical writers who proposed that the earth was the center of the universe, that below the surface were the infernal realms, and above it, the celestial spheres, leading ultimately beyond to the various levels of purgatory and heaven. The earth itself was populated with all sorts of legendary and mythic beasts that lived in the skies, upon the earth, in the waters, and under the earth. The medieval mind saw the earth in a very archetypal manner, mixing the fabulous with the mundane, so that practical knowledge was allowed to coexist with myth and superstition.

For the modern magician, the antique definition of the world that was used in the Middle Ages by savants, clergy, and sorcerers would no longer be a useful model since it has been profoundly overturned by the discoveries of modern science. It has been supplanted in the study of magick with a new model, which is based upon an occult perspective of the Inner Planes or dimensions that exist wholly within the domain of Spirit and Mind and are not found within the physical world. This new model of the Inner Planes represents the relationship that exists between the domains of spirit and the mind, and how they can manipulate, shape, and change the physical world through that relationship. This is undoubtedly a model of consciousness, not cosmology.

The basic model of consciousness has seven planes, and one can find explanations for this model in many occult books.[71] The Seven Planes are the Absolute, Spirit, Mind, Higher Astral, Lower Astral, Etheric, and the Physical. The Absolute plane has powerful numinous threads that bind all the six lower planes into a continuum, so that all things can be said to be connected to the One. This is a very different model than what was used in medieval times and represents a synthesis of Eastern and Western occult theosophies.

The Seven Planes also represent a spiritual hierarchy since the higher planes represent a higher order of being than the lower planes. Thus, at the highest or Absolute plane are the various facets of the Godhead, which is indivisible and always in union. Below the Absolute plane is the

---

71 I have produced a list to identify these books in the bibliography under the heading "Magick."

plane of Spirit, and here we have the various angelic spirits, daemons, and demigods, who can appear to function apart from the unity of all being, but who are actually as much a part of it as the facets of the Godhead itself—they are just easier for us to connect with than the unified whole. Within the levels of the Mind, Higher Astral, and Lower Astral are the various spirits and entities, from abstract symbolism and philosophic archetypes to heroes, heroines, legendary personages, and spirits of the four Elements (Elementals), as well as lower forms, such as various entities and monsters of nightmare—devils, vampires, werewolves, medusas, fabulous creatures (unicorns, basilisks, winged horses, and so on), etheric larvae, ghosts, disembodied thought forms, and many other entities and fragments of consciousness. All these entities are arranged in a hierarchy from lowest to highest, and all are controlled and even commanded by their higher superiors. Some entities are too dormant and have no intelligence at all, and cannot be commanded but just driven away (such as larvae and other spurious thought forms); others display a great deal of intelligence and even seem autonomous. The magician commands and controls these various spirits from the highest levels of the Absolute plane, where they have assumed the Godhead of their alignment. The magician acts as the Deity and accesses all these entities in their magick, or at least the ones that can produce constructive and positive magickal outcomes.

The structures of the Inner Planes that are used by magicians today consist of variations on this model of the Seven Planes. Principally, the Qabalah, astrology, and the Tarot determine most of these structures, and instead of Seven Planes, there are four Qabalistic Worlds (Assiah, Yetzirah, Briah, and Atziluth) and various attributes of these four worlds. The first and most obvious structure is the forty Sephiroth domains of the Qabalah of the Forty Worlds, which represents the ten Sephiroth projected through the four Qabalistic Worlds. Extracted out of these forty domains are the thirty-six Decans, which are represented by the zodiac divided into sections of ten degrees each, and the four primary Elemental Worlds; these can also be associated with the forty cards of the Lesser Arcana of the Tarot (Ace through 10 of the four suits).

Associated with the thirty-six Decans are the seventy-two Quinarians, or the five-degree segment partitioning of the zodiac. The thirty-six Decans are associated with specific Angelic Rulers, and the seventy-two Quinarians are associated with the seventy-two Angels of the

Shehemphorash and the seventy-two Daemons of the Goetia. Because of the relationship between the Decans and the Quinarians,[72] the Angelic Rulers of the Decans would have rulership over both the Angels of the Shehemphorash, as well as the Daemons of the Goetia. The Angelic Rulers of the twelve signs of the zodiac would have rulership over the thirty-six Decans and would represent the higher spiritual authority.

There are also the inner plane structures associated with the twenty-eight Lunar Mansions, and these are arranged in a matrix of the seven planets and the four elements. Two other structures that should be mentioned are the sixteen Elementals, which represent a matrix of the four Elements, and the forty-nine Bonarum or Good Spirits, which represents a matrix of the seven planets. These inner plane structures derive different qualities for the domains that they define, but all of them serve to determine the inner occult worlds of the Spirit, Mind, Astral, and the Etheric body. One can create a series of qualifying correspondences that define the analogous symbolic characteristics of these domains and all the spiritual entities associated with them. A modern theory of theurgical and goetic magick would declare that if the magician can fully define these worlds and, through trance and ritual techniques, enter into them, then all their associated powers and wisdom and the entities that populate them would become revealed, and ultimately subject unto them. This is the objective of the modern magician, who practices a form of magick called Archeomancy, the *magick of the source* ($\alpha\rho\chi\eta$— *arche*—meaning principle, origin; and $\mu\alpha\nu\tau\epsilon\iota\alpha$—*manteia*—meaning prophetic power).

ANALYSIS OF THE SEVEN WORLDS OR PLANES OF THE MAGICIAN

The first plane or world is the Absolute. This is the domain of super consciousness where everything exists in its purest and most symbolic form of expression, the causal world of archetypes. These abstract symbolic qualities don't exist in isolation but are part of a unified network which produces archetypal patterns and symbolic relationships. No single symbol can be evaluated without considering its relationship to the whole of the others.

---

72   The Quinarians are a subset of the Decans.

The easiest way to express this concept is to consider any system of divination. Although there are specific symbologies that must be learned and understood, the power of a system of divination lies in the relationship between the symbolic components and the context they establish. It's the context of symbolic meaning that the diviner attempts to interpret so that a reading may become understood. The Absolute plane is purely representational of all the other levels but must be translated in order for us to comprehend it. This is why the magician seeks to manipulate the Absolute plane through magickal symbols and actions, representing the components of the archetypal plane and their relationships.

The second level is the World of Spirit, or the subtle Spirit plane. This level represents the first expression of individuality, although it is still very much a part of the unified whole. Thus, the qualities found within the World of Spirit consist of mythic images or masks of reality, and the mythic patterns or stories that represent their interrelationships. The Spirit plane gives definition to the Absolute plane, making it intelligible to the individual. Yet the spiritual level is only a mask that the Absolute wears to assume individuality. While it is inherently illusory and only approximates the absolute truth, the level of Spirit assists the seeker in perceiving the divine, even though it is through the guise of a mask.

The third level is the Mental plane that represents the domain of egocentric individuality; within it is found the living matrix of thought and language, the core of individual consciousness. The mind and its world of words is the most familiar domain of consciousness for the average Western educated person, but as a fish is unaware of the water that it swims in, so the average person is unaware of the linguistic web that tightly binds them. Whether or not people are aware of the fact that their senses are being continuously bombarded by the multimedia of Western culture, this process is constant and thorough in its effectiveness. If one wishes to see the stars more clearly, they go out to the country where there are no city lights. Similarly, if one wishes to experience the subtle linguistic web that binds us, then one must step outside the continuous stream of media that bombards our conscious minds. We must temporarily allow our minds and body a rest from the media blizzard.

Magick and mysticism are artifices of symbolic language. The terminologies they employ become the very same metaphoric symbols that affect the magician and cause them to assume the associated states of consciousness they describe. Words wield a great power over the stuff of the conscious mind, and language is the very structure of one's social existence. One merely supplants one medium and its values for another in order to assume a magickal or mystical perspective. The seeker eschews the material world and its values and embraces the values of the spiritual world. However, either perspective is still a product of the mind and requires language and culture to make it real.

The direction people choose for their life's orientation already has an embedded background of belief and expectation. It will consist of either traditional or alternative values. Therefore, ideals that do not have cultural precedence cannot endure. However, we choose to direct our lives; we are using beliefs and ideas already deeply embedded in our culture. Only a few people ever really conceive of something totally new. If something new is invented and it's accepted by social convention, then the novelty wears off and it quickly becomes part of the cultural consensus. Certainly, the paper clip and the staple are considered rudimentary items in the domain of the office, but they were invented at some point, and prior to that event they didn't exist, even though now they are an indispensable part of our everyday world.

The emotional body is divided into two related but distinct planes known as the Higher and Lower Astral. These two planes occupy the fourth and fifth levels, and they share characteristics associated with the emotional body. The word astral, which is from the Latin astreas or "star," represents the domain of emotions, the world of dreams, fantasy, desire, and sentiments. It's the lower compliment of the mind. In spiritually advanced people, the mind and emotions are perfectly integrated. However, for the purpose of our understanding, the Astral levels are examined separately, for the Astral is where magickal power and its transformative effects are most profoundly experienced. The spirit will imprint upon self-transformational experiences using symbols and beliefs, imbuing them with a transcendental quality. The emotions easily assimilate such occurrences directly; therefore, the heart is said to be the most direct receptor of all spirituality.

The Astral plane is the place where duality is directly experienced as the qualities of good and evil. Where the mind can easily argue the merits or vices of any specific subject, rationalizing through a process of intellectual philosophy; the emotions can't be so ambiguous, and therefore a person develops likes and dislikes. This isn't to say that one's emotions can never be confused or conflicting, but feelings can't be dismissed or ignored as inconsequential thoughts.

The higher Astral holds the power of transformation and is populated by visual images, impressions, and fantasies that make for an effective medium, which the mind uses to create. The lower Astral contains the desires and passions that act as either a compliment or a contrary force to the world of the mind. The lower Astral also has a strong connection to the unconscious mind, acting as a gate to the lower sensations of the body and its vital forces. The higher Astral has a strong connection to the collective unconscious, and it is powerfully influenced by the mythic background of society, of which one is always a part. The magician focuses upon the higher Astral as the world of myth and magick, projecting the dream image of themselves therein; but they also harness the emotional powers of the lower Astral, joining the dream images of magick with the heartfelt forces of inspiration and enthusiasm. Therefore, the key to unleashing magickal powers lies in the effective integration of dream and emotion, the higher and lower Astral planes.

The physical world is also split into two different levels consisting of the plane of energy, called the Etheric plane, and the plane of matter, called the Physical plane. Thus, the Etheric and the Physical planes are the sixth and seventh levels. These two planes are not essentially distinct and separate in the real world, but as a complement to the Lower and Higher Astral planes, they can be perceived as operating on different vibrational levels. To the physicist and the occultist, particles of energy vibrate at a higher frequency than particles of matter because they have different densities. Various psychic incidents are directly associated with the action of the Etheric plane and are of interest to the practicing magician, such as the manifestation of ectoplasm, psychokinesis, fire-walking, and other types of psychically related physical phenomenon. It's the integration of energy and matter that produces living organisms; the vital forces that cause organic life are almost indistinguishable from the matter that they animate. With the advent of death, the energy of the etheric is released from the embrace of matter, and the material substances return to their original inanimate state.

The vital energy of the Etheric plane also represents a source or reservoir of physical power. This resource can be directed to heal and restore the vitality of a sick or injured person or animal. The practice of sexual magick uses this reservoir of power to impact physical reality and alter or bend it in a different direction, allowing for a direct manipulation of the physical world. The only practical limits to the use of this power are found in an individual's ability to harness this energy and efficiently direct it.

All physical effects of magick are caused by the interaction of the Etheric plane and the Physical plane, especially when projected by the combined potency of the emotions and mind. When the integration of these five levels occurs, they will ultimately cause a profound transformation within the individual, opening one up to experiencing the domain of the spirit that is the sixth. When these six levels are joined together, they will impact the highest level of the Absolute plane and establish, however temporary, a unification of the Archetypal Self (Self as Deity) throughout all the seven levels. This represents the ultimate goal of the magician, to establish a unified expression of the self throughout the Seven Worlds.

THE MICROCOSM AND THE MACROCOSM

In addition to the conceptual model of the Seven Worlds, the magician also works with the dual states of the Macrocosm and Microcosm. These two terms represent the differences between the levels of the individual and the unified collective, or the Deity.

These two opposite states are the polarities that define the dynamism of magick, the ascending and descending emanations of consciousness that characterize the processes of individual enlightenment and incarnation of Spirit. The ascending and descending emanations are the cyclic processes of the evolution of consciousness. The magician, being aware of and open to these processes, becomes an accelerated part of them, an agent of these processes as well as a beneficiary of them.

The model of the Macrocosm and Microcosm also instructs the magician that the highest and most abstract level must be altered before the effects of magickal manipulation can be experienced on the lowest and most dense physical level. This is why the magician works with symbolic tools, performing mythical actions within a symbolic environment; they seek to impact the Macrocosm through the artifice of the Microcosm and so transform them both.

The relationship between the Microcosm and the Macrocosm was first revealed in an ancient paradigm that was reputed to be part of the Hermetic philosophy and later incorporated into the discipline of Alchemy.

However, it is a universal theorem, and it is translated from the Latin in the following manner:

"Verum sine mendacio, certum et verissimum quod est inferius est sicut quod est superius, et quod est superius est sicut quod est inferius, ad perpetranda miracula Rei Unius."

"Tis true, without falsehood, and most real: that which is below is like that which is above, and that which is above is like that which is below, to perpetuate the miracles of the One thing."

—Hermes Thoth Trismagistus[73]

The above quotation comes from the Emerald Tablet of Hermes and contains a formula revealing the continuity between heaven and earth. It is similar to the pronouncement made to St. Peter by the Christ: in being given the keys to both heaven and earth, whatever was loosed in heaven would be loosed on Earth, and vice versa. This revelation was a profound occult precept that had its origin in the first century CE but is still relevant today.

The Emerald Tablet was supposedly found in a cave by Galienus the physician, clasped by the hands of the unspoiled corpse of Hermes Trismagistus. The tablet was variously referred to as the Tablet of Zaradi or Smaragdina, and the discoverer was credited as Galienus (Galen or Balinas, a possible corruption of Apollonius of Tyana), or Sarah, the wife of Abraham, or even Alexander the Great.[74]

The Underworld allusions to the hiding place of the tablet suggest that it was perhaps an important piece of secret lore (the emerald, as a precious stone found deep in the earth) that was revealed in the liturgy of an initiation mystery (the underground tomb). A similar treasure of knowledge was associated with the underground tomb of Christian Rosenkruetz, and its dissemination purportedly culminated in the spread of Rosicrucianism in the seventeenth century. It's possible that the recurring mythic motif cited above was not accidental, for

---

73 Gilchrist, Cherry, *Alchemy: The Great Work* (Aquarian Press, 1984) p. 55.

74 Gilchrist, Cherry, *Alchemy: The Great Work* (Aquarian Press, 1984) p. 57.

the emergence of the tablet coincided with the dissemination of the Hermetic philosophy that culminated in the third century CE.

The words of the tablet indicate that the Microcosm and the Macrocosm are one and the same, yet the word "like" denotes that the similarity is not to be confused with equivalency. Through a symbolic artifice, the Macrocosm mirrors all that is physically manifest in the Microcosm.

The miracles of the One are the arts of *Telesma,* the method of producing wonders by magickal artifice. The methodology is clearly established by the first statement of similarities: that a symbol can become that which it represents, and a material object can become imbued with spiritual power. The cycle of ascending and descending divine grace is nothing more than the continuing process of the Absolute (the "One" referred to above), and the miraculous is shown to be the action of subtle but natural laws.

The medieval depiction of the magician (as illustrated in any period Tarot deck), who stands before a table holding their right arm aloft and pointing to the sky and the other down to the earth, is an amalgam of this formula of the relationship between the Absolute and the Manifest. The magician's body acts as the mediator of these two worlds, where their forces converge and meet to produce the human spirit, which is the principal mediator of unity and diversity. But the Absolute isn't to be experienced outside of the body, for the inner infinite reaches of the mind represent the dimension of the Absolute within human nature. The magician seeks to unite the Microcosm and the Macrocosm within themselves, producing the spiritual analogue of both worlds. It's the conscious merging of these two worlds that offers the magician the boon of redemption defined as becoming whole and one. It is assumed in the Western tradition that the natural state of humanity exists as one where the spirit and the body are separated, and their integration is the natural remedy. The search for redemption is the primary quest of the magician. Although it's usually disguised in symbolism or depicted as a great feat or impossible accomplishment, it is actually a very simple act.

The path of the mystic is distinct from the path of the magician, for the mystic is concerned with only achieving union with God, having renounced the material world. Where the mystic, who has persevered to make themselves perfectly empty and selfless, surrenders to their Deity, the magician takes the initiative and acts as a creative agent, boldly assuming the highest state of being. The Absolute descends to a personal level and becomes what was called the Holy Guardian Angel and is now called the Higher Self. The magician seeks this Higher Self and merges themselves with it in the ultimate sacrifice of the individual ego, and the task of redemption is nothing more or less than realizing oneself as God. The magician must remain clear and sane, balanced and deeply aware of the human condition while in this sublime state. They don't seek to destroy the human side of themselves, as some disciplines seem to teach. The magician must become more human than humanity, thus revealing the truth behind the title *Son of Man* given to Christ.

The realization of the union of everything causes one to understand—perhaps for the first time—how important everything has become, particularly when one is personally attached to it. Thus, the plight of the garden spider becomes as important as the impending war between nations. The selfless state of union has no need to differentiate or discriminate, for everything is equal and one with it.

The polarities of the Microcosm and the Macrocosm are also represented by the shift in personal perspective between objectivity and subjectivity, the inner and outer realities of the mind. The truth is that people live inside their minds, but they also live in the world at large. They experience outer occurrences, and they process them through their thoughts and feelings. There is an established theoretical border between the internal awareness of the body and the outer world in which it exists.

The inner domain of the mind is referred to as the *subjective world* and the outer world in which we live is considered the *objective world*. All internal psychic events are therefore subjective because they are privately perceived, and all outward occurrences are objective because they can be perceived by more than one person. This border between objective and subjective occurrences is indistinct and arbitrarily determined by society, for both perspectives are products of the mind.

The magician discovers very early in the practice of magick that these two perspectives are actually one. People may project their various beliefs and illusions onto the world, and others will not only perceive them but believe that they are objective reality. Such a process continuously supports all the arts, religion, politics, and even science. Human nature is not immune to either the follies or brilliant insights caused by the projection of the subjective mind upon objective reality. The theory that objective reality is not an infallible construct but is, in fact, a socially generated and agreed upon illusion was well stated by Emmanuel Kant in the eighteenth century and came to be known later as transcendental philosophy. Yet in antiquity, this process of projection was called magick. Projection is still a fundamental concept in the practice of ritual magick.

However, when one organizes and applies an objective value system upon the internal subjective world of the mind, one experiences the acquisition of self-knowledge and, ultimately, wisdom. This form of inward projection is called *self-analysis* or *introspection,* and it's a process of internalizing values and order upon the chaotic world of the subjective mind. It's the most important task that a magician can undertake, aside from ascending to the plane of consciousness of the Absolute.

The processes of consciousness associated with the Microcosm and the Macrocosm represent the mainspring of the operation of magick. The magician must understand their interaction to grasp their cyclic and dynamic nature.

CHAPTER SIX

CONCLUSION: THE PRACTICE OF RITUAL MAGICK

We've now covered the entire spectrum of concepts and ideas about ritual magick that allows a beginner to proceed from the theoretical discussions to actual ritual practice. What we will provide in the next section of this book is a set of eight completed rituals and the directions for performing the four basic magickal workings. This book is not meant to be comprehensive but is a definitive outline of what the magician needs to know in order to practice magick. Obviously, a magician learns about magick by practicing and not merely reading about it. It would be like trying to learn how to play a musical instrument by just reading books about it. At some point, books and reading material become superfluous to learning by experience, and this is very much true with the practice of ritual magick. The magician learns primarily by doing, and so a book on magick must include an extensive set of rituals for the student to prove the basic injunctions of the author: that ritual magick does indeed work and is relevant to the practical study of occultism in the Western Mystery tradition. Such a collection of rituals is classically referred to as a *grimoire*,[75] and we will refer to it as such in this book.

The fact that many books lack an extensive set of rituals represents the bankrupt state of the art of magick. In my humble opinion, a book on magick that doesn't contain a method for proving the author's

---

75   From Old French *gramaire*, translated as "grammar" —a book of basic instruction.

assertions (such as actual rituals that can be performed) could be considered suspect at best and even fraudulent at worst. This statement doesn't cover authors who actually made oaths about revealing their lore to the public, but today there are few such proscriptions and really no excuses for not revealing a body of lore that the average individual may use outside of any traditional magickal organization. Some may dispute this issue, but in my opinion, the secret societies of the past are no longer valid in the age of rapid information dissemination and openness. The veil of Isis has been removed, and the only secrets are those things that are of Spirit (and completely inexplicable anyway).

The practice of ritual magick takes the student out of the domain of theory and places them into the practice of building a spiritual and magickal discipline. This doesn't mean that the student no longer reads or studies any books or performs any kind of research, for this activity will undoubtedly become even more important once the magician is working ritual magick and experiencing phenomena that needs to be explained and understood. The information in this book will aid in that quest, but it'll require the student to develop more than a passing knowledge of the basic occult studies associated with the practice of ritual magick.

The occult disciplines that the magician needs to study beyond the boundaries of this book are within the subject areas of magick, Qabalah, Tarot, astrology, Eastern Yoga, Hermetics, occult history, and philosophy. I have provided a bibliography at the end of this book that can be used as a recommended reading list, and the student should attempt to read all the books listed there. I have made certain that these books are relevant and currently available, whether as published books or as online books, since some of the out-of-print classics have found their way into the online eBook collections. The student is advised to study other pertinent subject areas, such as classical psychology, integral psychology and philosophy, anthropology, ancient history, archaeology, biology, astronomy, and the history of philosophy. There are other areas as well—too numerous to list here—but leave no stone unturned in the quest for knowledge.

The practicing magician assumes the legacy of magick as it has been practiced through the ages, but they are not bound by that tradition. The tradition of magick is part of what is called the *perennial philosophy*, a term coined by the eighteenth century mathematician Gottfried Leibniz, where he defined it as the common and eternal philosophy that underlies all religions and spiritual traditions, particularly representing those hidden mystical streams that are embedded in the deep structure of all spiritual experiences.[76] A perennial philosophy is neither a static nor changeless system, since it represents a living, dynamic, and holistic expression of all spirituality at the present moment. The perennial philosophy of past ages is not the same as the perennial philosophy of today, nor should it be. Continuity for the perennial philosophy is *change*, since nothing stays the same; some could say that the evolution of ideas represents a change from a lower ordered system to a higher ordered one, so there is a spiral of evolving development that is constantly occurring within the perennial philosophy. These streams are indicative of a mutable gnosis that is always available to the seeker, and what they do with this illumination becomes a legacy for the future perennial philosophy—it is a system that perpetually adds to itself and grows. Perhaps the greatest relevancy for ritual magick is that it partakes in the perennial philosophy, since it's indeed one of the mystical streams that embeds many religions, and that to invest oneself in it is a truly great and holy vocation.

There's also a difference between being a mystic and a magician. Organized religions tend to favor the mystic over the magician, for the obvious reasons that the mystic is usually passive and operates through a religion instead of against it. On the other hand, organized religions tend to condemn the magician because they are generally perceived as an impious and aggressively immodest self-promoter. However, the path of the magician, contrasted against the path of the mystic, has some notable distinctions. The magician and the mystic both start from the same place, except the magician uses ritual mechanisms in addition to meditative ones (of course, this is not too far out from the Sufis). Both the magician and the mystic seek to gain the vistas and immerse themselves in the Spiritual domain, obtaining the higher forms of consciousness as a permanent part of their normal conscious selves. However, where they part ways is the next stage in the magickal cycle of initiation, since the one and only goal of the mystic is to obtain union with the Godhead and remain in that state indefinitely. The magician must continue the cycle and translate what they have obtained through their spiritual union for the benefit of others and the world itself. The magician must

---

76 Vicente Hao Chin Jr., "Perennial Philosophy," Theosophy World Resource Center, www.theosophy.world/encyclopedia/perennial-philosophy. Accessed May 12, 2024.

manifest and enact in this world the reality of the Godhead, and it must be intelligible to others, but it can only be communicated through direct experience. Therefore, the magician has a duty to humanity and the world to return from their spiritual sojourn and bring their visions and their revolutionary teachings to the average person. This is known as the Magnum Opus, the Great Work of the magician. It's also obvious that all the world's religions were founded by individuals who functioned as magicians in the world, bringing forth their teachings for all humanity and starting traditions that became world religions.

In the manner of the magician's cycle of illumination and communication, I have written this book to assist others in adopting and practicing the art of ritual magick. I have put into it all the knowledge and experience that I collected over the years, but I've also had to select specific topics and exclude others in order to build a core tradition that would be immediately useful and easy to master. The magician acquires knowledge in a direct and holistic fashion, and then must express it in a linear fashion so that it is intelligible to others. This will undoubtedly cause distortions and raise the possibility of being misinterpreted, or perhaps it may even allow misstatements, considering how inaccurate and incapable language is in describing higher states of consciousness. My hope is that the rituals themselves will be the focus of this book, and that students will attempt to use these rituals to prove whether I am correct or mistaken in my assertions about ritual magick. I am confident that an open-minded approach in using them will certainly be met with some degree of success. The rest is in the hands of the student, aided by their talents, virtues, and brilliance, and detracted by all their flaws and foolishness, which is what every human being has to deal with in the long course of a productive and eventful life.

PART II

THE GRIMOIRE

CHAPTER ONE

INTRODUCTION TO THE GRIMOIRE

This section contains the rituals, ritual workings, and directions that the beginner will need to know to get down to the real business of practicing magick. After all, that's likely why you, the reader, bought the book in the first place. (I typically zoom to the actual written rituals in a book that I am perusing.) If you have read this far into the book and done some deep thinking about the things that I have imparted to you, you will no doubt have a lot of questions. Unfortunately, the only way that any of your questions will be truly answered is to perform the magick yourself. Hopefully, if the magick is successful, then you will be transformed from someone who is interested and curious about the subject to someone who actually knows something about it through that priceless commodity called *experience*.

This section is essentially divided into two major parts. The first part (Chapter Two) reveals the techniques and methods of controlling the mind and assuming the altered states of consciousness that are required for magickal phenomena to occur. These techniques are incorporated into the meditation and trance session, both of which are used to prepare the mind for working magick. Mental discipline is an essential part of the preparation of the self, which is the first step in performing ritual magick. The second part (Chapters Three through Ten) contains the basic rituals that are required for a magician to practice ritual magick as a discipline. The rituals that are part of the grimoire cover the six basic categories for the performance of the ritual of acquisition, as well as the three mysteries of the Moon, Sun, and Self. These rituals are the Circle Consecration rite, the Pyramidal Pentagram rite, the Rose Ankh Vortex rite, Assumption of the Godhead, the Lunar Mystery rite, the Solar Mystery rite, and the Self-Initiation Mystery rite. The Circle Consecration rite is used to make sacred space, and the Pyramidal Pentagram rite and the Rose Ankh rite are the creative and receptive methods of generating magickal power, also known as the rites of self-empowerment. The Assumption of the Godhead assists the magician in developing a powerful alignment with the Deity, which becomes the central rite that assists the magician in attaining personal self-transformation, a prerequisite for initiation. The mysteries of the Moon and Sun represent the use of the Gateway ritual structure in its alignment to the Western Gateway into the Underworld and the Eastern Gateway out of the Underworld. The mystery of Self-Initiation uses both gateways to facilitate the complete cycle of initiation. There is also an ancillary ritual that assists the magician in consecrating the five basic magickal tools, and this is the eighth ritual in the series.

The combination of mental discipline techniques and the eight basic rituals represents a complete methodology for practicing an elementary level of ritual magick. Using this system of ritual magick, the magician will be able to develop a magickal and spiritual discipline, which is the most important and basic achievement that they can attain, and one that's oddly not often emphasized in other systems of magick. They will be able to perform rituals to acquire and achieve goals in the physical plane, as well as begin to discover their own inner nature and their connection and affiliation to the Deity. Once this magickal process begins and the magician is performing daily meditation sessions and weekly, monthly, and seasonal magickal workings, they will experience a greater sensitivity to all things of a spiritual and magickal nature, and their own internal mysteries will begin to emerge from their deeper unconscious mind. Their greatest achievement will be when they are finally able to perform the Self-Initiation mystery, making the transition between a mere practitioner and an initiate. Although they would be considered a first-degree initiated neophyte in most magickal organizations, they would actually be more proficient than most individuals who are initiated to an even higher degree and part of a popular occult organization. The magician who uses these rituals will also discover other lore through their studies and workings, accumulating new insights and developing new mechanisms for performing rituals. The ritual patterns and structures used in this system of magick represent only the most simplistic mechanisms. There are certainly many more structures of greater complexity that can be discovered and developed over time.

There's another series of books that represent the next step or stage in the development of the magician: *Mastering the Art of Ritual Magick*. The lore of this work begins where the current book leaves off, and all three books were written for the intermediate level magickal practitioner who seeks to master the art of building their own magickal system. There is, of course, intersecting lore between these two books, and the rituals that are part of the grimoires for each are similar. But *Mastering the Art of Ritual Magick* is much more extensive in its presentation of ritual magick, and the rituals are more complex, detailed, and require a greater degree of ability than the rituals that are part of this book. The three books of the *MARM* series are also published, so as students progress from the beginner to intermediate level, they are there to be used if the student has need for them or seeks to write their magical system.[77]

Another important consideration is that the eight rituals in this book are written within a specific occult context: the Grail Mythos of the Western Mystery tradition. Although virtually everyone knows about the Quest for the Holy Grail as found in the various Arthurian romances that popularized it several centuries ago, there's a powerful spiritual motif that underlies those stories. Once this motif is realized, the fictional works become allegorical and spiritually instructive. The theme of these stories is still quite relevant today, despite all the obvious changes and differences between today and the world of the twelfth century.

The Grail symbolizes a powerful transformative spiritual agent that's both material and immaterial, representing a spiritual immanence symbolized by the sacred feminine that is missing from our communal religious organizations and theological doctrines. This is similar to the beliefs held about the Grail in late twelfth century romances, so it is indeed a timeless and relevant spiritual allegory for today's world. It also means that we haven't resolved the issue of the missing feminine spiritual agency in our religious world today. The popularity of the DaVinci Code and the controversial reinterpretation of Mary Magdalene in the New

---

77 *MARM* is now published as a single omnibus edition.

Testament have shown this to be true. Since we've long since passed out of the harsh, barbarous world of the twelfth century and are now entering the lofty twenty-first century, one would assume that this issue of the missing feminine aspect would finally be resolved, but it still haunts us. The Grail Quest represents one avenue for the resolution of that issue, reintegrating the feminine into our religious systems.

The Grail Mythos as it's presented in this series of magickal rituals uses a polarity of four and three legendary personages, which is to say that there are four masculine and feminine characters that qualify the four Watchtowers, Angles, and Element powers, and three masculine and feminine characters that qualify the Lunar and Solar Gateways. There are four warriors or knights of the Grail, four Grail queens, and eight qualified powers that are represented by the eight Pagan gods and goddesses that underlie the Grail mythology.[78] There are also three Grail maidens or priestesses, and three Grail masters that represent the core of the Grail mysteries. The Grail Quest follows the typical cycle of the hero traveling into the Underworld (the Grail chapel), where certain trials are encountered and ultimately mastered. It's followed by a return to the world of light, where the sickness, injustice, and imbalance of the world are corrected by an administration of the Grail in its various forms. The quest is necessary because the implied vitality of the world has vanished, making it a great and terrible wasteland. The Grail knight must perform the quest to find the missing elements symbolized by the Grail, which are embodied in the archetypal feminine spiritual qualities of grace, creativity, compassion, love, and revitalization. The Grail must be returned so the world may be healed and restored to its formal glory.

The Grail manifests in five different forms—the four Elements and Spirit—and these different forms of the Grail express the full spectrum of spiritual transformation. Since it's always changing its form, appearing and reappearing in various legends, the Grail is a symbol of transformation par excellence. The five different forms of the Grail are the lance, the sword, the chalice, the dish, and the stone. These forms have a specific Christian interpretation: the lance is the javelin that pierced the side of Christ on the cross, the sword is the weapon used to decapitate the head from John the Baptiste, the chalice is the cup of the last supper

---

78 The Ogdoadic God and Goddess invocations used in the Pyramidal Pentagram rite.

and also the container that was used to capture the blood of Christ on the cross, the dish is the same as the platter that held the severed head of John the Baptiste, and the stone is the emerald that fell out of the tiara of Lucifer as he was cast out of heaven. These relics are later reinterpretations of the twelve Pagan Celtic treasures of ancient Briton, which are the underlying sacred items later assimilated and associated with the Holy Grail. Thus, the magickal sword and lance or spear represent the tools of the holy warrior king and the powers of justice, protection, invincibility, and an eternal destiny of greatness. The magickal cup and dish, which are also represented as the cauldron and the cornucopia, are the dispensers of an endless supply of drink and food, as well as the receptacles of eternal health, wealth, inspiration, wisdom, and the power of bodily resurrection. The magickal stone is, of course, the stone that acts as the throne or seat of power, the foundation of the sacred kingship. This stone is reputed to magically cry out to indicate whenever a truly ordained and rightful king has been coronated upon it. The famous Scottish Stone of Scone is one good example, the Irish Lia Fáil is another, but it is known simply as the *Stone of Destiny* and represented an important component of sacred kingship.

All these Grail Hallows, as they are so called, represent the elements of sacred kingship, and at least the sword and lance could be interpreted as having masculine qualities. But they are all considered feminine, dispensed by feminine agents that grant the sacred connection between the king, his people, and the land. The true mystery associated with these hallows is the sacrament of the *Hieros Gamos,* where the king must either marry or mate with a goddess in order to be considered truly anointed and graced to be the sacred king. Once this sacred act is performed, then the king and the land are one, and whatever fortunes or misfortunes occur to one also occurs to the other. This theme is found throughout the Arthurian romances and the Grail legends. Thus, when the kingdom is rendered a wasteland, it is because the king has been wounded, and the king must be healed in order for the land to be restored. This is the central motif of the Grail legends, and one that we endeavor to include as a theme in our rituals.

Much more could be said about the Grail mythos, and, indeed, one could easily write an entire book just on this topic alone, but I believe that I have included the basic background and understanding required for the student to make some sense out of the ritual themes. I recommend that the student perform more thorough research on this topic, consulting other books referred to in the bibliography included in this book. However, the other method of understanding these themes is to perform the rituals and experience them within the context of the magickal visions generated. A combination of both methods will ensure that the student realizes the richness and depth of this legendary tradition and its powerful relevance in today's world.

In conclusion, the combination of the techniques of mental discipline and the eight rituals will allow the magician to master the basic practice of magick. It will unleash the magickal qualities of the higher states of consciousness through the artful combination of symbols of transformation and the controlled, altered states of consciousness produced by performing rituals while maintaining rigorous control of the mind. The combination of these tasks is no small matter to accomplish, and the magician achieves them through consistent practice and performance. The key to the mastery of ritual magick is the adoption of a magickal discipline. It's important to perform the meditation sessions and the magickal workings and mysteries at their appointed times without fail. There's no alternative to hard work and persistence, and no shortcut to spiritual mastery.

Chapter Two

TECHNIQUES OF MENTAL DISCIPLINE

INTRODUCTION

Throughout the process of mastering magick, the magician will practice the methods and techniques for the altering of consciousness. These techniques of mental discipline are necessary for the experience of ritual to be realized in its most spiritual and meaningful guise. The magician's normal conscious state must be expanded, making the perceptive faculties more sensitive and attuned to unconscious stirring and various psychic phenomena. Magick cannot be perceived unless one is in an altered state.

To become open to the preternatural influences of the spiritual world, the magician must be sufficiently detached from the mundane world so that they can discern the subtlety of occult phenomena. Despite the dazzling creativity displayed in Hollywood movies depicting paranormal activities, these occurrences are actually very faint and usually not noticed by most people. However, the use of techniques of controlled breathing, intoning mantras or chants, self-hypnosis or trance, body postures (asanas), hand gestures (mudras), and visualization allows the subtle influences of the unseen occult world to become readily perceptible. These techniques cause an altered state of consciousness to occur, and it is in this altered state that the reality of the paranormal is revealed. The techniques of mental discipline require no elaborate precautions, are very simple to learn and adopt, and can be performed anywhere as long as it is an appropriate time and place for their undistracted use.

However, students must practice and use these techniques regularly in order to develop their skills for the maximum effect in ritual.

The above techniques are organized around a ritual structure that's called the *meditation session*. The exercises that are part of the meditation session are practiced, then become part of the neophyte's discipline, and eventually become completely automatic—an unconscious part of the magician's process for the preparation of ritual work.

Essentially, these techniques redirect one's attention from the concerns, cares, and preoccupations with the outer world to one's internal mental and biological processes. This is done by emphasizing the processes of breathing, seeing, and listening, thinking, or moving. These processes can be presented in six categories: breath control, body postures, mantras and yantras, centering and grounding, trance, and visualization.

These practices have been considered the sacramental means of experiencing religious magick within most Western mainstream religions, especially Catholicism. However, to the student and the advanced practitioner of ritual magick, the need for deliberate use of these techniques arises in order to build the psychological basis for all magickal workings, so they become more of a means for doing magick rather than an end in themselves. The following sections consist of five of the six categories that represent the methods of mental discipline used in the rituals of the grimoire. The topic of visualization isn't covered in this text because it isn't an integral technique to the grimoire but can be researched using other source materials.

BREATH CONTROL

There are three basic techniques of breath control. The first technique is the deliberate regulation of breathing, in which the operator focuses their attention thoroughly upon the timing of inhalation and exhalation. This focus of attention should be so complete that one loses awareness of everything except the constant cycle of breath. The timing of the breathing can be arbitrary mental counting, or perhaps based upon the organic tempo of the body itself (that is, the heartbeat). Whatever method is used, the operator should employ a consistent and relaxed tempo with an equal number of counts required to inhale and exhale. There are also two periods of cessation positioned at the beginning and the end of exhalation. These are the still-points in the breathing cycle, and they require a regulated period of the same length as the periods for inhalation and exhalation. The four periods are mentally counted out as they occur. This method of breath control is called the *fourfold breath*. Usually, to maximize the significance of the number four, each of the four periods is restricted to the count of four: inhale to the count of four, hold to the count of four, exhale to the count of four, and hold to the count of four. This process is repeated for long periods of time. The fourfold breathing technique is used as the primary method of establishing the basic altered state that the workings of magick require, and it's used prior to all workings.

The second breathing technique consists of controlled exhalation and resonant breathing, which is accomplished by manipulating the mouth. Controlled exhalation is the use of exhaled breath to resonate some magickal action, becoming a kind of sound effect that expresses magickal power as a rushing sound. Another variation is one in which one forms the mouth as if to utter the vowel sound of "u," then sucks the breath in and blows it out through this reduced aperture of the lips, making a hissing sound. This is known as *cool breathing*, and usually accompanies a very significant magickal moment: that moment in the ritual when one seeks to resonate the established energies. These two methods of breath control are used in specific ritual circumstances, but the student should be made thoroughly aware of their effect through practice and constant exercise.

The third technique involves the process of hyperventilation. It's used to force a magickal event to its climax and cause a profound ecstatic release. This technique can be used to cause an exteriorization of the energy established in the Pyramidal Pentagram ritual or the Rose Ankh Vortex ritual, in which it produces a wave of transformation. The magician begins this technique with cool breathing, then increases the tempo and volume of the intake of the inhalation and exhalation using a method called the *bellows breath* until dizziness occurs. Then, the magician takes a final deep breath and holds it, locking their arms across the chest, and attempts to force out the breath. After a moment of sustaining this tension, they then violently exhale all the breath at once. This method is called the *lotus seven-breath*, referring to the lotus oil that the magician inhales through each nostril seven times just prior to beginning cool breathing.

The following are the specific instructions for the practice of each of these breath control techniques.

FOURFOLD BREATHING TECHNIQUE

The operator sits in a comfortable position, but not one that would allow the onset of sleep. They should then become aware of the normal and relaxed cycle of their breathing. Then, using either the technique of counting heartbeats or simple mental counting, they draw in a slow and gentle breath for four counts, hold it for four, exhale for a count of four, and then hold the empty lungs for a count of four. This cycle is continually repeated with the objective of focusing their awareness exclusively upon counting out the periods of breath. When a distracting thought occurs, they just gently disengage from it and continue to monitor the breathing cycle. After performing this exercise for a lengthy period, the breathing cycle will slow down to become ever more relaxed, and a noticeable change of awareness will occur. The operator will feel very relaxed and free from tension and stress, and the mind will assume a complete state of quiescence that will be alert and free of fatigue. An acute sensitivity will develop, and even minute and subtle changes in the environment will become very noticeable. This new sensitive awareness is the exact state that the magician seeks to establish before working a ritual.

COOL BREATHING

Where the fourfold breathing technique is used to relax and remove stress from the mind and body, cool breathing is used to intensify one's state of mind, focusing it outwardly upon a specific action or event. The technique of cool breathing is one in which the operator breathes through a reduced aperture formed by the lips, as described earlier.

The operator should be seated in a comfortable position, having already performed a period of the fourfold breathing technique, and thus establishing the basic mind-state. Then, the operator purses their lips and begins to slowly breathe through the "u" shape of the mouth. Where the fourfold breath allows the breathing process to be performed normally through the nostrils, the operator is now exclusively breathing through the mouth, increasing the flow of oxygen to the brain. The cycle of inhalation and exhalation should be continuous with no pause between breaths. In this practice, the breath should be drawn in and out in a relaxed and normal fashion as an extension of the fourfold breathing method. The cool breathing technique will cause the subject to feel slightly light-headed when performed. Thus, the operator should only perform this technique for short periods of time, ceasing before the onset of dizziness and returning to the fourfold breathing technique to relax and stabilize.

When cool breathing is used in ritual, the breath is sucked in and blown out quickly for a single to several breathing cycles, which is sufficient for the magician to alter consciousness in a quick and dramatic manner. Many times, cool breathing is accompanied by an involuntary body movement, such as a vibrating movement of the fingers accompanied with a rigid stance producing a potent dynamic of tension. This is the manner of increasing resonance and the level of magickal power. The magician also uses cool breathing to resonate the magickal power at precise moments, such as when drawing lines of force, drawing invoking spirals in the air with the wand, or the action of drawing an invoking pentagram. The use of this breathing technique at the climax of a ritual greatly increases the perceived empowerment, making it more profound.

LOTUS SEVEN-BREATH

This technique of breath control is a form of hyperventilation. It isn't advised for individuals who have chronic breathing disorders or heart problems. However, when used carefully, this technique will cause normal consciousness to be completely eclipsed by an ecstatic release. The rush of blood to the brain is accompanied by a profound slowing of the heart that, in many instances, can be heard slowing through the internal rushing sound of the blood coursing through the arteries past the inner ear and into the brain. There is a certain sensation of rapture at the moment the breath is violently released, and the mind is essentially wiped clear for a few minutes. A deep trance may then be assumed if the operator chooses to build upon the state already established.

The operator sits comfortably and engages in the fourfold breathing technique for around twenty minutes. Then, they apply a small amount of lotus oil (or some suitable alternative) to the upper lip below the nose and begin to slowly take in the scent in long, deep breaths, performing this action seven times. The operator then begins to hyperventilate, employing the cool breathing technique in a more rapid and vigorous manner. This process begins slowly and increases until the operator seems to pant through both the mouth and nose, quickening the onset of vertigo.

When dizziness occurs, the operator then takes a final deep breath and holds it in while attempting to force the breath out but resisting. This is accomplished by almost doubling over, holding the arms across the chest, and applying pressure to the lungs. Then after a period of extreme tension and strain, the operator violently and completely exhales their breath causing the onset of rapture and release. The operator may collapse and even momentarily lose consciousness, but if they have a healthy body and carefully apply the above steps, it is unlikely that this will produce any harmful effects. The period following the release is punctuated by a normal and relaxed rate of breathing, almost so relaxed as to mimic deep sleep; however, the operator is completely awake and alert.

ASANAS (BODY POSTURES)

During periods of working magick and in the discipline of meditation, the operator must sit completely still for long periods of time. They must be alert, awake, and very comfortable, but not comfortable enough to fall asleep. The legs and back must endure these long periods locked in a stationary posture without causing discomfort and distraction; this becomes quite a task.

The easiest posture to adopt is to sit cross-legged with one leg folded over the other. Many living in Asian cultures find it quite comfortable to kneel on a futon pillow, resting the buttocks upon the soles of the feet. However, Americans and Europeans will likely find either position tiring; thus, they may use a stool or a chair. The student of Hatha Yoga may assume any of the more elaborate poses, such as the full or half lotus position, ankle lock position, adept (genital guard) position, or the kneeling position. Whatever posture the magician uses or whatever aid is required,[79] it should be used consistently and become practiced to the point that the magician can assume it for long periods without fatigue. This is a very necessary part of a magician's discipline, for sitting very still and focusing the mind cannot be accomplished unless one is sitting in a reasonable degree of comfort.

Prior to meditation, the magician may wish to perform some stretching exercises to limber the body and relieve any accumulated tensions. This

---

79 Such as a chair, stool, or pillow, or with the back against a wall, and so on.

is also a good practice after the magician has sat in their asana for long periods of time, especially after performing trance.

The body is the principal vehicle for working magick and it is the place where spiritual knowledge is first realized. Magick must be experienced so that the body can grasp and know its mysteries. Therefore, the practice of magick requires that a body should be healthy and sound so that it can withstand the intense stresses associated with the controlled release of magickal powers and the exertion that ritual performance incurs. A magician should never undertake a magickal working when sick, in a weakened state, or emotionally disturbed. Working magick under such duress will certainly cause one to be drained and subsequently make the condition worse.

MANTRA AND YANTRA (MANDALA) TECHNIQUES

The word *mantra* refers to a technique of mental discipline that involves the intoning or monotonous vocalization of a single word or phrase, like *aum*. This process of intonation begins with the mouth open and the voice projected outward. Then, the mouth is gradually closed while the intonation is reduced to humming. The final internal vibration, which occurs with the mouth completely closed and before running out of breath, causes the sinuses to vibrate with the tone. This resonates throughout the skull of the operator, particularly stimulating the frontal lobes of the brain in my experience. As in the case of breath control, the operator focuses upon the intonation's sound so that the mind is dislodged from its normal processes. The operator is attentive to the intoning of the mantra and gently blocks out all other intruding thoughts. When extraneous thoughts do intrude, they should calmly refocus their attention back on the mantra. After a period, the vibrating hum causes the magician to feel very focused and alert. The use of the mantra as a form of mental discipline differs from breath control in that the sound it produces is loud and varied enough to easily capture the attention of the operator and keep them alert and awake.

In a typical meditation session using the mantra, the operator begins by using the fourfold breath technique to relax and prepare the mind. Then, the operator proceeds to intone the mantra, beginning with a solid projected tone and diminishing to a quiet, internalized vibrating, all within the exhalation cycle of the controlled breathing technique. The inhalation, of course, is silent and performed for a shorter amount of time, making the exhalation period much longer than the inhalation period.

However, when practicing the mantra technique in a group, individuals may wish to intone as a chorus of voices, creating beautiful and strange sounding harmonies. When the above pattern is followed, the group begins by vocalizing the mantra melodiously as a chorus. Then, as their lungs begin to empty, the intonation decreases in volume until only a low humming sound is heard. A continuous round of mantra intoned within a group can produce a wondrous chorus of rising and lowering tones. The group may desire to stagger the inhalation phase, thus minimizing the period of silence so that a continuous sound is created.

A group or individual can also practice a chant or mantric round by repeating a word or phrase continuously in a normal speaking voice, but with ever rapid execution until the speed reduces the word to a single hissing or susurration. This technique will cause the mind to be completely captivated and will also cause a potent resonance of magickal power. The mantric round can be used instead of ecstatic dance to exteriorize magickal energy, raising its basic level of intensity to a climax.

Another method of mental discipline is one in which the operator stares fixedly at a symbol, sigil, or some type of recursive-looking psychedelic illustration. The image the operator intently focuses upon is called a *yantra*, and the method of visually focusing on it is called *Yantra Yoga*. The yantra is an elaborate series of geometric patterns that symbolize the active agency of the divine. It captivates the mind through the instrument of the eye, imprinting it with the essence of the yantra's symbolic meaning. A yantra is not simply a clever illusion-producing diagram but a highly symbolic structure that has condensed numerous concepts and ideas into a single visual representation.

The shape of the yantra is recursive, as the Sri Yantra demonstrates (the yantra image most commonly represented, as shown on the right).

However, two factors are important for the magician to consider when using diagramed images for visual concentration. The diagram should be symbolic and meaningful, and it should cause visual illusions when stared at. The visual illusions cause the onset of a mild trance state, and the symbolic characteristics of the yantra affect a subtle programming of the mind. Thus, the magician becomes visually permeated by the yantra's significance. The image must symbolically denote some esoteric and spiritual property that is significant to the operator. The yantra should be illustrated in color combinations or contrasts that cause visual effects; that is, when the operator stares at it for a period, it should alter consciousness through the visual centers of the brain. This technique consists of focusing the eyes and awareness completely upon the yantra, allowing the image to captivate the mind and calm the internal mental processes. Usually, the yantra is fixed upon a wall or displayed as a mandala. There should be no distracting visual input as one is gazing; therefore, the background and adjoining area of the yantra should be neutral. Visual concentration is interrupted only by breaks in the focus and can be easily restored.

By its nature, a yantra causes visual illusions when gazed upon for a short period of time. Shifting visual focus and optical fatigue normally cause various visual distortions, but a yantra can cause this effect even when gazed upon momentarily. Therefore, a yantra is a powerful tool for the altering of consciousness. This explains why a magician has many such illustrations adorning the walls of their temple. However, to give a definition to the classical yantric configuration, one must merely consult a book on Eastern Indian meditation, particularly tantric literature.

The magician can stare at any monochromatic surface and achieve a similar state as using a yantra. In fact, a well-disciplined magician should be able to cause a visual trance by staring at anything for a period of time. The monochromatic background is called a *ganzfeldt* in the German Gestalt school of psychology, and it can cause hallucinations when the eyes are subjected to it for a long period of time. This was discovered by explorers who were subject to the monochromatic whiteness of snow in mountains or Arctic regions for long periods of time and verified by the meticulous experiments of German scientists in the early twentieth century. The ganzfeldt effect is actually a phenomenon that has been known about and used since ancient times for the establishment of a mild trance state in preparation for crystal scrying or other clairvoyant operations.

In a typical meditation session where the yantra is employed, the operator begins with the breath-control technique of the fourfold breath. When the operator achieves the proper base level of relaxation and inner stillness, they then direct the gaze to an illustration or a monochromatic background and stare fixedly at it. The image should become the complete focus of all of one's attention and breaks in concentration should be gently overcome. The operator should not become distracted by any visual hallucinations, but simply observe all that occurs in a detached manner. This technique can be continued until the eyes become too fatigued, at which point the operator should close their eyes and resume the fourfold breathing technique to become re-centered.

The methods of using a yantra or a ganzfeldt are numerous, and the student should experiment with the above exercise and attempt some variations. This method is an important one to master because the mind-state it causes is very useful for clairvoyance. The yantra or ganzfeldt effect is to the visual senses what mantra intoning is to the auditory senses. The operator seeks to captivate and control the mind so that it is more easily focused and capable of sensing paranormal phenomenon. Each of the above techniques produces a slightly different state of mind. They are not interchangeable, but are distinct tools used to enhance the faculty of perception that is engaged.

The final technique for affecting the visual perception of the operator is applying a moderate amount of pressure upon the closed eyes with the palms of the hands. This pressure is gently increased until the optic nerve is stimulated, producing an explosion of light and color that, if intently focused on, will assume shapes and forms (and even entire visual scenes). Once an image is formulated, the operator can release the pressure on their eyes and continue to focus on the afterimages. If carefully practiced, this method can be used as a good precursor for scrying or creative visualization, since it seems to purify the visual process for a moment and captivates the mind.

CENTERING AND GROUNDING

The two most important exercises that a student should know if they are seriously interested in practicing ritual magick are grounding and centering. *Grounding* refers to the act of draining surplus energy into the earth, thus relieving the body and mind of the stresses of magickal power and establishing a connection with the earth and the healing power of its living ecosystem. *Centering* is the technique whereby the energetic components of the magician's body are drawn into a unified whole. The axis of this alignment is drawn along the spine, unifying the whorls of etheric vital energy (chakras) into a single ray of lifeforce. This ray has two directions: the ascending arc of spiritual evolution, and the descending arc of spiritual benediction. Together, they represent the mediation of Deity and humanity through the body of the magician.

The actions of grounding and centering are used by the practicing magician in every working, both great and small. Even for meditation sessions, it is advisable for the operator to perform a centering exercise first, then meditate for a specific period, and follow the meditation session with a grounding exercise. This combination of exercises establishes a very potent flow of energy through the body and eliminates the potential for any physical or mental obstruction to act as a dam, blocking the natural flow of that energy into its primary reservoir—the earth itself.

It's very important for the student of magick to learn how to become an unbiased channel for the energies of the Deity and the life force of the planet. They become the very medium of their ultimate joining and are absorbed into the process of the incarnation of avatars. As the perfect channel of divine power, the magician becomes an incarnation of the Deity and assumes the mantle of authority and purpose that is the legacy of all humanity. The great secret truth of ritual magick is that all people are magicians. Yet only one who becomes aware of this fact and deliberately practice it comes to fully realize the essence of that legacy. However, the student must practice these techniques to the point that they become second nature. The greatest protection that any magician can adopt is the automatic responses of centering and grounding so that they are a kind of inhalation and exhalation of energy, allowing for a freely circulating flow of psychic power and vital forces. The state of being centered and grounded is the unassailable fortress that protects the disciplined magician.

The following are examples of centering and grounding exercises that the student can use to create their own tailored methods. The concepts of these exercises are universal to human life and are probably of ancient origin. They should be utilized in all serious magickal workings and become part of any serious magician's discipline.

CENTERING METHODOLOGY

The exercise of centering uses five body points usually referred to in yoga as *chakras* (with the exception of the feet), and it is necessary to briefly describe and explain these points. I use five points or chakras instead of seven (or more), since I base my model of the magickal body on the Qabalistic Middle Pillar, adding my own variations.

The first point is the crown of the head and the area just above it that represents the connection of the operator with the divine through the mediation of the higher self. It's, therefore, called the crown chakra. When this point is stimulated, it activates the connection of the mental and spiritual planes.

The second point is the area just above the point between the eyes, known as the third eye in yoga and other metaphysical systems. The third eye represents the sensitized vision of the spirit that compliments and augments the operator's normal vision. When this area is stimulated, the operator can see the world of the Spirit through the power of visions.

The third point is the area from the heart to the solar plexus, centered around and just above the navel, where there's a nerve juncture for the smooth muscle of the belly. The solar plexus represents the center of the volatile self and the will of the operator. The slang phrase "he hasn't the guts to do it" is actually making a metaphysical statement about one's will. The heart represents the love and compassion of the individual. The combination of the two chakras causes love to be tempered by the will. When this area is stimulated, the operator can exert a tremendous force of will that can cause all sorts of curious physical phenomena, such as miraculous feats of strength and even levitation. Yet it's also the area where all love and compassion find their origin; therefore, this emanation of personal strength and prowess is qualified by devotion and passion. It's taught in magick that the solar plexus is the place where the magician's power has its origin and that the heart is the place of the soul. Joined, they become the base of all spiritual alignment and power.

The fourth point consists of what are called the extremities—the anus and the genitals—and although most systems separate them into two distinct locations, this exercise uses them in conjunction as representing the desire center. The desire center represents the zone of energies most associated with the vital forces, creation, and excretion. In conjunction with the power of the will (the solar plexus), the power of desire is the cause of all change and transformation in the physical and psychic dimensions of reality.

The fifth point is the feet and their connection to the earth, representing the basis or foundation of all matters pertaining to the operator. When these are stimulated, the resultant movement causes a wave of force to be drawn up from the earth, cycled through the body, and then projected into the floor. It's for this reason that magick rituals should be performed with bare feet to allow the maximum circulation of energy. The connection of the feet to the earth is a measure of the strength of one's position and the certainty of one's chosen direction, reflected in the confidence of one's preparation.

These five points are used in the centering exercise, but don't exhaust all the possible body points. In yoga, there are seven chakras that include the throat, the heart distinct from the solar plexus and the base of the spine, and the separation of the genitals and the anus, while excluding the feet. Other systems include the hands, the thighs, and the back of the head. In some systems of magick, the chakras are called hot spots or power zones and there can be as many as sixteen or thirty-two of them. One must also consider that there are thousands of nerve endings in the human body accurately mapped in the discipline of acupuncture, thus representing a possible resource for determining potential magickal body points.

There are two basic directions to the flow and stimulation of the five bodily points in the exercise of centering. The first direction is known as the *ascending wave,* in which the points of the body are stimulated from the soles of the feet up to the crown of the head and beyond, representing the opening and aspiring will of the operator to connect with the Absolute Spirit. Conversely, the *descending wave* is where the points of the body are stimulated from the crown of the head and the area above it down through the body to the feet and out through the soles of the feet into the earth. The ascending wave is used at the beginning of a working and causes the operator to be centered and open to spiritual manifestations. The descending wave is used at the end of a working and causes the operator to be once again centered in the mundane waking world, allowing the powers experienced to become manifest. Stimulating each bodily point is accomplished through concentrating awareness on that area, and through vibrating the vocal cords while visualizing a colored light suffusing the area. The operator may also lightly touch or tighten the muscles in the area while performing the above actions. The light suffusing the body points is rose red when performing the ascending wave, and azure when performing the descending wave.

The Ascending Wave

The operator stands fully erect, motionless for a moment while gently breathing with the fourfold breath technique. Then they flex the feet and begin the process of vibrating the vocal cords while chanting a mantra (*aum*), concentrating on the feet, and visualizing a red light emerging from the earth and suffusing the feet with its energy. The operator visualizes the energy traveling up their legs to the genital/anal region and tightens the muscles of the anus while vibrating the vocal cords and visualizing the red energy suffusing them. The operator then visualizes the energy traveling up to the solar plexus region and touches or gently rubs that area while vibrating the mantra with the vocal cords and imagining the red light suffusing it. The operator draws the energy up through the heart where it expands and fills the body with love and vitality, then up past the throat to the third eye, where the operator increases the volume of the vibrating and very lightly touches the area while visualizing it being suffused with the energy of the red light. At this point, the operator draws all the energy up from the feet through the third eye past the crown of the head and beyond with a graceful sweeping motion of the arms while increasing the volume of the vibrating and imagining the red light rising through the body through the crown of the head. At the zenith of this movement, they exhale, release all the tension, and cease vibrating the vocal cords, saying the following small prayer:

Rooted in Certainty, Desiring and Daring to Know the Essence of my Being, I Ascend to the Summit of Spiritual Awareness to Connect with the Union of Being.

THE DESCENDING WAVE

The operator stands fully erect, motionless for a moment while gently breathing, using the fourfold breath technique. Then, they draw in a deep breath, vibrating the vocal cords with the mantric chant and concentrating on the area above the head while visualizing a blue light occurring therein. The operator imagines that blue light gently descending to the area of the third eye, where they intensify the vibrating sound and touch the point with the right hand while visualizing the energy suffusing it. Then, the operator visualizes the blue light descending down the throat to the heart, where they feel the love of the Absolute Spirit filling them with inspiration and connection. The operator visualizes the blue light continuing down to the solar plexus, where they lower the volume of the vibrating vocal cords, touch or gently rub that area, and visualize the point suffused with blue light. The operator then visualizes the blue light traveling down to the genital/anal region, where they tighten the muscles of the anus and vibrate the vocal cords while imagining the blue light suffusing the point with its gentle energies. Then, they visualize the blue light traveling down the legs to the feet, where it enters the earth, thus uniting spirit and matter through the body of the operator. They vibrate the vocal cords and imagine a continuous circuit of blue light descending from the crown and beyond to the soles of the feet and into the earth. Then, they position their arms above the head and slowly, with a sweeping gesture, draw the blue light energy from the crown of the head down through the body to the feet in a single motion, gently exhaling the breath as this is done. In the ensuing silence, the operator says the following prayer:

The Union of Being Seeks to Know the Essence of Individuality by Willing Desire into Physical Manifestation, Thus Establishing the Foundation of Spiritualized Existence.

GROUNDING

The method of grounding is a very simple but effective technique performed by the operator after all else is completed to end a working. Even with the performance of the descending wave centering technique, there may be some residual energies and a sense of "otherness" still pervading the consciousness of the operator, and the grounding exercise ensures that no such forces remain to cause a disturbance. An ungrounded individual experiences a certain discomfort analogous to a deep-water diver who has not adequately decompressed after a prolonged dive, causing serious psychic disturbances. It's important for the magician to return to this world after engaging with the spirit world. This enables the magician to transform the mundane world and assist them in coping with a return to normalcy. By following this cycle, the magician emulates the cycle of initiation and puts their power into the world. It's also important to decompress the psyche, removing from it the intense forces of ritual work to complete the magickal process. The following is a simple procedure that should be adequate for grounding any of the workings found in the grimoire.

After a period of peaceful meditation and unstructured breathing, the operator stands and performs a few natural stretching exercises to get the stress worked out of the body. Then they return to a seated posture and proceed to vigorously rub the hands together for a short period. They then rub the body, beginning with the head and face and proceeding down to the chest, abdomen, legs, and ending at the feet. The operator takes the accumulated energy and, leaning forward, places the hands on the ground while gently and completely exhaling, visualizing all the surplus energy being sent into the earth. Then the operator slowly rises to a normal sitting posture, while drawing a corresponding resonance of energy from the earth into the body, thus relaxing and stabilizing it. After a moment of reflection, the operator is ready for normal activities.

TRANCE METHODOLOGY: SIMPLE TRANCE

The final technique of mental discipline that a magician needs to master is the art of trance, or self-hypnosis. There are many different methods of trance induction, but only a few are proven to be both simple and effective.

Trance represents the pure mind-state of the phenomenon of magick, a state that is profoundly receptive to suggestion and concentrated in its narrow focus of awareness. Trance states occur normally in human consciousness, but they are spontaneous and usually undesirable. Anyone who has driven a motor vehicle for very long periods of time at night knows what it's like to become hypnotized by the road. Driving requires an acute focusing of the driver's attention, in constant battle with the effects of a monotonous journey over an endless highway. A trance produced by road fatigue is fraught with danger.

Trance occurs whenever we focus our attention exclusively on an object while successfully excluding all other distractions or interruptions. As fatigue sets in, the tension between remaining fixed on that object and staying awake causes a shift of consciousness in the individual. Their focus becomes locked, but their awareness becomes profoundly diffused even though the subject is not asleep. This shift of consciousness causes a state of mind that is highly suggestive and sensitive to outer stimuli, yet locked to the narrow focus of attention that has captivated it. This is known as the *hypnogogic state*. The subject's attention is still powerfully focused, but the object upon which they were focusing has been replaced by an internalization process that opens the individual's unconscious mind into consciousness, allowing for a submersion of the egoic identity. Consciousness is inverted, becoming a negative image of itself, and the awareness of the unconscious mind supplants the normal outward focus of consciousness, causing the world to be perceived in a sort of dreamlike manner.

The magician knows that the greater and higher aspect of themselves lies within the unconscious mind, and therefore is prepared to deal with inner devils to discover the Deity within. The magician enters this strange underworld and does not fear the darkness or the reputation of evil and danger that is rumored to lurk within its shadows. Like the primordial hero or heroine, they seek to enter the personalized domain of trials in order to discover the answers to the meaning of life as they are individually applied to them. Great knowledge and illumination reside therein, and the disciplined magician who is confident, resourceful, and creative can discover its secrets for themselves, as well as for the world at large.

This hypnotic state is the basis for all the subjective experiences of magick. But even though the modern Western world holds subjectivity to be of little value or veracity, subjective experiences forge all our beliefs, building up our hopes and ideals and causing us to remake ourselves, reestablish our identities, and inform ourselves of where we have been and to what goals we aspire. Considering that the phenomenon of subjectivity has so much personal importance and insight, it causes one to question the belief that objectivity is the sole arbiter of truth. The borders also blur between objectivity and subjectivity. The experience of ritual magick could certainly be considered subjective, yet magickal experiences can be shared between individuals, indicating that they all have a common experiential base. Ritual experiences could also be considered objective. It is also possible to export rituals from one individual to another, and for a similar experience to be gained when the ritual is performed anew. (Otherwise, the publication of this grimoire would certainly be folly.) The magician makes use of subjectivity without doubt or worry and, through trance, opens the doorways to the subtle reality of the World of the Spirit.

A simple method of trance induction uses the techniques of mental discipline already discussed (breath control, mantra intoning, and staring at a yantra or an illustration). These induce an altered state of consciousness while the mind is completely absorbed in the proper performance of these techniques. The key here is to resonate one's awareness and focus it while maintaining a continuous level of activity, thus accelerating the effects of the mental discipline technique used. This process is continued until a profound state of awareness and inward focus (into the unconscious mind) is achieved. The operator achieves the trance state by altering consciousness through breath control, intonation, and visual focusing.

After the trance state is achieved, the magician may allow a certain degree of normal consciousness to return so that they will be capable of performing an elaborate ritual but still be receptive enough through a mild trance state to perceive it. However, the derived state of consciousness will seem very different and very profound compared to the normal state.

When attempting these trance techniques, the operator may close their eyes after a period of intense staring and allow the eyes to rest, as well as to observe the optical afterimage. The operator should maintain this optical afterimage through visualization so that it remains clear in the mind's eye. This has the effect of causing the visual trance to become internalized and therefore more susceptible to internal mental alteration. The background of the mind becomes like a video screen, on which the visions of the spiritual world may be presented.

THE MEDITATIVE SESSION

Since we have already covered various techniques for mental discipline, we only need to demonstrate how they are assembled in a meditative session. All meditative sessions begin with some stretching and relaxing exercises to remove any tension from the body and prepare it for a concentrated period of sitting.

The operator assumes their chosen asana, and after a few minutes of relaxation and clearing the mind of mundane thoughts and sentiments in this posture, the session is begun with the fourfold breathing technique. The fourfold breathing technique is repeated for around twenty minutes (or more), until the subject feels relaxed and completely at peace. The pace of breathing is then gently slowed until it reaches a relaxed and natural rhythm, similar to the frequency of breathing during sleep. This is the mind-state that the magician should achieve prior to any ritual working. This exercise should be practiced daily.

When a working is performed, it's prudent for the operator to practice an enhanced version of the meditation session. The operator intones a mantra using all the breath and follows it with a period of slow inhalation. The mantra should be continued for several minutes or until the desired effect is realized. This technique will intensify the altered state of consciousness already established by breath control, causing a noticeable shift in awareness.

A period of silence should follow the intonation of the mantra as the operator attempts to listen to the internal musical resonance within the body. At this moment of silence and internal sensitivity, the subject is ready for the performance of ritual.

In addition, the subject can use cool breathing to sharpen the focus of awareness after the above periods of fourfold breath control, mantra intoning, and the period of silence that follows. Cool breathing allows the operator to awaken from the lower metabolic level of deep meditation without losing the sense of depth and inner connection that it causes.

TRANCE WORKING

The basic level of consciousness required for working a trance session must be achieved first. This can be accomplished by performing a meditative session. The subject should keep their eyes open and focused upon the scrying device. This device can be a crystal ball, a magick mirror, a yantra illustration, or even a blank wall. The subject's eyes should be wide open, locked into this object while engaging in a short period of cool breathing with blinking kept to a minimum. While the subject is focusing in this manner, they then begin a period of controlled breathing so the mind is kept from being distracted by extraneous stimuli. After about ten minutes, the subject's vision should begin to distort. It's beyond this threshold that the question or desire is allowed to cycle in the mind of the subject, singularly obsessing on it, while the eyes behold the visual formation of the responses as they emerge from the unconscious mind.

Once established, the trance state should last as long as possible, until all the questions and inquiries have received some kind of response. A scribe (if one is available, otherwise a small tape recorder will do) should note down the questions and answers the subject articulates. It's necessary for the subject to be able to narrate what they are seeing. This can be done by whispering or speaking in a subdued voice so that the act of talking does not become a distraction from what is being envisioned.

When the trance is complete, the subject performs a grounding exercise and stretches their body, rubbing the hands and feet to stimulate the circulation of blood.

CHAPTER THREE

CONSECRATION OF
THE GRAIL TEMPLE

PREFACE TO THE RITE

This circle consecration rite uses the Arthurian legends of the Four Hallows of the Grail and the Grail quest to qualify and configure this rite. We won't get too deep into explaining this tradition, since many people are familiar with the Grail quest and its various offshoots from books and movies. There are a few good reference materials that explain the Grail myth in great detail found in the bibliography. According to the legend, the Grail has at least four different forms that it assumes, and there is an implied fifth, representing the four Elements and Spirit. This is an excellent motif to use for setting the four Watchtowers and consecrating ritual space, so we use it here. We also use Latin god names, which seem to fit the ritual well, as it is a mixture of Paganism and Christianity. These can be replaced with whatever is more appropriate to the operator.

The Table of Correspondences used in this ritual is listed below. Note that they are in the order of Element, Grail Warrior, Hallows, Archangel, and cardinal direction.

Fire	Water	Air	Earth	Spirit
Galahad	Lancelot	Arthur	Gawain	Parzival
Lance	Chalice	Sword	Dish	Crystal
Michael	Gabriel	Raphael	Uriel	Raziel
South	West	East	North	Center (IP)

The ritual pattern consists of the following steps:

1. Introduction, Declaration, and Generation of the Lustral Water
2. Procession of the Four Elements
3. Tracing the Magick Circle
4. Setting the Four Watchtowers and Infrapoint/Ultrapoint
   a. Setting the Four Guardian of the Watchtowers (performed deosil)
      i. Invocation of the Grail Hallow
      ii. Drawing the invoking pentagram of specific Element
      iii. Summoning the Warrior Guardian of the Grail
   b. Setting the Four Grail Wardens (performed deosil)
      i. Drawing invoking pentagram of Spirit (archetypal masculine/feminine)
      ii. Summoning Archangelic Warden
      iii. Squaring the circle (creating the inner circle area)
5. Creating the Central Pylon: the World Tree

The outer circle establishes the magickal perimeter of the magickal reality, defining and activating the four Watchtowers and their Warrior Guardians. The mystery of the Hallows of the Grail is also introduced, sacring (consecrating) the circle. The inner circle, which is drawn as a square (uniting the Watch Towers to each other along a linear structure), becomes the inner domain of the circle, warded by the four Archangels of the Hallows, who are the emissaries of the Grail Godhead. The squaring of the circle represents the joining of the archetypal feminine with the archetypal masculine, thus symbolizing the charging of the magick circle with that magickal power.

INTRODUCTION TO THE RITE

On the altar should be at least two candles, a chalice containing water, and a pentacle with salt placed upon it. The chalice is usually placed upon the pentacle, so it is resting on it and covering the salt. There should be a censer to burn incense, a magick sword to draw the circle, a magick wand for invocations, and a dagger (athamé) to draw the lines of force; these tools don't necessarily need to be placed on the altar.

The circle may be one of various sizes. An eleven-foot diameter is the standard size for small group workings. For more individualized and special workings, it can be three, five, seven, or nine feet. The altar may be placed at any of the four quarters or in the center of the circle. However, the orientation will have a subtle effect in determining the quality of the temple's energy. One can discover this effect by varying how the temple and its furniture are arranged.

The altar candles should be anointed with a specially chosen scented oil. It may be a favorite scent, or one used for its magickal correspondence and sympathy with the magick to be worked. When anointing a candle, it is best to envision the purpose of the rite, thereby adding an intention to the anointing process.

There should be four candles placed in the four cardinal directions. The directions marked are called the four Watchtowers. The candles may be different colors, or they may be placed in tinted glass candle holders. The colors that correspond to the four Watchtowers are as follows:

- **North:** green (Earth)
- **East:** yellow (Air)
- **South:** red (Fire)
- **West:** blue (Water)

The workers may use this color scheme or another. The candles would be wisely placed up off the floor, resting on some suitable tables or stands. Seven-day vigil candles that are completely enclosed in glass except for an aperture at the top are an excellent choice for the Watchtowers. A naked flame on the temple floor is a profound fire hazard.

There should also be four candles placed at the cross-cardinal points (between the cardinal positions) representing the four Angles. These candles are usually neutral colored (white or the natural color of pure beeswax), for the Angles do not have any correspondences but merely reflect those applied to them from the four Watchtowers.

The Celebrant is cleansed, purified, anointed, robed, and has already assumed their magickal persona. The Celebrant then proceeds to the temple within the magick circle, where they sit comfortably and meditate using the fourfold method of breath control. Then, after a suitable time, they practice the intoning of the mantra chant *aum*. This period of meditation is important for properly setting the mood and mind-state required for all ritual workings.

After the above process is completed, the candles are lit, the incense charcoal started, and the ritual begins. A pause at this moment allows for the Celebrant to recall the purpose of the working. This may be stated aloud or pondered quietly.

When the Celebrant has fully resolved to perform the work, they sound the bell or gong three times, and the ritual is truly begun. Facing the East, the Celebrant intones:

> *Here is the Book of Thy Descent.*
> *Here begins the Book of the Sangreal.*
> *Here begin the Terrors.*
> *Here begin the Miracles.*[80]

Then there is a pause for a few minutes while the above quotation is meditated upon.

GENERATION OF THE AQUA SACRA

The salt is already deemed blessed, but the water needs to be consecrated. Pure water is poured into the chalice, and salt is portioned out on the graal-dish. The chalice is placed upon the graal-dish.

BLESSING THE WATER

The water is blessed first. The dagger is placed into the chalice:

> *I Bless and Consecrate Thee O Holy Water, which has come forth like the Hidden Stream of The Mysteries and which lieth Clear and Pure like the Sacred Lake of Beginnings.*

---

80 Originally from Godwin, Malcolm, "Chronicle of Helinandus," *The Holy Grail* (Viking Studio, 1994) p. 10.

INVOKING THE SALT

The chalice is removed from the dish, and the salt is invoked with the dagger:

O Spiritual Salt, I Conjure and Summon Thee to affirm our Integrity of Purpose in the Quest for Perfection.

COMMIXIO (LATIN FOR MIXING)

The Sangraal-dish of salt is poured into the chalice of water; the chalice is then placed upon the sangraal-dish. The dagger is used to stir the elixir five times:

O Lady Vivienne—Lady of the Lake, The Mistress of the Veils, and The Queen of Avalon. We beseech Thee to Manifest Thy Holy Current and open The Gates to Thy Blessed Isle.

THE LEYLINES OF AVALON (DRAWING THE MAGICK CIRCLE)

The Celebrant takes up the sword and draws a circle of power around the perimeter of the temple, beginning at the East and proceeding clockwise to return to the East:

By this Sword of Light, we etch this Ley Line of Mediation, between Avalon and Albion, between the World of Spirit and the World of Form.

Herein shall we commune with the Manifestations of God, and God shall Reveal The Mystery of the Hallows unto us. So mote it be.

Then the sword is grounded gently upon the stone which lies in the center of the circle.

PROCESSION OF THE FOUR ELEMENTS

The Celebrant then takes up the chalice of lustral water and asperges the circle (or sprinkles the lustral water lightly with the fingers while walking with the chalice in hand), then takes up the burning censer and incenses the circle, and finally the right altar candle, which they use to set an equal arm cross at each of the four wards. They take each one of these containers of sacrament and in the above order, circumambulates the circle once, beginning in the Eastern quadrant and proceeding deosil until completing the circuit in the East. At each Watchtower, they shall bow and give salute, asperging with the lustral water, swinging the censer four times, or drawing an equal arm cross with the altar candle. Then, the Celebrant reads the incantation below after they have purified the temple with the four Elements (salt is Earth, water is Water, incense is Air, and the candle is Fire). The incantation is as follows:

> *I Bless and Sanctify this Space with the Powers of Earth and Water conjoined with Air and with Fire; in the Names of the Goddess of the Graal and Lord of the World Tree. So mote it be.*

PRESENTATION OF THE FIVE HALLOWS AND SETTING THE FOUR WARDS

The Celebrant stands in the center of the circle and intones the following incantation:

> *The Grail appeared at the Sacring of the Mass, in five several manners that None ought not to tell, for the Secret Things of the Sacrament ought None to tell openly but he unto whom God hath given it.*[81]

The Celebrant proceeds to the Eastern Watchtower and stands before it. They take up their dagger and gives a salute to the East. Then, holding

---

81 *Perlesvaus* (thirteenth century), p. 368.

their magick dagger aloft, they invoke the Ward of the Eastern Watchtower with the following incantation:

And behold, the First Veil parted, and I saw The Sword of Light emerging from the Darkness, and I heard a Voice and it said:

"In the Realms beyond the Light of Truth, shall make the Unknown Revealed."

I invoke Thee, Arthur Rex! and behold, before me appears a Great Bearded Man, with fair hair, and grey blue eyes sitting upon a Throne.

Thou art the Just King and Head of the Round Table, and Lord of Camelot, armed with Excalibur. Thou art the Great Undying King who shall return when Briton once again needs Him.

Above His head is a Shield displaying a Green Dragon, rampant upon a Scarlet Field. He is wearing Robes of Purple and Gold.

The Celebrant and workers then draw an invoking Pentagram of Air, completing it with a final thrust as they exhale. They then draw an invoking spiral around the completed Pentagram, penetrating its center as a final gesture and exhaling as they do it.

The Celebrant proceeds to the Southern Watchtower and stands before it. They take up their dagger and gives a salute to the South. Then, holding their magick dagger aloft, they invoke the Ward of the Southern Watchtower with the following incantation:

And behold, the Second Veil parted, and I saw The Spear of Longinus which ran with the Sangreal, and I heard a Voice and it said:

"The Universal will lead the Sage to Realms Beyond."

I invoke Thee, Galahad! and behold, before me appears, a Youthful Knight, sitting astride his Charger, with golden hair, and a Beautiful Beardless Countenance.

Thou art The Pure Knight, who sits at the Siege Perilous Seat of the Round Table, who pulled the Sword from the Floating Stone, and Healed and Restored The Fisher King in his rightful place in Sarras.

He is the Falcon of the Summer, whose Shield displays the Grail Chalice, Golden on a Blue field. He is wearing Golden Armor and a Livery of Scarlet and Gold.

The Celebrant then draws an invoking Pentagram of Fire, completing it with a final thrust as they exhale. They then draw an invoking spiral around the completed Pentagram, penetrating its center as a final gesture and exhaling as they do it.

The Celebrant proceeds to the Western Watchtower and stands before it. They take up their dagger and give a salute to the West. Then, holding their magick dagger aloft, they invoke the Ward of the Western Watchtower with the following incantation:

And behold, the Third Veil parted, and I saw The Chalice of the Sangreal descending from the Heavens and I heard a Voice, and it said:

"I am the Grace that is the Fulfillment of the Quest, through Me is Resurrection and Redemption."

I invoke Thee, Lancelot Dulac! And behold, before me appears a tall and Mighty Warrior, with long red hair and beard, green eyes, and Regal Bearing.

Thou art the Romantic Warrior, for Compassion, Love, and Loyal Friendship are Thy Greatest Gifts. The Knight of the Greatest Honor and Greater Humility.

He holds a Shield which displays the Grail Chalice, Golden on a Dark Blue field. He is wearing Silver Armor and a Livery of Indigo Blue.

The Celebrant then draws an invoking pentagram of Water, completing it with a final thrust as they exhale. They then draw an invoking spiral around the completed pentagram, penetrating its center as a final gesture and exhaling as they do it.

The Celebrant proceeds to the Northern Watchtower and stands before it. They take up their dagger and gives a salute to the North. Then, holding their magick dagger aloft, they invoke the Ward of the Northern Watchtower with the following incantation:

And behold, the Fourth Veil parted and I saw the Graal Dish which gives Sustenance to the Spirit, and I heard a Voice and it said:

Whom does the Grail serve, from whence does it come and whither does it go?

I invoke Thee, Gawain! and behold, before me appears a Great and Mighty Warrior with curly black hair and beard, deep brown eyes and an Open and Friendly Bearing.

Thou art the Green Knight, the Oak Knight of the Sacred Earth, Thou art able to Restore Vitality to the Sick and Thou art Noble, Strong, and Wise of the Ways of the Earth and an Instrument of Earthly Justice.

He holds a Shield which displays a Wreath surrounding a Sacred Tree on a rich Green Field. He is wearing Black Armor and a Livery of Emerald Green trimmed with Crimson.

The Celebrant then draws an invoking pentagram of Earth, completing it with a final thrust as they exhale. They then draw an invoking spiral around the completed pentagram, penetrating its center as a final gesture and exhaling as they do it.

The Celebrant proceeds to the center of the circle and therein they stand. They take up their dagger and give a salute to the North. Then, pointing their magick dagger down, they invoke the Infrapoint with the following incantation:

And behold, the Fifth Veil parted and I saw The Holy Emerald Stone of Sion, which is the Key and Foundation to the Temple of the Grail, and I heard a Voice, and it said:

"The Mystery of the Grail is Resolved at the end, wherein is the Quest begun here Time and Space are One."

I invoke Thee, Parzival, Purest of the Knights, and the one who sought and obtained the Grail for his King and the Land.

And behold, before me appears a Noble Youth riding a white horse, with raven colored hair, and Beardless Face, he is Smiling, and a Radiance of Golden Light emanates from Him.

Thou art the Grail Knight and the Lord of the Quest, and Thou hast taken the Sins from the World and Purified it. Where the World is Complex, Thou art Simple and Straightforward.

He holds a Shield which displays a White Pearl held in a hand gloved in White Sammite on a White and Pale Azure Field.

He is wearing no Armor, but is clad in fine White Robes of Linen, having given up his World and Warrior Ways.

The Celebrant then draws an invoking pentagram of Spirit Feminine, completing it with a final thrust as they exhale. They then draw an invoking spiral around the completed pentagram, penetrating its center as a final gesture and exhaling as they do it.

SETTING THE GRAIL WARDENS AND THE GRAIL CASTLE

The Celebrant then replaces their dagger on the altar and takes up their wand. They resume standing in the center of the circle with their wand to perform the next part of the rite.

Facing the East, the Celebrant intones the Name of God (*Sanctus Deus Sabaoth*), then draws an invoking pentagram of Spirit Masculine above the pentagram inscribed therein with their wand and seals it with an invoking spiral. They then intone:

I invoke Thee, Raphael! O Thou who bears the Sword of Power and therein Reveals The Mystery of the Path of the Spiritual Healer. For through Selfless Service, Compassion and Love of God shall the Hallowed Sword return from Sarras to reside herein with us!

The Celebrant draws an invoking spiral around both pentagrams, drawing them together.

Facing the South, the Celebrant intones the Name of God (*Sanctus Dominus Sabaoth*), then draws an invoking pentagram of Spirit Masculine above the pentagram inscribed therein with their wand and seals it with an invoking spiral. They then intone:

I invoke Thee, Michael! O Thou who bears the Sacred Spear and therein Reveals The Mystery of the Path of the Spiritual Warrior. For through Pure Integrity, Truthfulness, and Obedience to God shall the Hallowed Spear return from Sarras to reside herein with us!

The Celebrant draws an invoking spiral around both pentagrams, drawing them together.

Facing the West, the Celebrant intones the Name of God (*Omnipotens Aeterne Deus*), then draws an invoking pentagram of Spirit Feminine above the pentagram inscribed therein with their wand and seals it with an invoking spiral. They then intone:

I invoke Thee, Gabriel! O Thou who bears the Chalice of Glory and therein Reveals The Mystery of the Path of the Sage of Devotion. For through the Divine Passion of the Highest Spiritual Love in the Quest for Union with God shall the Hallowed Chalice return from Sarras to reside herein with us!

The Celebrant draws an invoking spiral around both pentagrams, drawing them together.

Facing the North, the Celebrant intones the Name of God (*Dominus Mundi*), then draws an invoking pentagram of Spirit Feminine above the pentagram inscribed therein with their wand and seals it with an invoking spiral. They then intone:

I invoke Thee, Uriel! O Thou who bears the Dish of in Exhaustive Treasure and therein Reveals The Mystery of the Mastery of Life. For through Great Steadfastness Self-Awareness and the Maturity of Ages shall the Hallowed Paten return from Sarras to reside herein with us!

The Celebrant draws an invoking spiral around both pentagrams, drawing them together.

Facing the Ultrapoint in the center, the Celebrant intones the Name of God (*Lucis Deus Albus*), and then draws an invoking pentagram of Spirit Masculine in the Ultrapoint with their wand and seals it with an invoking spiral. They then intone:

> *I invoke Thee, Razael! O Thou who bears the Stone of Destiny and therein Reveals The Mystery of the Source of All. For through Openness and Pure Wonder, Spiritual Insight, and the Knowing found in the Light of Divine Reason shall the Hallowed Lapidus return from Sarras to reside herein with us!*

The Celebrant draws an invoking spiral around both pentagrams, drawing them together.

The Celebrant returns the wand to the altar, takes up their sword again, and proceeds to draw a line of force from Watchtower to Watchtower, producing a square, beginning with the East, and proceeding deosil, until they end in the East. They say the following incantation while performing this task.

> *I shall take my Sword and draw the Ley Lines of Force, so that the Magick Circle shall be Squared, and so the Divine Marriage of Opposites shall come to pass.*

> *In this manner, the Guardians and the Wardens of the Grail Watchtowers shall be joined within a Wall of Power, like the walls of a Mighty Castle of Sarras so the Grail Castle is therein Revealed, and all that occurs within it is a Mystery and a Wonder! So mote it be!*

Then the Celebrant returns the sword to the altar and returns to the center of the circle. Therein, they draw an equal arm cross in the Mesopoint, the place between the Ultrapoint and the Infrapoint. They then stand there, draw all of the powers of the three central nodes into themselves with arms outstretched, and say the final incantation.

The Crown of the Grail King shall Enlighten and Empower me in all the acts of Magick and Mystery that I shall now enact.

May the Hallows of the Grail Bless and Enrich my Body and Soul, and may I be a Servant to their Glory and Eternal Light. I have become the World Tree, whose roots are in the Source of all Earth, whose branches span the Starry Heavens, and whose trunk is found in the Center of the World. So mote it be!

The Celebrant then draws a cross upon their body, touching their head, genitals, right shoulder, and left shoulder, then focusing on their heart center, drawing all the nodes together. As they touch those points, they say:

Sanctus Deus Sabaoth! Sanctus Dominus Sabaoth! Omnipotens Aeterne Deus! Dominus Mundi! Lucis Deus Albus!

The rest of the ritual working is performed here.

RESTORING THE VEIL

This part of the rite is only performed if the Celebrant has not performed the vortex rite; otherwise, they must perform the sealing spiral task as written in that rite.

The Celebrant proceeds to the Eastern Watchtower, gives it salute, and draws with the dagger the banishing pentagram of Air and a banishing spiral around it. They extinguish the Watchtower candle and say:

Hail Arthur and Raphael! We Release our bond with you and bid you Depart for Avalon and the Heart of God in Peace.

The Celebrant proceeds to the Northern Watchtower, gives it salute, and draws with the dagger the banishing pentagram of Earth and a banishing spiral around it. They extinguish the Watchtower candle and say:

Hail Gawain and Uriel! We Release our bond with you and bid you Depart for Avalon and the Heart of God in Peace.

The Celebrant proceeds to the Western Watchtower, gives it salute, and draws with the dagger the banishing pentagram of Water and a banishing spiral around it. They extinguish the Watchtower candle and say:

Hail Lancelot Dulac and Gabriel! We Release our bond with you and bid you Depart for Avalon and the Heart of God in Peace.

The Celebrant proceeds to the Southern Watchtower, gives it salute, and draws with the dagger the banishing pentagram of Fire and a banishing spiral around it. They extinguish the Watchtower candle and say:

Hail Galahad and Michael! We Release our bond with you and bid you Depart for Avalon and the Heart of God in Peace.

The Celebrant proceeds to the center of the circle, standing before the shrine of the Stone. They gives it a salute, then, in the Ultrapoint, they draw with the dagger the banishing pentagram of Spirit Masculine and a banishing spiral around it. To the Infrapoint, they draw the banishing pentagram of Spirit Feminine and a banishing spiral around it, and then extinguish the candles upon the altar.

Hail Parzival and Raziel! We Release our bond with you and bid you Depart for Avalon and the Heart of God in Peace.

Until the Time when we again begin the Quest, we stand in the Center of Light in Veneration of the Fivefold Hallows of the Grail!

CHAPTER FOUR

PYRAMIDAL PENTAGRAM RITUAL

PREFACE TO THE RITE

The Pyramidal Pentagram ritual is essentially an extensive modification of the Cone of Power or Witches' dance and is used in conjunction with the circle consecration rite to perform a working of acquisition. The pyramid shape that the ritual assumes is determined by the ritual structure that the four Angles and the Ultrapoint create. In addition, there are pylons set to these five circle points, which would include the Infrapoint as the anchor of the central pylon. The circle is squared when the magician draws the four angles together within the magick circle. The Pyramid is aligned to the four Angles and fits perfectly into the circle consecration ritual structure, which is aligned to the four Watchtowers. The two rituals together produce an octagon, which is the overlay of the two squares occupying the circle, with one aligned to the Watchtowers and the other to the Angles. The octagon represents the premium magickal symbol for generating magickal energies, since it's the polarization of the number four, which represents the four Elements. The magician can choose to use this rite within the consecrated circle, or they can use it within a vortex as part of the Lunar Mystery rite. Either way, the octagon will be an active part of this ritual.

The Pyramidal Pentagram ritual generates eight different qualities of energies, which represent the four Elements qualified by either the masculine or feminine spirit, producing a spiritualized Element as a hybrid. These energies are further identified by the eight Pagan Deities that lurk behind the Grail Mythos, giving it that mysterious quality of deep Earth magick that seems to haunt the otherwise seemingly Christian Arthurian tales. These eight powers represent the full spectrum of energies that the magician can generate, and they choose the one that best matches their needs.

The mechanism for generating this power lies in the use of the invoking pentagram of a specific Element, joined with the Rose Cross device. The magician projects the device of the invoking pentagram of a specific element to each of the four Angles, establishing them as potent generators of magickal power. The magician also projects either the invoking pentagram of Spirit Masculine or Feminine, depending on the chosen power qualification, to the Infrapoint in the center of the circle. Each of the pentagram devices drawn to the four Angles and the Infrapoint are additionally qualified by a Rose Cross device drawn above it and joined within an invoking spiral, thus erecting a pylon structure at all four Angles and in the center of the circle, where the final Rose Cross is set to the Ultrapoint. The four Angles and the Infrapoint are qualified by the five mistresses of the Arthurian tales (Vivienne, Igraine, Morgane, Guinevere, and Nimue), who represent the five mysteries (the Mystery of the Spiritual Warrior, the Mystery of Holy Blood, the Mystery of the Earth Dragon, the Mystery of Sovereignty, and the Mystery of the Gnosis of the Grail Hallows). These five Grail mistresses and their associated mysteries represent the compliment to the Five Warriors found in the circle consecration rite, although they don't match the explicit elemental correspondence of the Grail Hallows.

The magickal power that this ritual produces is generated and resonated through the use of a deosil spiral that the magician performs as an ambulation, walking three times around the circle, starting at the periphery in the Northeast Angle and gradually moving in towards the center. By walking this pattern, they form an inward invoking spiral that starts on the outside and terminates at the center of the circle. They will also summon the associated godhead of the Grail Mythos in the center of the circle to qualify the energy with an imago of the Deity, so it can be given an image easily envisioned by the magician. Once in the center, they can imprint the power with their intention and release it.

Once the power is established, the magician uses the sigil previously fashioned to act as a link for the intent and the objective of the rite. The power is then exteriorized through a widdershins spiral that the magician performs as an ambulation three times around the circle, forming an outward spiral that starts in the center of the circle and terminates on the outer periphery. At this point in the ritual, this is when they project all the power accumulated in the circle and projects it out towards the intended objective.

When the pyramidal energy field is released, it becomes a *yod* or lightning bolt that quickly seeks its target through the magician's field of reality. This signifies that the power unleashed is only as effective as the will and insight of the operator and is dependent upon whether or not they are able to capitalize upon those opportunities that manifest.

The ritual has the following structure or pattern:

1. Declamation and Setting the Intention
2. Erecting the Pyramidal Base (done to each of the four Angles, starting in the Northeast)
   a. Setting the invoking pentagram device
   b. Setting the Rose Cross device above the pentagram device
   c. Drawing an invoking spiral to join both devices
   d. Summoning the Grail Priestess and declaiming the Grail Mystery
3. Erecting the Central Pylon
   a. Setting the invoking pentagram device to the Infrapoint
   b. Summoning the Grail Priestess and declaiming the Grail Mystery
   c. Setting the Rose Cross device in the Ultrapoint
   d. Drawing an invoking spiral to join both devices
4. Squaring the Circle and Erecting the Pyramid
   a. Drawing the Angles together with the sword (deosil arc beginning in the Northeast)
      i. Drawing the Angles to the center of the circle at the Ultrapoint
5. Winding up the Magickal Power
   a. Perform deosil spiral, starting in the Northeast and ending the center of the circle

b. Summoning the Ogdoadic Godhead
c. Imprinting the power with the intention and sigil
6. Exteriorizing the Magick Power
a. Performing widdershins spiral, starting in the center and ending in the Northwest
b. Projecting the power as a yod and final declamation

The use of the Rose Cross device with the invoking pentagrams within a pylon structure has the quality of highly spiritualizing the forces that are generated by this rite, making them sacramental and associated with the energy of the Deity. The Rose Cross can be perceived as a form of Celtic Cross, and does not have to be associated with Christianity, even though the Grail Mythos seems to seamlessly blend Christianity with Paganism. The combination of qualifying the Element power with either of the Spirit Masculine or Feminine invoking pentagrams, as well as the Rose Cross, makes the magickal power generated irresistibly intertwined with the fate of the Gods, and so it will certainly make the magician feel as though they were seeking a goal sanctioned by the will of the Deity. Therefore, it would be wise for the magician to make certain that their working is above board and completely within the bounds of all ethical considerations, since this combination of magickal structures and their close association with the Deity would make it perilous to work any kind of negative magick.

The eight Qualified Powers are listed below, along with their associated correspondences. The names that are bold faced are the names of the associated Pagan Deities.

Element and Correspondence	Masculine Spirit	Feminine Spirit
Fire ALHYM Lance	**Llew:** success, vitality, physical well-being, illumination (making the unknown known).	**Rhiannon:** passion, desire, love, magick of the grace and beauty of the Goddess.
Water AL Chalice	**Manawyddan:** wisdom, compassion, under-standing the Heart.	**Branwen:** insight, psychic sensitivity, nurturing, love, compassion.

ELEMENT AND CORRESPONDENCE	MASCULINE SPIRIT	FEMININE SPIRIT
Air YHVH Sword	**Gwydion:** cleverness, articulation, cunning, ambition.	**Arianrhod:** eloquence, beauty, integrity, purity, truthfulness.
Earth ADNY Dish	**Bran:** wealth, harmony, happiness, protection of home, good reputation.	**Cerridwen:** regeneration, fertility, healing, shrewdness, life wisdom.

When selecting a qualified power to use with a working, the magician should use a simple method to determine where to start. The four Elements have specific uses when it comes to working practical magick. They are as follows:

- **Fire:** inspiration, illumination, knowledge guided by wisdom, aspiration.
- **Water:** love, emotional wellbeing, emotional healing, joy, fulfillment.
- **Air:** activity, knowledge (information), cleverness, ambition, motivation.
- **Earth:** wealth, health, fertility, creativity, home, career, mundane sphere.

If the magician seeks to perform a working to help promote their career, then either Air (motivation) or Earth (mundane sphere) would be acceptable. If the magician seeks to perform a healing working, then Earth would be the best choice, and the same is true for money issues. The magician would use Water for a love spell or to perform a working for healing a bad relationship. The magician would use Fire to understand the basis of an issue or to cause inspiration in themselves or others, and it could also be used to inflame their passions as part of a love spell. The magician could probably determine many more categories for potential magickal workings when considering the four Elements, but these hints should help them get started in that direction.

In addition to the four Elements, there's also a consideration for a specific gender correspondence, and this is the manner in which the Element is qualified. The four categories associated with the four Elements are split into eight categories, allowing for a masculine and feminine characterization of these four forces. It's really not too difficult to conceptualize. When we were children, we were usually able to identify which parent would be most inclined to approve our request, and we would pick that parent to ask as opposed to the other. The same logic can be used in the use of either the masculine or feminine aspects of the four Elements. Just imagine (humorously) that if you were seeking a specific kind of working and it fell under one of the four Elements, which aspect would you wish to approach: the mother aspect (feminine spirit) or the father aspect (masculine spirit)? The masculine is more direct, intense, and extroverted, and the feminine is more subtle, gentle, and introverted. The qualified Element is therefore a bit more useful since it has more correspondence, producing harder and softer qualities to the four Elements. The key to this logic is that the more correspondences there are for a given type of magickal energy, then the greater its utilization. This is very much the case when we consider that there are sixteen Elementals (Element qualified by an Element), twenty-eight Talismanic Elementals (Planet qualified by an Element), and forty Qabalistic Powers (Sephirah qualified by an Element). In these systems, the more attributes there are in the matrix, the more refined and detailed is the definition of the magickal power.

The eight Pagan Deities associated with the eight qualified powers are used to give an image and characterization to the qualified power, and are not defined very extensively for this working, even though it could be an avenue for the further developing of this system of magick. The magician could also use a purely Qabalistic approach to the definition of the qualified powers instead of the Celtic pantheon used here (the masculine Element would be qualified by the Godname of Atziluth, and the feminine Element would be qualified by the Archangel of Briah), or they could use another pantheon altogether, depending on their personal magickal system and preferences. We will use an invocation to the godhead to qualify the eight powers that this rite generates, and that invocation will produce an adequate image of the Deity so we can manipulate the qualified magickal power that we seek to use. The qualified power is then merged with the sigil that represents the magician's objective, and then imprinted and made ready for use.

The magician symbolizes the energy of the intent by defining it in terms of the eight aspects of the Deity (the Ogdoad), which is produced by the division of the four Elements by gender. The magician chooses one of the eight qualities that best depicts the energy and nature of their desire. This process causes the intention to become transpersonalized, allowing it to become an archetype within the magician's unconscious mind. Then, the magician is ready to use their symbolized desire to design a sigil and draw it on parchment with ink. The creation of a sigil is a process that consists of condensing a word, phrase, or picture of the personal desire into a simplified drawn image or a word of power. This condensing process is little more than the elimination of all redundant forms. In the case of a word or phrase, only the unique letters are used, and the duplications are eliminated. To create a sigil, the unique letters are used to form a symbolic image using the form of the letter (such as a left or right curve, cross, straight line, or circle), and these are used to build a composite image, where the unique individual forms of the letters are melded into a new unified form. A magickal word derived in this manner, as opposed to a sigil, becomes a personal word of magickal power, a perfect symbol for the verbal expression of the magician's desire as an incantation. For a more thorough explanation of the art of creating sigils the student should read and study the book *Practical Sigil Magick*, written by Frater U. D.

Once the qualified power is chosen and the sigil created, then the magician is ready to perform the working. They should choose a date that is both practical and auspicious, such as a weekend night when the Moon is waxing but not yet full. The idea is that once the magickal working is performed and released, its powers and effect will grow with the waxing of the Moon. When the Moon is full, then the rite will be at its maximum power, allowing the magician to engage in the mundane actions that will enable the objective to be fully realized. The more complex or profound the change sought through the magickal working, the greater the required energy needed to fulfill the objective and the more time the desired change will need to be fulfilled (the more steps that will need to be followed in the mundane sphere). The magician may seek to perform their working before the full moon, perhaps a few days after the new moon, or they may perform multiple workings using the vortex as the container of the magick and not allow it to be exteriorized until all the parts of the working are complete and fully charged.

INTRODUCTION TO THE RITE

The Celebrant performs the circle consecration rite and fully erects the magick circle. They then sit in the center of the circle, holding in their hand the parchment sigil representing their objective. They should meditate deeply on this objective, letting their desire for it completely fill their mind and being, until nothing else is distracting them from performing the working. At this point, the magician may begin the working.

The Celebrant has already charged the magick sigil that embodies the purpose of this working. This was accomplished earlier by first holding the sigil in the incense smoke for a period of time, then placing it upon the altar and drawing an invoking spiral upon it with the wand, so it's sealed and ready to be used later in the ritual.

The magician takes up the wand and proceeds to the center of the circle. They face the North, bow, and draw a great equal arm cross. They say the following incantation:

> *In the Names of the Great Five Fiery Dragons of Arthur, Protectors of the Island of Avalon, and of the Pyramidal Temple that stands at its Summit.*
>
> *I perform this Working and Unleash these Forces in the Name of (personal God-name). So mote it be.*

At this point, the magician states their objective succinctly and without embellishment. The rite has begun. They may stand in the center of the circle for a few minutes longer while contemplating what they are about to set in motion.

BUILDING THE PYRAMIDAL PYLONS

The Celebrant, armed with their wand, proceeds to the Northeastern Angle and draws an invoking pentagram of the Element that they seek to generate. They then draw above it a Rose Cross device and connect the two devices together with an invoking spiral. They then say the following incantation:

> *I summon forth the Grace and Beauty of Guinevere, also known as the "White Phantom," who represents The Mystery of Sovereignty and who is the Throne of the Grail King.*

She is the Bearer of the Spear of Destiny, and Lance of the Grail Hallows, and who confers upon all who are Worthy of Her Grace, the Power of Kingship, and the Mastery of Fate.

Let all know and remember that She may be taken by Force, or Guile, or by Right of Succession but She is never Wholly Belonging to anyone forever.

Thus is the fate of all Kings, Madmen, Tyrants, and Usurpers, that what shall Ascend to Greatness in a moment shall also know the Fall of Ruin and the Legacy of Futile Emptiness.

The Lance belongs to no Man; neither does the Throne of the Grail.

The Celebrant proceeds to the Southeastern Angle and draws with their wand an invoking pentagram of the Element that they seek to generate. They then draw a Rose Cross device above it and connect the two devices together with an invoking spiral. They say the following incantation:

I summon forth the Nobility and Majesty of Igraine, Mother of Arthur, Morgawse, Morgane, and Elaine. She is the Descendent of Joseph of Arimathea, the Holder of the Sacred Cup, and is Mother of the Grail Lineage of Kings, Queens, Warriors, and Great Ladies.

She is also the Embodiment of the Mystery of the Sangreal, the Holy Royal Blood of Kings and Gods, and so She is the Spirit of the Life of the Grail, and its Progenitrix in the Magick of Arthur and the Grail.

She is undying since She lives in the blood of the Sacred Kingship for all time. For the Breath of the Gods blew upon the Waters, and it became the Holy Blood as Wine, and therein from that Sacrament came forth the Great Lady, who like a Chalice is its container, and who is known by many Names.

The Mystery of the Living Sacrament is herein revealed and then made Secret once again.

The Celebrant proceeds to the Southwestern Angle and draws with their wand an invoking pentagram of the Element that they seek to generate. They draw a Rose Cross device above it and connect the two devices together with an invoking spiral. They say the following incantation:

I summon forth the Powers and the Mystery of Vivienne, Lady of Lake, She who is dressed in White Samite and who bears the Great Sword of Mystery, Excalibur.

She is the Intuitive Wisdom, as Merlin is the Applied Wisdom and Her ways are the ways of the Spiritual Warrior. Purity of Intention, Singleness of Pursuit, Efficiency of Motion, and all Shrouded by Silence both within and without.

She was the Teacher of Lancelot, the Greatest Warrior of all time, and She was the Guardian of Parzival, the Purest of all Warriors.

For know that you cannot approach the Grail unless you meet the challenge of the Lady of the Lake, and thus you must be reduced to all Simplicity and Passionless Skill if you are to be worthy of beholding the Grail.

She is the Giver of the Hallows of the Sword, which is given to the worthy to use with Justice and Compassion, and it must be returned when the task is done, the Sun has set, and the King has passed from the World of the Living.

The Celebrant proceeds to the Northwestern Angle and draws an invoking pentagram of the Element that they seek to generate with their wand. They then draw a Rose Cross device above it and connect the two devices together with an invoking spiral. They say the following incantation:

I summon the Fey Magick and the Mystery of Morgane (Le Fey), Fairy Queen and Lady of the Other-World of Avalon.

You are the Mistress of the deep Earth Magick of the Grail, the Great Dragon of the Life and Fertility of the Kingdom of heaven and earth.

The Life of the Land is the Great Mystery of the Grail, and it is symbolized by the Dish or the Cornucopia, where the Hungry are fed, the Sick and Wounded are healed, and the Blessed Holder of this Hallow knows only Wealth and Good Fortune.

The Sacred Dish is also known as the Shield of Protection, the Symbolic Heraldry of the Great Houses, and the Lamen of the Magicians, it is depicted as a Pentagram and a Rose.

Morgan is the Queen of Witches and Sorcerers, and holds the Powers of the Fey, whose Realm she commands as her own.

Know that the base of all the Grail Hallows is the Great Dish, for without it, they would be Intangible and have no Material form. For the Dish is the Source of Material Manifestation (where Spirit becomes Matter) and is shared by all who are Worthy.

The Blessed Life is one that is Healthy and Wealthy, and so the Fulfillment of the Grail Quest is the Fulfillment of all Material Aspirations thus we eat and drink to Honor, Love and give Life to the Gods.

The Celebrant proceeds to the center of the circle and draws with their wand an invoking pentagram of either the Spirit Masculine or Feminine in the Infrapoint, setting the gender of the qualified power. They draw a Rose Cross device in the Ultrapoint and connect the two devices together with an invoking spiral. They then draw a small equal arm cross in the point between the two central nodes and say the following incantation.

I summon the Mystery and Gnosis of Nimue, Mistress of Magicians (Merlin), Lady of the Mastery of Fate, Water Nymph, and Princess of Avalon.

You are the Mistress of the Transformative Magick and Gnosis of the Grail, a Symbol of Transformation itself, since it is Multiform, and it Appears and Reappears in a manner imbued with the Mystery and Magick of the Gods.

You are the Quintessence; the blending of the Four Hallows into the Fifth, which is known as the Sacred Stone, The Emerald Eye of Lucifer, the Tiara of the Star Goddess.

From the Sacred Stone is also found the Stone of the Philosophers, that Great Achievement or Magnum Opus of Magicians and Alchemists, which produces Alchemical Gold and the Universal Medicine the Elixir of Immortality.

The Stone is the Mystery of Transmutation, and the Secret of Emanation that which changes the World is itself unchangeable but also ineffable.

SQUARING THE CIRCLE AND BUILDING THE PYRAMID

The Celebrant returns the wand to the altar, picks up the sword, and proceeds to the Northeast Angle, where they point it to the pentagram device drawn. They begin to trace a square, joining the four Angles together and proceeding in a deosil arc until they return to the Northeast Angle a second time. They take the sword and draw a line of force from the Northeast Angle to the center of the circle at the Ultrapoint. Once this is accomplished, they proceed to the Southeast Angle and draw a line of force from that Angle to the Ultrapoint. They proceed to the Southwest Angle and joins it with the Ultrapoint, and then finally proceeds to the Northwest Angle, joining it with the Ultrapoint. The pyramid is now created. The magician says the following incantation:

I draw the Lines of Force, to Square the Circle, to erect the Pyramidian Force that shall contain the Powers of my Desires and Aspirations.

The Circle squared is within the Circle Squared, and so the Ogdoad is the Secret Sign of the Mysterious Gods operating within the Core of the Grail Mysteries.

The Celebrant returns the sword to the altar, takes up the wand in their right hand and the sigil in their left, and proceeds to the Northeast Angle.

CHARGING THE SPIRAL
MYSTIKON OF THE GODS

The Celebrant circumambulates the magick circle deosil, holding their wand before them in their right hand and tracing a line of force with it (the left hand is holding the sigil at their side). Beginning in the Northeast, they chant the Power Chant as they trace a spiral path from the outside of the circle to the center, circumambulating the circle three times. Once in the center, the Celebrant draws the power in the Infrapoint through their body up into the Ultrapoint using the wand, thus becoming its master.

The drawing up of the power is conceptualized with the following gesture: the magician should bend over as far as they can with the wand touching the ground, then rise up, slowly raising the wand up until it is over their head. The Celebrant takes upon themselves the magick of the working by drawing the power from above their head with the wand down into their body, centering it around the heart. These two gestures are performed together as an expression of connecting the Infrapoint with the Ultrapoint through one's physical body. The following is the Summoning of the Power Chant (as taken from the *MARM* series):

I arouse the Power bold to kindle the Magick of Lily and Rose. This Force I wind-up, to cleave, where the Powers of Light and Darkness meet.

This Image I send. This Desire I Project. My Will to This End. To Fulfill my Object. So mote it be.

The magician takes out the sigil and places it on the ground in the center of the circle, drawing an invoking spiral around it with the wand, and potently visualizing the outcome of the magick working. The magician may also place their magick crystal upon the sigil to give it added power. The sigil is now set and charged in the center of the circle, where the confluences of powers exist. The sigil will act as a magickal link, imprinting the energy with the magician's intent.

The magician stands in the center of the circle before the sigil, with arms folded across their breast, visualizing their image of the Deity and silently summoning it with love and veneration. The Celebrant then performs a self-crossing, causing the chakras or power points to align in an equal arm cross over their body. This is done in the following manner.

The Celebrant touches the forehead and says:

From the Highest;

Touches the genitals and says:

To the Source of Life;

Then touches the right shoulder and says:

Through the Grace;

Then touches the left shoulder and says:

And the Power;

And then folds the hands before the heart and says:

Unified in Love, So mote it be.

The Celebrant meditates for a moment with their arms outstretched to form a cross with the whole body (holding the wand in a station keeping stance along their arm). In this posture, the power of the spirit of the Deity is internally summoned. After the meditation is completed, the Celebrant draws a triangle upon themselves (left breast, right breast, genitals) with the wand, representing the gateway through which the spirit of the Deity shall enter. The Celebrant intones a short silent invocation to their Deity. At this point, the Celebrant has assumed their godhead and is ready for the next phase of the working, which is to summon one of the eight gods or goddesses that will assist in qualifying the energy generated.

The Celebrant assumes the invocation stance with their wand raised above their head. They say the incantation of the Ogdoadic God or Goddess of the Qualified Power slowly and with a great deal of emphasis. (These invocative incantations are in the last section of this rite below.) The Celebrant may recite this invocation from memory, or they may use a cue card with the invocation written on it. Once this is complete, the Celebrant draws a line of force from the sigil on the ground to the Ultrapoint, the apex of the pyramid, while perceiving the qualified power being imprinted with the magickal link. All that's left to do is to exteriorize the imprinted power.

EXTERIORIZING THE PYRAMIDIAN FORCE

The Celebrant circumambulates the magick circle widdershins. They begin in the center of the circle, facing the Northeast Angle, chanting the Release Chant as they walk a spiral path, holding their wand before them in their right hand and tracing lines of force with it, using cool breathing to resonate the power. The Celebrant proceeds from the center of the circle to the outside periphery, circumambulating the circle three times. At each circuit of the circle, the energy becomes more intense, almost resisting their passage. At the end of the circuit, the Celebrant stops in the Northeast, sending the power out with a forced exhalation and projects the power with both arms extended. The following is the Release Chant:

I send this Power out—to do my Will!
I send this Power out—my Will to Fulfill!
I send this Power out—Three times Three to instill!

The work is now completed, and after a suitable period of meditation, the Celebrant proceeds to each of the four Angles (Southeast, Northeast, Northwest, and the Southwest) and draws banishing spirals. This is also performed to the Infrapoint and the Ultrapoint. Then the circle is banished in the traditional manner. The sigil parchment is retrieved from the center of the circle and burned to release the link and aid the magick to its goal.

THE OGDOADIC GOD/DESS INVOCATIVE INCANTATIONS

The following are the eight invocative incantations to the gods and goddesses, which are implicitly associated with the Grail legends. The Celebrant reads one of the incantations slowly, with a strong voice and clearly enunciated speech. They should visualize and project the image of the Deity as they are calling it, so that it is temporarily realized. Later, after the rite is over, the Celebrant should make an offering or libation to this God or Goddess, pouring some wine or such drink to the earth, after making it known that they are doing this for the good services of that Deity.

FIRE

MASCULINE SPIRIT: LLEW

I Summon and Call Thee, O Llew, Lord of Light, Brilliance of the Sun, O Golden Lion in the Sky, O Wise Salmon, O Courageous Eagle, cast down the Rays of Thy Light and Illuminate my Path.

Show me the Secret way of Rebirth, and the Waxing and Waning Powers of the Light as it moves from Solstice to Equinox to Solstice, to Equinox.

Whose Power, grows and diminishes, but never fails and always returns.

FEMININE SPIRIT: RHIANNON

I Summon and Call Thee, O Rhiannon, Lady of the Golden and Crimson Dawn, the Muse of the Sweet Singing Voice, known as the Birds of Rhiannon, and they sing of the changing of the Seasons, and all of the Secret Things that are in the Hearts of Humanity.

Her voice inspires Joy in those who harken to it, and it said to be able to Raise the Dead.

Thou art also the Great White Mare that is the Mother of all Mankind, and who Cares and Loves for all Her Children, who were born to Master the Darkness and Light.

WATER

MASCULINE SPIRIT: MANAWYDDAN

I Summon and Call Thee, O Manawyddan, Lord of the Underworld and the Seas, whose Dominion is Nowhere and Everywhere, O Master of Magick and useful Crafts, Inventor of Writing, Tabulating, and Teacher of all Mercantile Endeavors.

Cleverness is Thy lot, and Natural Wisdom, Compassion, and Loyalty, for Thou wert the Lifelong friend of Bran, and the Survivor of the Great War.

Thou art the Keeper of Grail as Cauldron of Wisdom, and Thou wert the First of all Fisher Kings.

FEMININE SPIRIT: BRANWEN

I Summon and Call Thee, O Branwen, Lady of the Lunar Tides and the Seas, Patron of Lovers and Mothers, for Thy Protection of the Innocent and the Unborn.

Thou art also the Sadness of Heartbreak, and the Grand Consoler, for the Seas are bitter and briny with Thy tears, and you shall Heal them, the People with the Hurt Passions and Destroyed Dreams.

Thou art also the Queen of Dreams, Fantasy, and Nightmares. Thou art the White-Breast, the Illumination of the Moon Light upon the calm Seas.

Thou art the Starling calling out its Sad Song, and beginning the Time of Darkness and Death (Winter).

Air

Masculine Spirit: Gwydion

I Summon and Call Thee, O Gwydion, Ash King, Protector of the Sun, Druid of the Gods and Mastery of Magick and Illusions.

Thou art the Great Magician Artificer, and Purveyor of the Goods of the Underworld, which you stole for the Benefit of all Mankind.

Thy Sacred animals are the Stag, Boar, and the Wolf, from which you derived with your Cleverness. The Deer, the Swine, and the Dog the Totem of early Humanity.

The Milky Way is Thy Mansion, and the Stars are the Torches that Illuminate Thy Great Halls thus Thou art the Astrologer and Wielder of the Stellar Destinies of all the Royal Houses.

Thou art also the One who made the Sacred Hallows, melding Spirit and Magick into Material Treasures.

Feminine Spirit: Arianrhod

I Summon and Call Thee, O Arianrhod, Silver Wheel, Circle of Light. Thou art the Full Moon in the Silver Sky, and Thy head is lit by the Northern Crown, which is the place where Souls gather for Rebirth.

You wield the Twin Powers of Light (Llew) and Darkness (Dylan), for these are Thy Children, and so you Sanction all Nurturing and Motherhood.

For Thou art the Fruitful Mother of the Wheel of Fortune and Destiny, and Thou art a fickle Mistress, one who tests her Children and withholds their Legacy if they are deemed unworthy.

EARTH

MASCULINE SPIRIT: BRAN

I Summon and Call Thee, O Bran, for Thou art the King of the Bounteous Realm of Goodness, Wealth and Health; for all Earthly Things wax and grow great when you touch or breath upon them (Wind and Rain).

Thou art the Tree God and Green Man of the Sacred Earth, the Paradise of Plenty. Thou art the Holder of the Great Cauldron, The Grail as Giver of Life Renewed and of Inspiration.

Thou art the Warrior of the Home and the Hearth, the Protector of the Fertility and Treasures of the Land, and you battle the Forces of Death, Misfortune, and Destruction, which are the Freezing and Killing Winds of Winter.

The Cauldron and its bounty is poured upon the Earth, and The Grail Power gives its Healing Forces to all who eat and drink of it.

Thy head is severed from Thy body at Harvest, like John Barleycorn, but still you give Life and Joy to those who gather to Sing and Remember.

FEMININE SPIRIT: CERRIDWEN

I Summon and Call Thee, O Cerridwen, Lady of the Bountiful Harvest, She who gives Life and takes it away, thus Thou art the White Lady of Life and Death, Inspiration and Ecstasy, the Womb and the Tomb.

Thou gave Humanity the Gift of the Grains and Honey from the Bees, and also Diseases and Plagues, so our numbers would not crowd and choke the Earth.

Thou art the Holder and Wielder of the Cauldron of Inspiration and Wisdom, the Grail of Gnosis, from which all Healing, Benison, Wisdom, and Poetry doth come.

Thou art the Mistress of all the Wise Men and Women of the Powers of the Earth the Source of all Life, Insight and the Wisdom of the Ages.

Thou dost wield the Power of Rebirth and Reincarnation, but in order to be Reborn, one must first Die thus the Fate of all Living is Death, and the Inspiration in Life called Ecstasy.

CHAPTER FIVE

ROSE ANKH VORTEX RITUAL

PREFACE TO THE RITE

The Rose Ankh Vortex is an unknown ritual since little is either known or written about it. It's the feminine complement to the Pyramidal Pentagram ritual and its polar opposite. Where the masculine magickal power moves clockwise and rises to the zenith of the magick circle as a pyramid, the feminine magickal power moves counterclockwise and is drawn down to the nadir.

The principal qualities of the vortex are containment and centering. It's used to contain and maintain other energy fields that can coexist in layers within the vortex itself. The vortex can also project energy outside of itself, creating a wave-form causality effect that is subtle, ultimately potent, and irreversible. The vortex causality wave is a continuous process with projections of energy timed at harmonic intervals. This pulsing effect can be used to overcome entrenched obstacles and create even seemingly impossible resolutions. But the force of a vortex is very subtle, and it requires several overlaid workings to reach an irresistible level of transformation.

The Rose Ankh symbol is a hybrid representing both the life-giving and eternally regenerating qualities of the Ankh and the sensual and passionate qualities of the rose. This combination symbolizes the sanctification of life, the essence of which is personified by a spiritual love that is sensual and expressed within the mysteries of romantic love.

243

The basic structure of the ritual is the drawing of the Rose Ankh device to the four Watchtowers and the Infrapoint. The Ultrapoint is set with an invoking pentagram of Spirit Feminine, thus drawing down the source of the archetypal feminine. The Watchtowers are drawn together through the Infrapoint, and the magickal power generated throughout is drawn from the Ultrapoint down through the body of the Celebrant and into the Infrapoint. This creates a kind of psychic black hole.

In addition, there are five very deep mysteries concerning the manifestation of the Grail and its associated graces. These are lengthy incantations and serve almost as a kind of sermon, so they are probably not capable of being memorized. The Celebrant should print them out on note cards and read them while performing the rite and, after each one is read, the content of the message should be briefly meditated upon.

The vortex ritual is completed with a widdershins circumambulation of the circle that is performed three times. This action generates the vortex energy field and is accompanied by a chant and mantric round.

The core of this ritual concerns itself with the Feminine Grail Mysteries as the fivefold spiritual manifestation of the Grail Spirit of Illumination. These mysteries are expressed as if spoken by the feminine Grail Spirit itself and are intoned at each of the four Watchtowers in succession. The four mysteries set to the four Watchtowers are resolved within a fifth that is represented by the archetypal Grail Spirit in its purest expression.

The magick circle has already been consecrated in either a temple or a grove. The circle must be already set, or the resultant structure would collapse. The magick circle assists in the containment of the vortex, keeping it from imploding.

MYSTERY OF THE FIVE HALLOWS OF THE GRAIL

The Celebrant, armed with their wand, proceeds to the Northern Watchtower and draws a great Rose Ankh device. The Celebrant says the following incantation:

Behold, I saw the Hallows of the Dish appear before me, and I felt a Presence, and a Voice spoke to me, and it said these words of the Mystery of the Grail.

I am the Pure and Lovely Spirit of She whose Heart is the Graal for all Humanity, the Manifested Grace of the Graal Spirit is given to you who Commune with my Essence.

The descending Blessing is the outpouring of Love for you from my Heart, the Source of Spiritual Love, for as Lovers, you are Impassioned and Bonded in Union with me, I am in you and you are in me.

This, my Gift, is Eternal for wherever shall you wander, I shall be there with you, and you shall not be alone. I am your Beloved and the Light of my Spirit shall not leave you ever. Thus is Revealed The Mystery of Spiritual Union.

Then, the Celebrant proceeds to the Western Watchtower and draws a great Rose Ankh device. The Celebrant says the following incantation:

Behold, I saw the Hallows of the Chalice appear before me, and I felt a Presence, and a Voice spoke to me, and it said these words of the Mystery of the Grail.

I am the Pure and Lovely Spirit of She whose Heart is the Graal for all Humanity. The Threefold Mystery of Spiritual Transformation is given to you who Commune with my Essence.

For in the beginning I draw you unto me with the Sweet Seduction that leads to Spiritual Inspiration and thence to Ecstasy, therefore are you Illuminated with the Grace of my Spirit and Consecrated to my Secret Service.

Then you become a Vehicle of my Light, sending forth the Sacrament which is my Life and my Love, for I dwell within you and you shall come to know me, and through Love, you shall come to know yourself and others.

Then, the Celebrant proceeds to the Southern Watchtower and draws a great Rose Ankh device. The Celebrant says the following incantation:

Behold, I saw the Hallows of the Lance appear before me, and I felt a Presence, and a Voice spoke to me, and it said these words of the Mystery of the Grail.

I am the Pure and Lovely Spirit of She whose Heart is the Graal for all Humanity.

The Blessings of the Dawn of the Glowing Spirit is given to you who Commune with my Essence. The Renewed Light has come forth and put away the Darkness of Material Ambitions and Pursuits.

Behold the Golden Light which shall warm your Heart and Guide your Ways for the Path is now Illuminated with the Fiery Spirit of Aspiration.

O my Beloved Seekers of Truth, walk always in my Ways, and when the time of the Quickening descends, when the Light is Reborn anew, there shall we meet again and through Love become One.

Then, the Celebrant proceeds to the Eastern Watchtower and draws a great Rose Ankh device. The Celebrant says the following incantation:

Behold, I saw the Hallows of the Sword appear before me, and I felt a Presence, and a Voice spoke to me, and it said these words of the Mystery of the Grail.

I am the Pure and Lovely Spirit of She whose Heart is the Graal for all Humanity. The Blessings of the Spiral Pathway to Attainment is given to you who Commune with my Essence.

The Way is pointed out by the Light coming forth from the Spiritual Dawn, you are drawn on the Pathway by me, tested by Trials and completed by your own Accomplishments. This is the Golden Path which leads to my Secret Embrace wherein the Light and Darkness merge into One.

They who follow the Trials of this Path are the Initiated and Anointed of Humanity who shall evolve through Selfless Love into the Vanguard of Holy Initiation.

The Celebrant proceeds to the center of the Circle and draws a great Rose Ankh device to the Infrapoint. The Celebrant then draws an invoking pentagram of Spirit Feminine in the Ultrapoint. The Celebrant says the following incantation:

Behold, I saw the Hallows of the Stone appear before me, and I felt a Presence, and a Voice spoke to me, and it said these words of the Mystery of the Grail.

I am the Pure and Lovely Spirit of She whose Heart is the Graal for all Humanity. The Love and Friendship of the Spiritual Society is given to you who Commune with my Essence. Be not alone on your Path of Transformation, for the Anguish of the Trials was never meant to be Borne without Comfort and Council.

For many Seekers are drawn to the same Source and they find the common Quest Strengthening and Reaffirming, for the Burden of your Fate is upon your shoulders, yet this Burden also belongs to all of the Sacred Company of Seekers.

Find Love and Friendship and therein you shall find me, and we shall become One in the fusion of the Multitudes, when all Humanity is Awakened.

The Celebrant takes the sword and joins the four Watchtowers to the Infrapoint, beginning in the North, moving to the West, the South, and then completing the process in the East.

The Celebrant circumambulates the circle widdershins beginning in the Northern Watchtower while chanting a mantric round (by lance, sword, chalice, dish, and stone). They trace a spiral path from outside of the circle to the center, circumambulating the circle three times. Once in the center, the Celebrant draws the power from the Ultrapoint through their body down into the Infrapoint, thus projecting the resultant force into a narrow, well-like form below the ground.

The vortex is now complete and whatever internal workings are desired can now be started, such as a specific Pyramidal Pentagram rite for acquisition; a divination session; the Lunar, Solar, or Self Initiation Mysteries; or the assumption rite. When these are completed, the Celebrant goes to the four Angles and draws a sealing spiral to the eight circle nodes in order of North, Northwest, West, Southwest, South, Southeast, East, and Northeast. The Celebrant then proceeds to the center of the circle and draws sealing spirals to the Infrapoint and the Ultrapoint.

The vortex is now sealed but is still marginally activated. It requires only the consecration of a new magick circle, the establishment of the proper mind-state, the raising of another vortex, and the drawing of unsealing spirals to the eight positions (beginning in the North and proceeding deosil) for the vortex to be reactivated to its original level of power and intensity.

Chapter Six

ASSUMPTION OF THE GODHEAD

PREFACE TO THE RITE

The rite of the Assumption of the Godhead is used to satisfy all four of the requirements for alignment. As the reader will recall, the four requirements for alignment are devotion, invocation, assumption, and communion. This rite will embody all of these elements and is to be used as a separate ritual that is performed fully at least once a month (or, even better, once a week). The key to this rite is the ability for the operator to enter a deep trance and effect a temporary transformation of consciousness within themselves, such that they can identify completely with their personal concept of the Deity. The performance of this rite requires that the magician identify their personal Deity and develop the theological and mythological context in which that Godhead has relevance and life. This is a large undertaking, and it must be completed to some degree for the magician to make use of this ritual, which is central and critical to the entire set of rituals in this grimoire. We have already gone over the importance of this ritual and the necessity of spiritual alignment as the core tradition or keystone of the practicing ritual magician regarding this system of magick. This ritual is not pre-packaged and ready for immediate use; it represents an intimate operation that no author could possibility anticipate. The magician must develop the pattern and follow the instructions that are provided here to produce the actual ritual that will be used.

What is required to fill out this ritual pattern and its associated detailed suggestions is the fully defined aspect of the magician's personal Deity. This includes a developed image of this Deity that would aid the magician in visualizing it. The rite is not complex by itself, and in fact, the magician can incrementally approach its development, starting out with a simple definition and description of the Deity and later deepening it for a greater impact on the magician when it is performed. The magician's personal Deity can be based on modern or ancient Pagan gods or goddesses but should be the same sex as the magician, no matter their sexual preference or mundane gender. The godhead consists of a description of the elected Deity and includes the cultural context of that Deity as well. For instance, if the specific Deity is from the Welsh tradition of Christianized Paganism, such as the Grail Mythos, then the other mythic heroes, heroines, gods, and goddesses could play a role involving the magician's chosen Deity. This is also true if the Deity is from ancient Egypt, where there would be other gods and goddesses that would be part of same theological tradition (such as Heliopolitan, Theban, and Osirian). These issues should be considered when developing a concept and image of the Deity that is meaningful for the magician.

The ritual is divided into four basic events: the primary invocation, the secondary invocation, the trance and affirmation, and the communion and final blessing. The entire ritual can be broken into four distinct parts that can be performed separately at different times, if required. This would allow the magician to focus on one of the specific areas and devote a greater degree of attention to it than it would receive if it were performed as part of the whole rite. The preliminary meditation can also be performed as a meditation session apart from the assumption rite. It serves as a mechanism of devotion, since it is where the magician worships and adores the Godhead, giving it an offering of incense, sprinkling lustral water in the area, and deeply meditating upon its image. The centering exercises and the primary invocation can be performed separately, as can the self-crossing or mantle of glory. The opening of the heart gateway (self-invoking triangle) and the second invocation, which produces the Image of the Deity, are the preliminary steps to performing the assumption rite and properly belong to it. The assumption of the possession trance state, which is the next step, triggers the process of assuming the Godhead and is also part of the assumption rite proper.

Communion is performed when the magician is fully possessed by the Godhead. The sacrament that is produced can either be offered immediately or saved for future use. Communion can be given and received at any time deemed auspicious using the saved sacrament, freeing up time that would normally be used for the Celebrant to assume the Deity and charge new sacraments. For instance, a quick communion can be given during the devotional meditation session or the Pyramidal Pentagram rite.

The ritual, when performed in its entirety, assists the magician to assume the Godhead through a process of possession trance, so being able to achieve this state is important to the successful outcome of the ritual. It will take the magician some time, practice, and experience before this ritual becomes the power center of their spiritual tradition, and it needs to become that to facilitate the magician's spiritual process and inaugurate the beginning of the initiatory cycle. The magician uses the fully developed version of this rite as the centerpiece for the self-initiation ritual that is the final stage of development in this system of magick. After that achievement, they will need to graduate to more advanced systems of magick to continue the transformative initiatory process. However, elements of this ritual will be found in other traditions and rituals, most notably Alexandrian or Gardnerian Witchcraft, Neo-Pagan magickal systems, and other earth-based spiritual traditions that simultaneously use magick and assume the Deity. The Assumption of the Godhead ritual has the following structure or pattern:

1. Primary Invocation (Deity Devotion and Invocation Meditation Session)
   a. Meditation and Deity devotions
   b. Centering exercise (crown of head to the feet)
   c. First invocation of Deity (summoning and description of qualities)
   d. Self-crossing or mantle of glory
2. Secondary Invocation (first stage of assumption process)
   a. Drawing invoking triangle on self (heart gateway), second invocation of Deity (Creating visual imago)
   b. Drawing down and identification
3. Trance and Affirmation (second stage of assumption process)
   a. Assumption of deep trance state

      b.   Affirmation of Godhead (affirmation that the magician is the Godhead)

  4.   Communion and Final Blessing (Sacramentation)

      a.   Communion

      b.   Final blessing

PRIMARY INVOCATION

The Celebrant performs the circle consecration rite, so the following actions are done in a sacred space. Once these are completed, the Celebrant begins their devotional meditations. If there is a shrine to their Deity, they approach it with the chalice of lustral water, bow low, and sprinkle it around the area of the shrine to specifically sacralize that area of the temple. They light incense sticks within the shrine, as well as candles—the more the better. There can be a statue of the God, a picture, or even some kind of symbolic illustration, like a diagram or a yantra, but there should be something for the Celebrant to focus on. Other offerings can be made, such as flowers, a small glass of wine or beer, and even a small plate of food. Whatever is offered to the Deity cannot be used for any other purpose and should be discarded as an offering to the Earth when no longer needed.

The Celebrant either sits before the shrine or sits in the center of the circle, assuming their most comfortable asana. They begin to perform a meditation session, beginning with breathing exercises before moving on to mantra intonation. All the while, they are staring at the fixed point of the shrine where the image of their Deity is ensconced, and they restrict themselves to dwelling only on the awesome qualities and supernatural powers that their Godhead possesses. They could also recite a psalm-like meditative prayer about their God, but they should be projecting feelings of awe, love, and veneration, knowing that, as a magician, they are giving devotions to what is really a godly image of themselves. The Celebrant should perform this devotional meditation session for at least several minutes, or at most thirty minutes, which is the maximum for a meditation session.

Once the meditation session is completed and the Celebrant is feeling a powerful connection with this Deity, they should rise and perform a centering exercise while standing in the center of the circle. The Celebrant begins by focusing upon the magickal chakras from crown to foot (crown, forehead, heart and solar plexus, genitals and anus, and feet). The Celebrant then reads or recites the first invocation, which is the Summoning. A solitary worker can use a recording of the invocation, and the accompanied worker can have a narrator read it. After it's completed, the Celebrant performs another centering exercise, this time from foot to crown.

EXAMPLE OF SUMMONING INVOCATION

I Summon Thee, O Great God [Godhead name], to appear to me, who is Thy Devoted Child and Disciple.

Come to me, who yearns for Thy Sight and Touch. Come unto me as a Lover and a Great God, and take me into Thy Power and Majesty, the Sphere of Thy Heart and Soul, so that I may become One with Thee.

I see Thee, and exult in Thy Beauty and Awesome Presence Thou art like to me. [Descriptions of Deity and other such adoration follow.]

I Summon You to appear through words of Love and the overpowering Desire that draws Us together.

Come down to me, O Beauteous Being of Light and Love! Shed your Light and Commune with me, revealing your Wisdom. for I offer unto you the Gift of Life, of which you shall partake when in Union with me.

The Celebrant performs the self-crossing operation, which is also called the *Mantle of Glory*. This operation is a form of self-sacralization, since it joins points on the body that correspond to a symbol of transformation (in this case, a cross).

The Celebrant touches the forehead and says:

From the highest;

Touches the genitals and says:

To the source of life;

Then touches the right shoulder and says:

Through the grace;

Then touches the left shoulder and says:

And the power;

And then folds the hands before the heart and says:

Unified in Love, So Mote It Be.

The Celebrant meditates for a moment with their arms outstretched to form a cross with the whole body. In this posture, the power of the spirit of the Godhead is internally summoned.

SECONDARY INVOCATION

The Celebrant recites the second invocation and summons the Deity into manifestation, linking it with their body. The second invocation is called *the Glorification* because it celebrates the merging of the Godhead and the Celebrant.

After the invocation is completed, the Celebrant draws a triangle upon themselves, representing the gateway through which the Spirit of the Godhead shall enter.

EXAMPLE OF SECONDARY INVOCATION

Oh my God, Thou art my God, in Thy image and in Thy flesh I am made, Thee and I are One and the Same. Enter into me, that you may See with my Eyes, Hear with my Ears, and Live through my Flesh.

Thou art the Beauteous God of Light and Power, Graceful and Wise above All Other Beings, Compassionate and Merciful, a Power of Love and Justice in the World of Humanity.

I Summon Thee and I call Thee, O Great God, who art within me and all around me, Guardian and Guide, Empower me with Thy Aid and Preternatural Abilities, Inspire me and Enlighten me!

Come to me! Come to me! Come to me! At once, and without delay!

The Celebrant touches their left breast, right breast, and forehead, and says while they trace this triangle upon their body:

The Great God lives through me, and I, through Him. Thus our Wills are United, our Goals are One Goal, My Heart is His Heart, and my Wisdom comes from His Infinite Source of Wisdom.

What Magick I work, I do not work alone, for Thou art with me and in me whenever I am living in the World or standing in Sacred Space.

The Celebrant then crosses their arms over their breast and completes the glorification:

Thus is the image of Thy Glory, Great God.

Here, build the image of the Godhead.

TRANCE AND AFFIRMATION

The Celebrant enters into a light trance if standing, or, if reclining, a full trance is possible. They draw the Godhead into their being, feeling its power and glory enter within. As this occurs, they raise their arms up, as if reaching for the Ultrapoint.

The Celebrant quietly chants the associated name of the Deity as this sensitive process of identification occurs. If others are present, they will bow before the Celebrant as Deity and adore its Spirit as if it were the God incarnate. Once this trance state is fully realized, then the Celebrant will recite the words inspired directly from the Deity (these can be spontaneous or spoken from memory):

I am the Spirit of the Great God, come to Reside for a moment in this Body, who is my Priest and Chief Devotee.

I come to give Blessings, to Instruct and Guide the Seeker on the Path to Enlightenment.

The Celebrant can remain standing or sitting for as long as the trance state lasts, absorbing the spiritual qualities of their Godhead into themselves.

COMMUNION AND FINAL BLESSING

When the trance has reached its maximum effect and begins to recede, the devotees (if any are present) become silent and bow before their Deity. The Celebrant as Deity steps forward and gives a blessing (laying on of hands and blowing the breath into the crown of the head) to those devotees who come before them.

The Celebrant proceeds to the altar where food and drink are set. They lay their hands upon them and breathes upon them, saying the following blessing:

> *I, as the Spirit of the Great God, do Bless this food and drink as the joining of Spirit and Matter; thus will this food and drink Sustain our Bodies and the Spirit will Fortify our Souls.*
>
> *And the joining of Spirit to Spirit shall be the Joy of the Realization of the Individual within the Embrace of All. So mote it be.*

The Celebrant partakes of the food and the drink, and then passes them to the devotees (if any), who reverently consume them as sacraments. This is the feast of the Agape. When all the food and drink have been consumed or saved, the Celebrant will perform a final meditation. This allows the last of the spiritual energies of the Godhead to be absorbed.

When all is accomplished, the Celebrant shall arise and recite the following thanksgiving prayer:

> *Let us open our Hearts and be Pleased with our Communion of Life, Spirit, and Love, may we come to know the Wholeness of the Great God, as it enters our Lives and gives us the Blessing of the Fivefold Treasures of Human Life: Wisdom, Compassion, Justice, Fortune, and Serenity. So mote it be.*

The assumption rite is completed.

CHAPTER SEVEN

LUNAR
MYSTERY RITUAL

PREFACE TO THE RITE

The ritual pattern for the performance of the Lunar Mysteries brings the waxing and waning powers of the Moon into the working of the magician. The Moon represents the powers of the unconscious mind as it pertains to both the individual and the social collective. The Moon's influence causes potential desires and aspirations to be realized. It also causes the emergence of unwanted desires and fantasies that are illusory or even self-destructive, so the magician would be advised to treat it with caution and respect. The Moon is the healer of the psyche of the individual. It is also the cause of the eruption of unconscious forces that have been repressed in the mind. Thus, the Moon is the great revealer of inner truth, whether or not one is prepared for its revelation.

The psychological associations of the Moon are centered on the menstrual cycle. The Moon also has a corresponding impact upon those who do not menstruate. This is perhaps why the full moon is considered responsible for attacks of "lunacy" and irrational impulses principally found in men, who likely have their own much less known cycle. The lesson here, of course, is about self-control and the constructive channeling of such forces.

The waxing and waning of the Moon illustrates the states of contraction and expansion associated with life force as it affects those who menstruate. The purpose of working the Lunar Mysteries, however, is to take control of these powers inherent in human existence and harness them for constructive uses. It isn't by mere chance that some ancient farming communities planted tubers in the darkness of the new moon and harvested them by the light of the full moon. This is still practiced by many people today.

The cycle of the planting season is a symbolic process that begins with the establishment of a potential idea (a seed), and when it has reached its maximum level of growth, the emergent desire becomes capable of realization (harvesting). This symbolizes the cycle of the Moon waxing from the darkness of the new moon and increasing its light to fullness. The other side of the lunar process is where the Moon's light is diminished into darkness. There, it becomes the internalization of the lunar power and the revelation of the inner mysteries of the darkness of the soul. These cyclic changes continuously affect all life on this planet. The magician should learn to align with the positive projections of the lunar cycle, thus profiting from them as they occur. The art of magick attempts to reveal and use the inherent patterns found in existence for the purpose of self-direction, control, and the spiritualization of one's life.

The basic ritual pattern of the lunar mysteries consists of performing the Rose Ankh vortex ritual to establish the sacred field of containment for the mysteries to be presented. These mysteries are primarily about the mysterious psychic life cycle symbolizing the balance of light and darkness; thus, the vortex acts as a personification of the receptive powers of the feminine archetype. The Lunar Mystery ritual uses a combination of Rose Ankh Vortex and the Western Gateway to produce a magickal domain that allows for the mystery of the Moon and inner psyche of the magician to be experienced. When it's used to anchor a personal working for acquisition, then that working becomes imbued with the psychic nature of the inner mind. A series of such workings will not only assist the magician in acquiring those things that they need to ensure survival and develop their level of wisdom, but it will also trigger the magician's spiritual process of conscious evolution.

The pattern for the Lunar Mystery rite is very simple, since it contains rituals that are already written and defined so far in this grimoire. The only addition is the Western Gateway and the Lunar Mystery meditation. The Western Gateway uses the Grail motif and focuses on the trials of obtaining the Grail that each of the Grail knights had to undergo.

The Western Gateway is the gateway into the Underworld, and in the case of the Grail Mythos, it is the Chapel Perilous warded by the three Grail maidens who act as the arbiters of fate. The maidens are Elaine, Kundrie, and Dindrane, who are known as the scarlet, black, and white priestesses of the Grail, respectively. These three roles can also be seen as Mother, Crone, and Maiden, or Incarnation, Gnosis, and Redemption, as they relate to these three priestesses. Once the ordeal of the gateway has been achieved, then the magician enters the Underworld proper, where they encounter the supreme ordeal, and the psychic quality of the Lunar Mystery is revealed. We have written a meditative mystery, but there is certainly more that can be done with the Lunar Mystery in a more advanced system of magick.

The Grail is the feminine spirit haunting an overly masculine world that has lost its wit, wisdom, charm, compassion, and nurturing; this is still as much an issue today as it was in the twelfth century. Thus, in the Underworld, the hero is accosted with many expressions and variations of the lost and repressed feminine aspects, even and including their dark shadowy self, which can appear in many guises, genders, and shapes. The quest is for healing, regeneration, and wholeness; this cannot be accomplished without a rediscovery of the feminine aspect and spiritual quality of the physical world. The mystery of the Underworld process consists of the lesser trials of life and death, and then the supreme ordeal, where the hero meets their differently gendered unconscious counterpart, what Jung would have called the *anima* or *animus*. The hero or heroine must discover the manner in which they may be reunited with their feminine or masculine dark half in order for regeneration to take place. The feminine cycle of initiation and transformation is different than the masculine, but they are similar enough that a woman can work with it as a beginner, and she can differentiate when she advances to the point of being able to take on her own initiatory mysteries.

The Lunar Mystery rite has the following pattern or structure:

1. Circle Consecration
2. Rose Ankh Vortex
3. Western Gateway Erected
   a. Setting the Three Gate Nodes
      i. Southeast: Guide of the Mysteries

ii. West: Guardian of the Mysteries

iii. Northeast: The Ordeal

b. Opening the Portal Gate Expression

4. Lunar Mystery Meditation

5. Magickal Working (Acquisition or Godhead Assumption)

6. Closing the Gateway

7. Sealing the Vortex

ERECTING THE WESTERN GATEWAY: ENTERING THE GRAIL CHAPEL

The Celebrant performs the Consecration of the Grail Temple rite and the Rose Ankh Vortex rite as they are written. Then, armed with their wand, the Celebrant proceeds to the East, turns, and faces the West. They bow and proceed to erect the Gateway ritual structure. They say the following incantation:

> *There upon I saw a Great Cart approach, most Wondrously and Richly appointed, pulled by Three White Harts. Within it were Three Maids, a young Fair Queen, a Pure and Blessed Virgin, and a Plain Maid of Dark and Terrible Countenance.*

> *Within the Cart were the Heads of 150 Knights, some were sealed in Gold, some in Silver, and others in Lead. Therefore, the Plain Maid of Terrible Countenance announces the Beginning of the Quest of the Grail, and the Advent of its Appearance and Disappearance, and the Ordeal of the Grail Chapel, The Chapel Perilous or Castle of Marvels.*

Facing the Southeast, the Celebrant draws an invoking spiral, projects it into the Angle, and then says the following incantation:

> *I call upon Thee, O Elaine, Guide of the Grail Quest, and Fair Maiden of Spiritual Service, Incarnation and Sanctification the Love of the Goddess is poured out for all to share.*

> *Thou art adorned in Scarlet Robes, with Scarlet Tresses. Thou art the Mother of the Greatest Grail Knight, and Priestess of the Grail in its Physical Manifestation.*

Beloved Priestess of the Scarlet Way, show us the mysteries of the Grail and aid us in our Quest to be Whole and Perfect Graced by the Manna of the High Holy Grail!

Facing the West, the Celebrant draws an invoking spiral, projects it into the Watchtower, and then says the following incantation:

I call upon Thee, O Kundrie, Guardian of the Grail Quest, and Dark and Plain Maiden of Spiritual Trials, Transformation and Gnosis achieved through Suffering and Abstention.

Thou art adorned in Black Robes, with Black Tresses. Thou art the Announcer of the Grail Quest, and the Herald of the Trials of the Path of Initiation the Priestess of the Pitiless Darkness.

Respected Priestess of the Black Way, Test and Ward us in the Mysteries of the Grail, and Aid us in our Quest to be Whole and Perfect Tempered and Annealed by the Powers of the High Holy Grail!

Facing the Northeast, the Celebrant draws an invoking spiral, projects it into the Angle, and then says the following incantation:

I call upon Thee, O Dindrane, Embodiment of the Grail Quest, and Pure Maiden of the Spiritual Ordeal to join with the Feminine Spirit and to be Redeemed and made Whole.

Thou art adorned in White Robes, with Fair Blonde Tresses. Thou art the Bearer and Mystikon of the Grail, Manifesting in Five Different Manners that None ought to talk about, and Thou art the Spiritual Queen of the Grail Mystery, to whom we must Realize and Swear Fealty towards.

The Mystery of Purity and Virginity is that the Vessel of the Grail is a Woman who has United with the Gods, and thus become their Agent and Medium in this World.

Sacred Priestess of the White Way, show us the Mystery, so we may ask the Questions that begin the Resolution of the Wasteland, thus we are made Whole and Redeemed by the Wisdom of the High Holy Grail.

The Celebrant draws the three gate nodes together in a triangle by drawing a line with the wand from the Northeast to the West, then to the Southeast, and again to the Northeast. They draw the three gate nodes to the Ultrapoint, in the order of Northeast, West, and Southeast. The Gateway is now established. They set the wand carefully aside to begin the next task unencumbered.

The Celebrant proceeds to walk very slowly from the East to the West, imagining that they are proceeding down a dark and forbidding passageway, feeling their way with their hands before them, and, halfway across, they pause and put their finger to their lips in the sign of silence, then proceeds until they are standing before the Western Watchtower. There, they bow and then carefully place their hands forward, flattening them against an imaginary curtain or veil. They grip the imaginary seam in the middle, and then carefully rend the curtain or veil and opens it up, to reveal the glorious light and power emanating behind it. They behold the light, embrace it, and turn to face the East, imagining a great shower of light cascading down from the ceiling and covering their body with a brilliant illumination. Once this experience is completed, they proceed to the center of the circle, imagining a steep stairway that takes them down to center of the circle in the Infrapoint. They have now entered the depth of the *mystikon*, where the rest of the mystery shall take place. They say the following incantation:

We have met the Guide, and been Tested by the Guardian, and have undergone the Ordeal.

We have entered the Chapel of Perils, and herein seek the Source of the Mystery, the Bond that links The Sword, Lance, Chalice and Dish with the Stone.

The Three Grail Priestesses appear before us, the Hallows are unveiled, Blazing with a Glorious Illumination, and the Angels and Gods are seen Transfixed by Visions of Euphoria and Bliss.

Yet all is Silent, waiting for us to act, to Ask the most Terrible Three Questions that shall Release the Healing Powers of the Grail upon the Land.

Failure to ask these Questions shall Doom everyone to the ever Growing and ever Destroying Wasteland.

For Whom does the Grail Serve? From Whence did it Come? And to Whither does it Go?

This being said, the Celebrant sits in the center of the circle and meditates for a short period of time before continuing with the rite.

LUNAR MYSTERY

The Celebrant rises and proceeds to the altar, where they pick up their sword and draw an inner circle, beginning in the North, proceeding widdershins, and ending again in the North. The inner circle will assist in establishing the domain of the Lunar Mystery.

Then the Celebrant sits down in the center of the circle, laying their sword before them, and recites the following short Lunar Meditation. They meditate on this for a time until beginning the next phase of the working. (Other poems can be used for this meditation, depending on your tastes, but this example may suffice.)

The Moon shines down its pale Silver Light, so Darkness obscures the details from our Sight. Lighting the Way of the Occult Paths of the Weird, and the Absence of Life fills our Hearts with Fear.

But the Moon is our Guardian and our Guide, we follow its Cycle, from Full to Waning Scythe. It leads us through the Labyrinth of the Twisting Tree, and back again to Full, its Fortune our Fate to see.

We summon the Lunar Aire, to come to us this Night, we plant our Desires in the dew, of the Shining Astral Light, to aid our Works of Magick, to Unleash our Mystic Word, and to Realize them all by the Powers of Wand and Sword!

The Celebrant performs another brief meditation, beginning with an acknowledgment of the phase of the Moon, its zodiacal sign, and the work that is being contemplated. Once this is completed, then the mystery is done.

The Celebrant may now perform an inner working, such as the Pyramidal Pentagram ritual or the Assumption of the Godhead rite. When this is completed, the Celebrant, taking up their wand, performs a circumambulation of the circle deosil, starting in the East, proceeding around the circle, and ending in the East, where they return the wand to its place. The Celebrant faces the West, and performs the closing threshold gesture, as if they were closing a curtain or veil in the Western Watchtower, and then draws a sealing spiral over it, thus closing the Gateway completely.

The Celebrant performs the closing rite for the Rose Ankh vortex rite and does not perform the closing for the Consecration of the Grail Temple rite, since a vortex was generated for this working and cannot be banished anyway.

Chapter Eight

SOLAR MYSTERY RITUAL

PREFACE TO THE RITE

As the Lunar Mysteries make people aware of the inner process of growth and transformation, so the Solar mysteries make them aware of the changing cycles of the entire world. While the Moon is the cause of many internal cycles, the Solar Wheel of the Year represents the external life cycle of the world—and particularly of humanity. Everyone experiences the stages of birth, growth, formation, procreation, love, fulfillment, old age, and death. Through the constant cycle of the renewal of life that is represented in the Wheel of the Year, the mystery of rebirth and reincarnation is revealed.

The four seasonal quarters are represented as the midpoint of each season in turn, for there is midsummer and midwinter and the equinoxes (or "equal nights"). Although the equinoxes are periods of equal day and night, they occur at times when the light or the darkness is ascending into prominence. Therefore, the Vernal Equinox occurs as the light is waxing, and the Autumnal Equinox occurs as darkness is waxing.

The solstices are the longest and the shortest days of the year. The Winter Solstice is the day of the longest night, a time when the light is at its lowest ebb. Conversely, the Summer Solstice is the time when the day is the longest, the light having reached its highest expression. The four seasons are stages in the continual mythical contest between light and darkness, life and death. The magician must heed the wisdom that darkness folds into light and light folds into darkness. They aren't in battle with each other, but they are in a cycle of waxing and waning that is ultimately balanced.

The Solar Cycle of the Year consists of four festivals, which are the four quarter seasonal festivals celebrated when the calendric day of the Sun enters the boundary of one of the four seasons. However, the background correspondences to the Wheel of the Year are determined by astrology, the only occult system in the Western tradition concerned with time. Each of the four quarter seasonal festivals are determined by exact positions in the zodiac, which the Sun enters at a specific time during the special day. The four quarter seasonal festivals always occur at the first degree of each of the cardinal signs of the zodiac. The astrological correspondence determines the magickal significance of each of the four Solar festivals. The magician scrutinizes them to understand their essential importance aside from folk custom and tradition.

The four quarter-seasonal festival days are associated with the four cardinal astrological signs: Aries, Cancer, Libra, and Capricorn. The cardinal signs represent the elemental energies in the state of dynamism; thus, the balance of light and darkness are profoundly shifting at these periods. The quality of cardinal Fire is represented by the fertile potential of the Vernal Equinox, for this fire is the creative vital force, freshly released as spring. Likewise, the quality of cardinal Air is represented by the harvest and diminishing light of the Autumnal Equinox. The quality of Cardinal Water is represented by the Summer Solstice, and the quality of Cardinal Earth is represented by the Winter Solstice.

The Solar Mystery rite uses the Eastern Gateway as its focus, and like the Lunar Mystery, it consists of performing the Rose Ankh Vortex ritual in order to establish the sacred field of containment for the mysteries to be presented. These mysteries are primarily about the creative life cycle, represented by the four seasons and focused on the Sun; thus, the vortex acts as a personification of the powers of the masculine archetype. The Solar Mystery ritual uses a combination of Rose Ankh Vortex and the Eastern Gateway to produce a magickal domain that allows for the mystery of the Sun and the celebratory persona of the magician to be experienced. The Solar Mystery is healing, redemptive, revelatory, joyous, and generous, representing the happiness of the gift of life and the realization of spirit in nature.

The pattern for the Solar Mystery rite is also very simple, since it contains rituals that are already written and defined in this grimoire. The only addition is the Eastern Gateway and the Solar Mystery Meditation. The Eastern Gateway uses the Grail motif and focuses on the greater trials of light and darkness, which are redemption (becoming whole) and revitalization. The Eastern Gateway is the gateway out of the Underworld, and in the case of the Grail Mythos, it is the Grail Kingdom and its restitution, presided over by the three Grail masters who act as the instruments of the healing process. These masters are Calixtus the Grail Hermit, Amfortas the Fisher King, and Merlin the Magician, who are known as the three mages of the Grail (thus the Mystic, Sacred King, and the Magician). The Mystic and Magician represent the two opposing paths of renunciation and transmutation that are embodied in the Sacred King, who is both mystic and magician in one body. The declarations to the three gate nodes are long, so the magician should read them from cue cards if they are not memorized.

The mystery of the Eastern Gateway is that the seeker must learn the answer to the questions about their own soul and be able to translate them in such a way that they are intelligible to others. The process of translation and objectification is the secret manner in which the seeker can once again enter into the world of light and the living. The domain of darkness is opened up to the light of the new dawning day, and the seeker walks out into the world, seeming as if newly remade and revitalized. The central mystery is the celebration of the seasonal meditation, which recaps an aspect of the Grail Mythos. The Grail story begins with the wasteland of winter, and then the glorious visitation of the Grail in the spring. The Quest proceeds until summer, where the Fisher King is healed and restored, and the Grail's glory departs this world, setting up the season of autumn, where the Fisher King is wounded, and the land begins its decline into waste and despair, which is the season of winter. The entire Grail cycle is represented by the four seasons and the four Solar mysteries. However, the Solar Mystery rite is not used to perform an internal working, since the emphasis is first on the seasonal meditation and then celebrating a feast. However, it can be used to experience one's personal Godhead, so the alignment rite can be incorporated if no one else is accompanying the Celebrant in the performance of the Solar Mystery.

The magician should keep in mind that the Eastern Gateway is a gate of revelation, which means that there are no deep and internal mysteries or processes present when the Solar Mystery is performed. It isn't appropriate for a personal working of acquisition to be performed during this mystery rite. The Solar Mystery requires some kind of celebration, so a feast is recommended. This means that the magician should plan some kind of commemorative meal, either for themselves or for friends and magickal companions. The magician should make some kind of declaration or speech before the meal is commenced (or as a silent prayer, if they are alone), and then the meal is enjoyed with pleasure, laughter, and pure enjoyment, since this is the tenor of the Solar Mystery—that life is to be lived in full enjoyment without inhibitions, restrictions, and false piety.

The Solar Mystery rite has the following pattern or structure:

1. Circle Consecration
2. Rose Ankh Vortex
3. Eastern Gateway Erected
   a. Setting the three Gate nodes
      i. Soutwest: Purification and Atonement
      ii. East: Healing and Translation
      iii. Northwest: Liberation and Revelation
   b. Opening the Portal Gate expression
4. Solar Mystery Meditation
5. Godhead Assumption (optional and only if alone)
6. Closing the Gateway
7. Sealing the Vortex
8. The Solar Feast

ERECTING THE EASTERN GATEWAY AND REVEALING THE GRAIL KINGDOM

The Celebrant performs the Consecration of the Grail Temple rite and the Rose Ankh Vortex rite as they are written. Then, armed with their wand, the Celebrant proceeds to the West, turns, and faces the East. They bow and proceed to erect the Gateway ritual structure. They say the following incantation:

I saw the Grail Kingdom unfold before me, that Ancient place Called Sarras, the Land of the Midnight Sun, and therein, the place was filled with Disease and Devastation, the Crops, Animals and People Suffering from the Great Wasting Desiccation, and the Land was filled with Plague and Pestilence, War, Famine and Death.

There was a Great Sorrowful Cry coming from all Directions, and I heard it as distinctly as if it were declaimed before me and it said:

"Woe unto the World where the Grail has Vanished, and where the Fisher King lies Wounded, Suffering but not Dying.

The Mystery requires a Hero who shall have the Purity and Wisdom to Realize the Grail Manifesting in its Five Forms, and Know when to ask the Three Questions that shall Release the stasis of Suffering, and cause a Great Healing and Restitution to occur.

For behold, the Sun shall Wax and Wane, and the Grail shall Appear and then Disappear, but the Mystery lives on Forever aided by the Youthful and Pure Hero Warrior of the Sun."

Facing the Southwest, the Celebrant draws an invoking spiral, projects it into the Angle, and says the following incantation:

I call upon Calixtus, Hermit of the Grail, that Great Sage who Knows the Right Action and the Proper Piety to gain the Vision of the Grail in the Darkening Times of Death and Despair.

His word is heard, and that word is Atonement! He calls us to Forsake the Ways of the World and turn within, so we might Rediscover our Spiritual Center, and be Redeemed for our Faults and Mistakes, our Sins against our Spiritual Selves.

We must Purge ourselves of the Distractions of our Mundane Life, to Immerse ourselves in our Spiritual Light, long Dimmed by the cares of Life to become Purified, Refreshed and Revitalized.

O Calixtus, Thou art a Crude Hermit living in a cave, Having Renounced the World, and barely any decent clothes To cover your body.

Thou art tall, thin, ascetic, bearded and of most Stern Countenance. Thy Voice is Loud, Crying out to the Grail Knights to mend their Ways and follow the Inner Light of the Grail.

Facing the East, the Celebrant draws an invoking spiral, projects it into the Watchtower, and says the following incantation:

I call upon Amfortas, The Fisher King whose ancestor is Joseph of Arimathea, or he who brought The Grail from the Holy Land to Britain.

Thou art the Sacred King who never Dies, but who is Wounded and requires Healing, he is the Source of the Mystery of the Grail, and his Wounding is the Source of the Wasteland that afflicts his most Holy Kingdom of the Grail.

His Wound is the Loss of Goodness and Fertility, Vitality and Ambition and these must be Renewed every Cycle, where the Grail appears, is Revealed, and then Disappears again. He cannot Die, but in His Wounded state, the World is Cursed and without the aid of Spirit or Renewal thus an Eternal Winter or Desert afflicts His Domain. The Mechanism of His Healing is simple but daunting except to the most Pure and Exalted Warrior, for many have failed the Quest.

The first task is to Realize the Nature of the Grail and to cause it to become Revealed to all the Senses, and the second task is to Ask the Three Questions at the appropriate Time.

And once Answered, these Three Questions will Reveal the Nature of the Grail within One, and so it will never truly Depart, but be with the Wise Grail Knight forever.

So the Wounded King must drink and eat from the Chalice and the Dish, and He must be aided by the Wisdom of the Lance and the Power of the Sword in order to be Healed so the Stone will Manifest and Heal the Land and its People once again.

Facing the Northwest, the Celebrant draws an invoking spiral, projects it into the Angle, and says the following incantation:

I call upon Merlin, the Great Magician, who is the Mystikon of the Grail, and who represents the Great Revelator and the Power that resides behind the Grail Quest.

For it is the Mystery and might of Magick that causes the Grail to be revealed to all, and for the Internal Mysteries to become realized in the Vicissitudes and Trials of Life, to be applied as the means for Revitalization and Restitution.

It is Magick that Heals the Grail Kingdom and make right all of the wrongs throughout that Domain and Merlin is the Wielder of that Sacred Magick.

For to ascend to the Spirit, we must be as the Mystic, and to draw down that same Spirit, we must be as the Magician, and to embody the goodness of Spirit in Life, we must be as the Sacred King, dispensing the Sacraments of Spirit through Compassion, Justice, and the Love of Harmony.

The Feminine Spirit of the Grail is revealed through the Sacred Marriage of the Sacred King and the Land, and the Goodness that Emanates from that Harmonious Liaison is the perfect joy of Spirit joined with Matter and thus, in such wise, we live in the Joy and Greatness of the Gods.

May the Powers and Wisdom of Merlin guide us in all that we do, whether in Darkness or in the Light.

The Celebrant draws the three gate nodes together in a triangle by drawing a line with the wand from the Northwest to the East, then to the Southwest, and again to the Northwest. They draw the three gate nodes to the Ultrapoint, in the order of Northwest, East, and Southwest. The Gateway is now established. They set the wand carefully aside to begin the next task unencumbered.

The Celebrant proceeds to walk very slowly from the West to the East, imagining that they are proceeding up a dark passageway that is becoming progressively filled with light, at first carefully proceeding and then, as it becomes more illuminated, with greater confidence. They proceed with their ascent until they are standing before the brilliant Eastern Watchtower. They bow, and then carefully place their hands forward, flattening them against an imaginary curtain or veil. They grip the imaginary seam in the middle and carefully rend the curtain or veil to open it up, revealing the blazing light of the rising Sun. They behold the Solar light, embrace it, and turn to face the West, imagining a great tall shadow of their form projecting into the West by the brilliance of the Sun. Once this experience is completed, they proceed to the center of the circle, imagining a gentle path up a great mound of earth that takes them up to center of the circle in the Ultrapoint.

They have now come forth like the dawning of a new day into the powerful revelatory light of logic and reason. They say the following incantation:

We have come forth, from the Darkening abode of the Inner Sanctum of the Mysteries, into the brilliant Light of the Dawn. The Solar Disk rises Majestically in the East and casts its Light into the Darkness, briefly Revealing the Mysteries of the Underworld. The Grail Mystery has reached its culmination, The Five Hallows are shown to the Hero, who then remembers to ask the Three Questions.

Thus I reveal their Answers herein, and seek to meditate deeply on their Revelation.

Whom does the Grail serve?

It serves the initiate upon the path of spiritual union.

From whence did it come?

From the womb of the Great Mother.

To whither does it go?

To the salvation of all humanity, It appears and then disappears.

Thus is the Mystery!

This being said, the Celebrant sits in the center of the circle and meditates for a short period of time before continuing with the rite.

SOLAR MYSTERY

The Celebrant rises and proceeds to the altar, where they pick up their sword and draw an inner circle, beginning in the South, proceeding deosil, and ending again in the South. The inner circle will assist in establishing the domain of the Solar Mystery. The Celebrant sits down in the center of the circle, laying their sword before them, and recites the following short Solar Meditation, depending on the Solar seasonal event. They then meditate on this for a time before beginning with the next phase of the working.

Autumn Equinox

The failing Light of Sun King has reached its terrible threshold, and thus He has received the Dolorous Blow and is Wounded.

The wasting begins, and the land is haunted by the increase of Darkness, as all Life departs this World.

The Grail has already departed, and all hope of Restoration is lost in the Despair of the Winter's approach.

Although it is a Time of Sadness, since Life is Dying and Disappearing, we shall Light the Fires and Candles of Hope for the Harvest is complete and shall see us through this marginal time.

Winter Solstice

The Darkness has achieved its complete Victory, for the Sun King has Died as the Sun set this Day, and we face the Peril of the Wasted land without Hope of any Renewal.

The Grace of Life and Warm Days are long past us, hardly remembered as we endure the hardships of Potential Loss and Misfortune. However, on the Dawning of the next Day, the Sun King us Reborn, and the Breath of Hope and Promise fills our Spirits with Joy and Happiness.

The Wheel has turned, and the Light increases, Promising to Restore us to our former State of Grace and Abundance.

SPRING EQUINOX

The first Manifestation of the Grail Has occurred, showering us with the Blessings of Life Renewed, and even the Land, still locked in the Wasteland of Winter's Embrace, shows signs of Stirring and Revitalization. The Light is in its ascendance over the Darkness, and we stand at this point of Balance, knowing that the Grail is near and within our grasp.

Let us seek the Greening of the Earth, to prepare for the Planting and the Bountiful Growth that the Fullness of Summer shall bring!

SUMMER SOLSTICE

The Grail has appeared in Five Distinct Forms, The Lance of Wisdom, The Sword of Justice, The Chalice of Spiritual Love and The Dish of Healing and Fulfillment, The Stone has Healed the Land and all is alive with Life and the Promise of a Bountiful Harvest.

The Grail has showered its Bounty upon the Earth, and all Darkness and Despair is long gone, a fleeting memory of other times. yet we should be Vigilant for The Grail has now departed this World having completed its task of Healing and Revitalizing, and the Light is beginning to Dim and Diminish.

Let us Renew our tasks and seek to complete all endeavors while the Life of the World is still abundantly present.

The Celebrant performs another brief meditation, beginning with an acknowledgment of the position of the Sun, its zodiacal sign, and the work that has been accomplished during the previous season. Once this is completed, the mystery is done.

The Celebrant may now optionally perform the Assumption of the Godhead rite if they are celebrating the Solar Mystery alone. Otherwise, they will defer any inner workings and proceed with the closing spell. The Celebrant, taking up their wand, performs a circumambulation of the circle widdershins, starting in the West, proceeding around the circle, and ending in the West, where they return the wand to its place. The Celebrant faces the East and performs the closing threshold gesture, as if they were closing a curtain or veil in the Eastern Watchtower, and draws a sealing spiral over it, closing the Gateway completely.

The Celebrant performs the closing rite for the Rose Ankh vortex rite and does not perform the closing for the Consecration of the Grail Temple rite, since a vortex was generated and cannot be banished anyway. Once this is completed, they (and any others who may be in attendance) proceed to the feast, making certain to either declare or silently meditate on the Seasonal Mystery, and to thank the Deity for the abundance and goodness of life. A libation may also be given to the earth later if the alignment rite is not performed.

CHAPTER NINE

SELF-INITIATION
MYSTERY RITUAL

PREFACE TO THE RITE

The ritual of self-initiation is probably the most important mystery of this book, but it's the last that is mastered by the magician. An initiation always represents what has already been accomplished, requiring skills and knowledge that one must already possess. It may also release the knowledge that was locked up and hidden from the candidate-initiate. Thus, an initiation may open new doors to greater awareness and ability.

However, an initiation cannot make anything occur within an individual unless it has already been realized on some other level. Spiritual development occurs on many levels at once, but an initiation brings these otherwise-subtle changes down to the level of the body, causing an indelible and permanent change to ultimately occur within the core of one's being.

An initiation seeks to cause three things to occur within the candidate. The first thing is, of course, a profound self-empowerment caused by the process of assuming the Godhead and expressing it through the self. The candidate takes on a magickal persona and, through it, channels the spiritual powers of the Absolute. The second consists of the forging of a new life perspective, life history, identity, and destiny. The candidate not only becomes the assumed magickal persona, but also emulates the

Deity who is behind the mythic image of the assumed magickal being. The third is the establishment of an alignment to a specific Deity, for in this manner one becomes a priest/ess, the perfect channel for the Deity to fulfill its cycle of manifestation. The ultimate spiritual discipline that develops from one's relationship with the Deity becomes the essential quality of an initiatory lineage.

The Self-Initiation Mystery ritual uses the double gateway to create a complete cycle of transformative initiation, representing the archetypal descent and return of the hero-initiate from the Underworld. This ritual uses the lunar and solar gate structures together and enacts an empowered dedication and godhead assumption within the central chamber of initiation. It's important for the candidate initiate to have at least one witness to this self-initiation, and they should also celebrate a feast afterwards, as if it were one of the four Solar celebrations.

The main consideration for the performing of this rite lies in the specific preparations that the candidate must undertake. The magician shouldn't celebrate the self-initiation rite until they have fully mastered the Assumption of the Godhead rite and is able to completely assume their chosen godhead to such an extent that there is little left of their normal self to interfere with the channeling. The candidate should also prepare a dedication speech that they can either read or memorize, depending on whether it is brief or detailed, poetry or prose. The dedication is a speech whereby the initiate dedicates their life to the practice and mastery of magick, and to the service of their personal Deity. They also state their ultimate objectives and goals that they seek as an initiate of the first degree, or the element of Earth. The empowerment that is used within the chamber of initiation is based on the element of Earth, and the magician will set invoking pentagrams for Earth at the four Angles and in the Infrapoint. These devices will be drawn together with the sword to create a kind of inverted pyramid, which is the symbolized magickal structure of the initiatory chamber. The magician must have practiced and be quite proficient with these magickal structures, as well as the other structures of the system, such as the Lunar Mystery, the Solar Mystery, and the Rose Ankh Vortex rite. The magician should probably work with this magickal system for at least a year before attempting the self-initiation rite.

The Self Initiation Mystery ritual has the following structure.

1. Circle Consecration
2. Rose Ankh Vortex
3. Western Gateway Erected
   a. Setting the Three Gate Nodes
      i. Southeast: Guide of the Mysteries
      ii. West: Guardian of the Mysteries
      iii. Northeast: The Ordeal
   b. Opening the Portal Gate expression
4. Setting the Internal Vortex of Earth
5. Dedication and Meditation
6. Godhead Assumption Rite
7. Eastern Gateway Erected
   a. Setting the three Gate nodes
      i. Southwest: Purification and atonement
      ii. East: Healing and translation
      iii. Northwest: Liberation and revelation
   b. Opening the Portal Gate expression
8. Closing the Gateway
9. Sealing the Vortex

ERECTING THE WESTERN GATEWAY AND ENTERING THE INITIATION CHAMBER

The Celebrant performs the Consecration of the Grail Temple rite and the Rose Ankh Vortex rite as they are written. Then, armed with their wand, the Celebrant proceeds to the East, turns, and faces the West. They bow and proceeds to erect the Gateway ritual structure. They say the following incantation:

Thereupon I saw a Great Cart approach, most Wondrously and Richly appointed, pulled by Three White Harts.

Within it were Three Maids, a Young Fair Queen, a Pure and Blessed Virgin, and a Plain Maid of Dark and Terrible Countenance.

Within the Cart were the Heads of 150 Knights, some were sealed in Gold, some in Silver and others in Lead.

Therefore, the Plain Maid of Terrible Countenance announces the beginning of the Quest of the Grail, and the advent of its Appearance and Disappearance, and the Ordeal of the Grail Chapel, the Chapel Perilous or Castel of Marvels.

Facing the Southeast, the Celebrant draws an invoking spiral, projects it into the Angle, and says the following incantation:

I call upon Thee, O Elaine, Guide of the Grail Quest, and Fair Maiden of Spiritual Service, Incarnation and Sanctification, the Love of the Goddess is poured out for all to share.

Thou art adorned in Scarlet Robes, with Scarlet Tresses. Thou art the Mother of the Greatest Grail Knight, and Priestess of the Grail in its Physical Manifestation.

Beloved Priestess of the Scarlet Way, show us the Mysteries of the Grail and aid us in our Quest to be Whole and Perfect, Graced by the Manna of the High Holy Grail!

Facing the West, the Celebrant draws an invoking spiral, projects it into the Watchtower, and says the following incantation:

I call upon Thee, O Kundrie, Guardian of the Grail Quest, and Dark and Plain Maiden of Spiritual Trials, Transformation and Gnosis achieved through Suffering and Abstention.

Thou art adorned in Black Robes, with Black Tresses. Thou art the Announcer of the Grail Quest, and the Herald of the Trials of the Path of Initiation, The Priestess of the Pitiless Darkness.

Respected Priestess of the Black Way, test and ward us in the Mysteries of the Grail, and aid us in our Quest to be Whole and Perfect Tempered and Annealed by the Powers of the High Holy Grail!

Facing the Northeast, the Celebrant draws an invoking spiral, projects it into the Angle, and says the following incantation:

I call upon Thee, O Dindrane, Embodiment of the Grail Quest, and Pure Maiden of the Spiritual Ordeal to join with the Feminine Spirit and to be Redeemed and made Whole.

Thou art adorned in White Robes, with Fair Blonde Tresses. Thou art the Bearer and Mystikon of the Grail, Manifesting in Five Different Manners that None ought to talk about.

And thou art the Spiritual Queen of the Grail Mystery, to whom we must Realize and Swear Fealty towards. The Mystery of Purity and Virginity is that the Vessel of the Grail is a Woman who has United with the Gods, and thus become their Agent and Medium in this World.

Sacred Priestess of the White Way, show us the Mystery, so we may ask the Questions that begin the Resolution of the Wasteland, thus we are made Whole and Redeemed by the Wisdom of the High Holy Grail.

The Celebrant draws the three gate nodes together in a triangle by drawing a line with the wand from the Northeast to the West, then to the Southeast, and again to the Northeast. They draw the three gate nodes to the Ultrapoint, in the order of Northeast, West, and Southeast. The Gateway is now established. They set the wand carefully aside to begin the next task unencumbered.

The Celebrant proceeds to walk very slowly from the East to the West, imagining that they are proceeding down a dark and forbidding passageway, feeling their way with their hands before them. Halfway across, they pause and put their finger to their lips in the sign of silence, and then proceed until they are standing before the Western Watchtower. They bow and carefully place their hands forward, flattening them against an imaginary curtain or veil. They grip the imaginary seam in the middle, carefully rend the curtain or veil, and opens it up, revealing the glorious light and power emanating behind it. They behold the light, embrace it, and turn to face the East, imagining a great shower of light cascading down from the ceiling and covering their body with a brilliant illumination. Once this experience is completed, they proceed to the center of the circle, imagining a steep stairway that takes them down to center of the circle in the Infrapoint. They have now entered the depth of the mystikon, and herein the rest of the mystery shall take place. They say the following incantation:

We have met the Guide, and been tested by the Guardian, and have undergone the Ordeal. We have entered the Chapel of Perils, and herein seek the Source of the Mystery the bond that links the Sword, Lance, Chalice and Dish with the Stone.

The Three Grail Priestesses appear before us, The Hallows are unveiled, Blazing with a Glorious Illumination, and the Angels and Gods are seen Transfixed by Visions of Euphoria and Bliss.

Yet all is Silent, Waiting for us to act to Ask the most Terrible Three Questions that shall Release the Healing Powers of the Grail upon the Land. Failure to Ask these Questions shall Doom everyone to ever Growing and ever Destroying Wasteland.

For Whom does the Grail serve?

From Whence did it come?

And to Whither does it go?

This said, the Celebrant sits in the center of the circle and meditates for a short period of time before continuing with the rite.

SETTING THE CHAMBER OF INITIATION

The Celebrant takes their magick dagger and proceeds to the Northeast Angle, where they draw an invoking pentagram of Earth. They then proceed widdershins to the Northwest Angle and perform the same action. They proceed to the Southwest Angle, doing the same action, then proceed to the Southeast Angle, doing the same. They return the dagger to the altar, take up the sword, and draw the pentagram devices in the four Angles together in the Infrapoint. They begin with the Northeast Angle, drawing a line of power from that Angle to the center of the circle in the Infrapoint, and repeat this action at the Northwest,

Southwest, and Southeast Angles. They draw the four Angles together, starting in the Northeast, and proceeding widdershins around the circle, drawing each of the four Angles into a square. They then draw an inner circle with the sword within the square, beginning in the Northeast and proceeding deosil around the circle. The chamber of initiation is now erected.

The Celebrant puts away their sword and proceeds into the center of the circle and sits comfortably, having in their hand the written dedication (or not if they have memorized it). After a period of internal soul searching, they bow their head and read or recite the dedication, slowly and with great emphasis. Once completed, they will meditate for a period of time, carefully reviewing in their mind all that was said and revealed in the dedication declaration. They may then perform the lotus seven-breath exercise, pausing for a period of time afterward to recover from it.

The Celebrant may now perform the inner initiatory working, which is the Assumption of the Godhead rite. When this is completed, the Celebrant, taking up their wand, performs a circumambulation of the circle deosil, starting in the East, proceeding around the circle, and ending in the East, where they return the wand to its place. The Celebrant faces the West and performs the closing threshold gesture, as if they were closing a curtain or veil in the Western Watchtower, and draws a sealing spiral over it, thus closing the Gateway completely.

ERECTING THE EASTERN GATEWAY AND REVEALING THE GRAIL KINGDOM

The Celebrant, armed with their wand, proceeds to the West, turns, and faces the East. They bow and proceed to erect the Gateway ritual structure. They say the following incantation:

> *I saw the Grail Kingdom unfold before me, that Ancient place called Sarras, the Land of the Midnight Sun, and therein, the place was filled with Disease and Devastation, the Crops, Animals and People Suffering from the Great Wasting Desiccation, and the Land was filled with Plague and Pestilence, War, Famine and Death.*

There was a Great Sorrowful Cry coming from all Directions, and I heard it as distinctly as if it were declaimed before me, and it said:

"Woe unto the World where the Grail has Vanished, and where the Fisher King lies Wounded, Suffering but not Dying.

The Mystery requires a Hero who shall have the Purity and Wisdom to Realize the Grail Manifesting in its Five Forms and Know when to ask the Three Questions that shall Release the stasis of Suffering, and cause a Great Healing and Restitution to occur.

For Behold, the Sun shall Wax and Wane, and the Grail shall Appear and then Disappear, but the Mystery lives on forever, aided by the Youthful and Pure Hero Warrior of the Sun."

Facing the Southwest, the Celebrant draws an invoking spiral, projects it into the Angle, and then says the following incantation:

I call upon Calixtus, Hermit of the Grail, that Great Sage who Knows the Right Action and the Proper Piety to gain the Vision of the Grail in the Darkening Times of Death and Despair. His word is heard, and that word is Atonement!

He calls us to Forsake the Ways of the World and turn within, so we might Rediscover our Spiritual Center, and be Redeemed for our Faults and Mistakes, our Sins against our Spiritual Selves.

We must Purge ourselves of the Distractions of our Mundane Life, to Immerse ourselves in our Spiritual Light, long dimmed by the cares of Life to become Purified, Refreshed and Revitalized.

O Calixtus, Thou art a Crude Hermit living in a cave, having Renounced the World, and barely any decent clothes cover your body. Thou art tall, thin, ascetic, bearded and of most Stern Countenance.

Thy Voice is Loud, Crying out to the Grail Knights to Mend their Ways and follow the Inner Light of the Grail.

Facing the East, the Celebrant draws an invoking spiral, projects it into the Watchtower, and says the following incantation:

I call upon Amfortas, the Fisher King whose Ancestor is Joseph of Arimathea, or He who brought the Grail from the Holy Land to Britain.

Thou art the Sacred King who never Dies, but who is Wounded and Requires Healing. He is the Source of the Mystery of the Grail, and his Wounding is the Source of the Wasteland that afflicts His most Holy Kingdom of the Grail.

His wound is the loss of Goodness and Fertility, Vitality and Ambition and these must be Renewed every Cycle, where the Grail appears, is Revealed, and then Disappears again. He cannot Die, but in His Wounded state, the World is Cursed and without the aid of Spirit or Renewal thus an Eternal Winter or Desert afflicts His Domain.

The Mechanism of His Healing is simple but Daunting except to the most Pure and Exalted Warrior, for many have failed the Quest. The First task is to Realize the Nature of the Grail and to cause it to become Revealed to all of the Senses, and the Second task is to ask the Three Questions at the appropriate Time.

And once Answered, these Three Questions will Reveal the Nature of the Grail within One, and so it will never truly Depart, but be with the Wise Grail Knight forever.

So the Wounded King must drink and eat from the Chalice and the Dish, and He must be aided by the Wisdom of the Lance and the Power of the Sword in order to be Healed so the Stone will Manifest and Heal the Land and its People once again.

Facing the Northwest, the Celebrant draws an invoking spiral, projects it into the Angle, and says the following incantation:

I call upon Merlin, the Great Magician, who is the Mystikon of the Grail, and who Represents the Great Revelator and the Power that Resides behind the Grail Quest.

For it is the Mystery and might of Magick that causes the Grail to be Revealed to all, and for the Internal Mysteries to become Realized in the Vicissitudes and Trials of Life, to be applied as the means for Revitalization and Restitution.

It is Magick that Heals the Grail Kingdom and make Right all of the Wrongs throughout that Domain and Merlin is the Wielder of that Sacred Magick.

For to Ascend to the Spirit, we must be as the Mystic, and to Draw down that same Spirit, we must be as the Magician, and to Embody the Goodness of Spirit in Life, we must be as the Sacred King, Dispensing the Sacraments of Spirit through Compassion, Justice, and the Love of Harmony.

The Feminine Spirit of the Grail is Revealed through the Sacred Marriage of the Sacred King and the Land, and the Goodness that Emanates from that Harmonious Liaison is the perfect Joy of Spirit joined with Matter and thus, in such wise, we live in the Joy and Greatness of the Gods.

May the Powers and Wisdom of Merlin Guide us in all that we do, whether in Darkness or in the Light.

The Celebrant draws the three gate nodes together in a triangle by drawing a line with the wand from the Northwest to the East, then to the Southwest, and again to the Northwest. They draw the three gate nodes to the Ultrapoint, in the order Northwest, East, and Southwest. The Gateway is now established. They set the wand carefully aside to begin the next task unencumbered.

The Celebrant proceeds to walk very slowly from the West to the East, imagining that they are proceeding up a dark passageway that is becoming progressively filled with light, carefully proceeding at first and then, as it becomes more illuminated, moving with greater confidence. They continue with their ascent until they are standing before the brilliant Eastern Watchtower. They bow and carefully place their hands forward, flattening them against an imaginary curtain or veil. They grip the imaginary seam in the middle and carefully rends the curtain or veil open, revealing the blazing light of the rising Sun. They behold the solar light, embrace it, and turn to face the West, imagining a great tall shadow of their form projecting into the West by the brilliance of the Sun. Once this experience is completed, they continue to the center of the circle, imagining a gentle path up a great mound of earth that takes them to center of the circle in the Ultrapoint. They have now come forth like the dawning of a new day into the powerful revelatory light of logic and reason. They say the following incantation:

We have come forth, from the Darkening abode of the Inner Sanctum of the Mysteries, into the Brilliant Light of the Dawn the Solar Disk rises Majestically in the East and casts its Light into the Darkness, briefly Revealing the Mysteries of the Underworld.

The Grail Mystery has reached its Culmination, The Five Hallows are shown to the Hero, who then remembers to ask the Three Questions. Thus I reveal their Answers herein, and seek to meditate Deeply on their Revelation.

Whom does the Grail serve?

It serves the Initiate Upon the Path of Spiritual Union.

From Whence did it come?

From the Womb of the Great Mother.

To Whither does it go?

To the Salvation of all Humanity, It Appears and then Disappears.

Thus is the Mystery!

This being said, the Celebrant sits in the center of the circle and meditates for a short period of time before continuing with the rite.

The Celebrant, taking up their wand, performs a circumambulation of the circle widdershins, starting in the West, proceeding around the circle, and ending in the West, where they return the wand to its place.

The Celebrant faces the East and performs the closing threshold gesture, as if they were closing a curtain or veil in the Eastern Watchtower, and draws a sealing spiral over it, closing the Gateway completely.

The Celebrant performs the closing rite for the Rose Ankh vortex rite and doesn't perform the closing for the Consecration of the Grail Temple rite, since a vortex was generated and cannot be banished anyway. Once this is completed, then they (and any others who may be in attendance) proceed to the feast, making certain to either declare or silently meditate on the personal Mystery of the candidate's initiation, and to thank the Deity for the abundance and goodness of life. A libation may also be given to the earth later.

Chapter Ten

CONSECRATION OF THE HALLOWS: THE FIVE MAGICKAL TOOLS

PREFACE TO THE RITE

The final ritual in this set is used to consecrate the five basic magickal tools: the dagger and sword, the wand or staff, the pentacle or dish, the chalice, and the crystal. Although all magickal tools become ultimately consecrated by use and approximation to the temple area, the magician can also deliberately consecrate their tools to imbue them with greater power and value. Usually, in a typical magickal lodge, the magickal tools are consecrated immediately after the neophyte's first initiation, but in this book, the magician may perform this rite as often as required until all their tools are consecrated, or they can consecrate them all at once. This can be accomplished long before they actually undergo the initiation mystery rite.

The ritual of the Consecration of the Hallows is used to charge and consecrate the five principal magickal tools, making them ready for magickal use. Each tool is charged and blessed by its associated Element, establishing a connection with all the Elemental symbolic correspondences. The physical tool is transformed from its mundane association and becomes the physical embodiment of the archetypal tool. Once consecrated, a tool must be treated with the veneration and respect due to a sacred object and must never be used for any purpose other than ritual magick. In this manner, the magickal tool becomes dedicated to the use of ritual.

The ritual pattern for this rite is very simple and direct. The magician begins the ritual by performing a self-crossing to sanctify themselves in preparation for the rite of consecrating the tools of the art of magick. The magician then blesses the tool with sacraments of lustral water, incense smoke, and oil. The magician may use a surrogate cup to hold the lustral water while blessing the chalice that is the focus of the consecration rite. The tool that is to be consecrated is dedicated to magick with a short incantation that associates it with the Element and the archetypal weapon of ritual magick. Air is associated with the dagger/sword. Fire is associated with the wand/staff. Water is associated with the chalice. Earth is associated with the pentacle/dish, and Spirit is associated with the crystal or stone.

The power used to consecrate the tool is generated through the artifice of a simple Element vortex. The magician intones the personal name of the Deity and draws an invoking pentagram of the corresponding Element. The pentagram device is sealed with an invoking spiral, and the magician intones a formula letter and word (in Greek) denoting the five qualities of the Grail.

The structure of the ritual uses the four Angles connected to a pylon in the center of the circle. The magician draws the invoking pentagrams to each Angle from Southeast to Northwest in a deosil circuit. The pylon, which consists of an invoking pentagram of the corresponding Element drawn to the Infrapoint and an invoking pentagram of Spirit Masculine or Feminine to the Ultrapoint, forms due to the duality of the highest and lowest points in the circle. The four Angles are then joined to the pylon through the Infrapoint, creating a hybrid of both the pyramid and vortex ritual structures. The Angles are connected to the Infrapoint from the Northwest to the Southeast in a widdershins circuit. Both types of energies are represented by the ritual actions and incantations of the magician. When setting the device in the Infrapoint, the magician also intones the personal name of the Deity. The choice of using either the archetypal masculine or archetypal feminine spirit is determined by the spiritual focus of the rite, whether it represents the creative or receptive energies, and this choice depends on the adopted spiritual characteristics of the magician performing the rite.

The final actions of the ritual consist of the magician drawing the powers of the Infrapoint and the Ultrapoint together through their body. The magician invokes the blessing of the Archangel associated with the tool and the Element. The magician directs the imprinted field of magickal power through their body into the tool that is to be consecrated, blowing their breath (pneuma) upon it. The magician intones the formula letters and words in the order which they were established to the four Angles and joins them to form the word *Calix*, which means "Grail" in Latin. The unified formula joins all the positions of the four Angles into a harmonious and completed field of magickal energy, thus assisting it to emulate the nature of the Spirit of the Deity. The tool, so imbued with significance and meaning, is charged and consecrated.

The theme of this ritual is concerned with the Grail, which represents the five archetypal tools as a fivefold manifestation of the powers of the Deity. The Grail, as a symbol of transformation itself, also symbolizes the five tools of ritual magick that are used to alter reality; it is an apt symbol to be used in a ritual which aims to charge and consecrate the magician's tools. I've also incorporated the use of the five Archangels to act as emissaries for the magickal blessing of the tool, but the magician can choose other types of spiritual beings to accomplish this task. The five emissaries are associated with the respective five manifestations of the Grail and connected with the blessing of the Spirit associated with each of the five Grail images.

BLESSING OF THE HALLOWS

The Celebrant consecrates each one of the five tools of magick. These will become their expression of the newly gained virtues of the Grail and their continued cultivation. These are each charged with a specific Element and identified with the corresponding archetype.

Fire	Water	Air	Earth	Spirit
Wand/ Staff	Chalice	Dagger/ Sword	Pentacle (Dish)	Crystal (Stone)
Michael	Gabriel	Raphael	Uriel	Raziel

The Celebrant stands before the altar. If the tools are a dagger, sword, or wand, they are placed upon the altar directly sitting upon the pentacle.

The chalice contains lustral water and sits behind the crossed dagger, sword, and wand. The staff is placed leaning against the center of the altar in the midst of the other tools. The crystal is carefully placed upon the stacked triune of wand, sword, and dagger. This ritual may be worked for each tool separately in the following order:

1. Chalice
2. Pentacle
3. Dagger
4. Wand
5. Sword
6. Staff
7. Stone

Each charging would utilize the other tools, whether consecrated or not. The result is the complete charging of all tools.

The Celebrant blesses each tool with lustral water, incense, and oil. The following prayers are used for each:

Fire

O Wand/Staff of Living Wisdom! You were born Centuries past and now Illuminate with the Sacrifice of your Long Life and Greater Rebirth. You call and the Spirits listen. May you be Blessed.

Water

O Chalice of Reflection! You are shaped in a form Loving and Giving. The Moon is your Heart and the Water of Life is the Fluid of your Strength. May you be Blessed.

Air

O Dagger/Sword of the Will! You were made of Air and Fire and to such you will Return. You are a Star-Metal Seed that etches the Lines of Power. May you be Blessed.

EARTH

O Pentacle Image of Cosmos! You are the Great Edifice of all Peace and Resolution. The Center does not Spin, the Knowing and the Righteous do not bend. May you be Blessed.

SPIRIT

O Crystal Stone of Creation! You are the Mind that Perceives and the Soul that Receives from the Source of all Being. Through you are the Currents made Visual and Physical. May you be Blessed.

ESTABLISHING THE ELEMENT VORTEX

The Celebrant stands in the center of the circle and faces the four Angles, starting from the East and proceeding clockwise, to invoke the four Archangels who each bear in their hands one of the four Grails from their resting place in Sarras (the ultimate hiding place of the Grail).

To the Southeast, the Celebrant intones the Name of the Deity, then draws an invoking pentagram of the corresponding Element and seals it with an invoking spiral.

They say the letter *Chi* (Charites, The Grace).

To the Southwest, the Celebrant intones the Name of the Deity, then draws an invoking pentagram of the corresponding Element and seals it with an invoking spiral.

They say the letter *Ioata* (Iudex, The Judgment).

To the Northwest, the Celebrant intones the Name of the Deity, then draws an invoking pentagram of the corresponding Element and seals it with an invoking spiral.

They say the letter *Xi* (Xoanos, The Crucible).

To the Northeast, the Celebrant intones the Name of the Deity, then draws an invoking pentagram of the corresponding Element and seals it with an invoking spiral.

They say the letter *Alpha* (Arcana, The Mystery).

To the Center, the Celebrant intones the Name of the Deity, then draws an invoking pentagram of the corresponding Element in the Infrapoint and seals it with an invoking spiral.

They say the letter *Lambda* (Lux, The Light).

The Celebrant draws an invoking pentagram of Spirit Masculine or Feminine in the Infrapoint and seals it with an invoking spiral. The Celebrant proceeds to connect the four Angles together through the Infrapoint, beginning in the Northwest and finishing in the Southeast, making a widdershins circuit. They then return to the center of circle and stand, drawing the pentagram in the Ultrapoint, connecting it in a downward arc of force, joining it with the pentagram in the Infrapoint to form a pylon of unifying light through their body.

The Celebrant says for the selected Element/tool:

FIRE

I invoke Thee, MIChAEL! O Thou who bearest the Sacred Spear and therein Reveals The Mystery of the Path of the Spiritual Healer. For through Selfless Service, Compassion, and Love of God shall the Hallowed Spear Return from Sarras to Reside herein with us!

AIR

I invoke Thee, RAPhAEL! O Thou who bearest the Sword of Power and therein Reveals The Mystery of the Path of the Spiritual Warrior. For through Pure Integrity, Truthfulness, and Obedience to God shall the Hallowed Sword Return from Sarras to reside herein with us!

WATER

I invoke Thee, GABRIEL! O Thou who bearest the Chalice of Glory and therein Reveals The Mystery of the Path of the Sage of Devotion. for through the Divine Passion of the Highest Spiritual Love in the Quest for Union with God shall the Hallowed Chalice Return from Sarras to Reside herein with us!

EARTH

I invoke Thee, URIEL! O Thou who bearest The Dish of Inexhaustive Treasure and therein Reveals The Mystery of the Mastery of Life, for through Great Steadfastness, Self-Awareness, and the Maturity of Ages shall the Hallowed Paten return from Sarras to Reside herein with us!

SPIRIT

I invoke Thee, RAZIEL! O Thou who bearest The Stone of Sion and therein Reveals The Mystery of the Source of All. For through Openness and Pure Wonder, Spiritual Insight, and the Knowing found in the Light of Divine Reason shall the Hallowed Lapidus return from Sarras to Reside herein with us.

The Celebrant stands in the pylon, facing the altar and breathes in the force of the vortex, letting it flow from them, through their hands to the tools upon the altar and says:

Charites, Arcana, Lux, Iudex, Xoanos, C.A.L.I.X:
The Five Hallows appear!

The Celebrant approaches the altar and blows the spirit breath or pneuma upon the tools, blessing them and sealing the charge. The Celebrant should use each charged tool (individually or in sequence immediately following the charging and blessing, as it is traditional and locks in the consecration for that tool.

WHAT WE
HAVE LEARNED

I have now presented both parts of this work, giving the student a background and the rituals so they may begin the work of practicing ritual magick. It's my hope that the student will actually assemble the items and space needed to practice magick and subject my rituals to experimentation. This is the only way that they will ever know if I'm on target with all the assumptions and assertions that I've made in this book. To understand ritual magick, one must practice and experience it—there's no other way in which it can be realized.

One of the most important topics covered in this book was the definition and examination of the nature of the seeker. I also defined initiation and transformation, and how magick plays a role in the conscious evolution of the magician. We examined the spectrum of consciousness and saw that there are levels far beyond what is considered normal in our culture. I included material from Ken Wilber's books, *Eye to Eye* and the *Atman Project,* to clearly show the nature of these higher states of consciousness. The reason I included an examination of this material is because practicing magick will ultimately cause an individual to experience these higher states of consciousness and consciously evolve, even if that is not their intention. It's important to know that these higher states exist and that they have a direct effect on the consciousness of the magician, being the primary cause of transformations and deep personal insights into the nature of one's spirit. If the student undertakes to practice these rituals as they are presented and forges a magickal discipline, then they will begin to undergo the first major transformative stage that Wilber talks about. The practicing magician, once they have developed the self-alignment rite of assuming Godhead and undergone self-initiation, will undoubtedly begin the transformation to the Centauric level of conscious development. This is a great achievement, and one that some practitioners—but not all—achieve. Yet the higher states of consciousness, those that are located in the subtle and causal levels, continue to effect and influence the student long before they ever encounter them directly. As I have pointed out, the nature of magick is that higher states of consciousness, when triggered, momentarily overwhelm the normal egoic levels of consciousness and cause all sorts of paranormal phenomena. It's for this reason that I sought to define these higher levels of consciousness and acquaint the student with their experiential effects to know when and how they are encountered in ritual practice.

Another important topic was the master pattern of ritual performance. The seven categories of self, space, power, alignment, the link, exteriorization, and insight represent the necessary components of the basic ritual working of acquisition. We covered the two methods of empowerment, which are the Pyramidal Pentagram (cone of power) and the vortex, representing the archetypal masculine and feminine aspects of magickal power. Also included were the Lunar, Solar, and Initiation mysteries, which round out the basic set of magickal structures. The mysteries incorporate the ritual structure of the Gateway, which allows a passage from the outer world to the inner world and back again: the cycle of light and darkness.

Other topics included the four Elements and their symbolic correspondences, the four magickal tools, and the magickal environments of the temple and the grove. We examined the magick circle and its variations, as well as the basic magickal devices of spiral, pentagram, and the Rose Cross and Rose Ankh. We also examined all the practical considerations needed in order to prepare for actual ritual practice.

The domain of Spirit was also examined since it's the world that the magician seeks to enter and engage with as part of the practice of magick. We saw that this world is protean and can be defined in several manners, all of them representing a different perspective on the same world. This domain is called the Inner Planes, and it can be defined as a symbolic matrix of Elements, planets, and astrological qualities, or as different layers of being—the Seven Planes of Consciousness. The domain of Spirit can also be seen as the Macrocosm, symbolically reflecting our world, which is the Microcosm.

The practice of magick, as defined in this book, is divided into two areas: the techniques of mental discipline and the rituals that constitute magickal workings. Mental discipline is essential, as previously explained, and represents what the magician does to achieve the altered states of consciousness necessary to help trigger the normally dormant spiritual dimension of the magician. The rituals supply the symbols of transformation within the context of sacred space and, in combination with the altered states of consciousness, produce the phenomena of magick.

The eight rituals and the meditation, as found in the grimoire, are used to satisfy all the categories of the master pattern. The rites of Circle Consecration and the Pyramidal Pentagram are used to perform the basic ritual working of material acquisition and change. The rites of the Rose Ankh Vortex and the three mystery rites represent the workings of the magickal discipline, which concerns itself with the internal workings of the self-existing in a spiritual context of the outer world. The meditation session and the alignment rite (assumption of the Godhead) are integral to the immersion of the magician within their definition of Godhead. These practices are the most important ones in this book, since they will guarantee that the magician will experience a profound conscious transformation over time. Obtaining personal transformation and conscious evolution is the reason for practicing magick, in my opinion, and something that is thoroughly defined and developed in this book.

What you have learned in reading this book isn't as important as what you will experience when you adopt a magickal discipline and begin to practice magick as a magician. There can be no greater exemplar of magick than practicing it, and it is my hope that I have given you, the reader, a passion for seeking what lies beyond the veil of normal perception. May you also gain a desire to pass into the realms of magick, exploring its mysteries and obtaining its secret visions, where dreams become reality and reality is nothing more than just another dream.

BIBLIOGRAPHY

The following is a list of books that I have assembled for suggested reading for the beginning student. It's necessary for the student to be proficient in several disciplines to become a master of ritual magick. Therefore, this list will provide them with a brief list of corresponding material that will augment the material presented in the *Disciple's Guide to Ritual Magick*. This list is by no means exhaustive, and it represents a selection of books from my own personal library. It is divided into eight different categories, covering the topics that I felt were vital to the study of ritual magick. These categories are Alchemy, Astrology, Holy Grail Mythology, Magick, Mythology, Philosophy, Psychology, Qabalah, and the Tarot.

Note: Some of these books are quite dated, but there are new and revised versions of them out on the market, and they can be considered of such value as to be indispensable.

ALCHEMY

Gilchrist, Cherry. *Alchemy: The Great Work*. Aquarian Press, 1984.
Regardie, Israel. *The Philosopher's Stone*. Llewellyn Publications, 1970.

ASTROLOGY

Hand, Robert. *Horoscope Symbols*. Para Research, 1981.
March, Marion D. and Joan McEvers. *The Only Way to Learn Astrology*, volumes I–III. ACS Publications, Inc., 1982.
Sakoian, Frances and Louis S. Acker, *The Astrologer's Handbook*. Harper & Row, 1973.

Holy Grail Mythology

Godwin, Malcolm. *The Holy Grail: Its Origins, Secrets & Meaning Revealed.* Viking Studio, 1994.

Mathews, John & Marian Green. *The Grail Seekers Companion.* Aquarian Press, 1986.

Magick

Butler, W. E. *The Magician: His Training and Work.* Willshire Book Co., 1969.

—. *Apprenticed to Magic & Magic and the Qabalah.* Aquarian Press, 1981.

—. *Practical Magic and the Western Mystery Tradition.* Aquarian Press, 1986.

Crowley, Aleister. *Book 4.* Sangreal, 1972.

—. *Magick in Theory and Practice.* Castle Books, 1991.

—. *Magick: Liber ABA, Book Four,* Second Edition. Red Wheel/Weiser, 2002.

Fortune, Dion. *Psychic Self-Defence.* Samuel Weiser, 1977.

Grey, William. *Magickal Ritual Methods.* Samuel Weiser, 1969.

Knight, Gareth. *The Practice of Ritual Magick.* Samuel Weiser, 1980.

Regardie, Israel. *Ceremonial Magic: A Guide to the Mechanism of Ritual.* Aquarian Press, 1980.

—. *Foundations of Practical Magic.* Aquarian Press, 1979.

—. *The Complete Golden Dawn System of Magic.* Falcon Press, 1984.

—. *The Tree of Life: A Study in Magic.* Samuel Weiser, 1972.

Stewart, R. J. *Living Magical Arts.* Blandford Press, 1987.

Versluis, Arthur. *The Philosophy of Magic.* Arkana, 1986.

Mythology

Campbell, Joseph. *The Hero with a Thousand Faces.* Bollingen Press, 1973.

—. *The Masks of God: Primitive Mythology.* Bollingen Press, 1974.

—. *The Masks of God: Oriental Mythology.* Bollingen Press, 1974.

—. *The Masks of God: Occidental Mythology.* Bollingen Press, 1974.

—. *The Masks of God: Creative Mythology.* Bollingen Press, 1974.

Philosophy

Wilber, Ken. *Eye to Eye: The Quest for the New Paradigm.* Shambhala Press, 2001.

—. *The Eye of Spirit: An Integral Vision.* Shambhala Press, 1998.

—. *The Atman Project: Collected Works*, Volume II. Shambhala Press, 1999.

—. *A Sociable God: Toward a New Understanding of Religion*. Shambhala Press, 2005.

PSYCHOLOGY

Jung, Carl G. *Man and His Symbols*. Doubleday & Co., 1964.

—. *Archetypes and the Collective Unconscious*. Bollingen Press, 1975.

—. *Symbols of Transformation*. Bollingen Press, 1976.

QABALAH

Crowley, Aleister. *The Qabalah of Aleister Crowley*. Samuel Weiser, 1973.

—. *Liber 777*. Level Press, 1970.

—. *777 and other Qabalistic Writings of Aleister Crowley*. Samuel Weiser, 1994.

Davidson, Gustav. *A Dictionary of Angels*. Free Press, 1971.

Fortune, Dion. *The Mystical Qabalah*. Ernest Benn, 1974.

Gray, William. *The Ladder of Lights*. Helios, 1971.

Halevi, Z'ev ben Shimon. *Psychology and Kabbalah*. Samuel Weiser, 1991.

Knight, Gareth. *A Practical Guide to Qabalistic Symbolism*, Volume I and II. Helios, 1972. (New version published in one volume by Samuel Weiser, 2001.)

Regardie, Israel. *A Garden of Pomegranates*. Llewellyn Publications, 2002.

—. *The Middle Pillar*. Llewellyn Publications, 2003.

Scholem, Gershom. *Kabbalah*. New American Library, 1974.

Whitcomb, Bill. *The Magician's Companion*. Llewellyn Publications, 1993.

TAROT

Campbell, Joseph and Richard Roberts. *Tarot Revelations*. Vernal Equinox Press, 1979.

Crowley, Aleister. *The Book of Thoth*. Samuel Weiser, 2000.

Hoeller, Stephan A. *The Royal Road*. Theosophical Publishing House, 1988.

Pollack, Rachel. *Seventy-eight Degrees of Wisdom: A Book of the Tarot, Parts I and II*. Aquarian Press, 1980.

Walker, Barbara G. *The Secrets of the Tarot: Way of the Great Oracle*. Merrill-West, 1989.